GREAT DECISIONS 2022

P9-CDF-351

About the cover

A Long March-2F carrier rocket, carrying the Shenzhou-12 spacecraft and a crew of three astronauts, lifts off from the Jiuquan Satellite Launch Centre in the Gobi desert in northwest China on June 17, 2021, the first crewed mission to China's new space station. (GREG BAKER/AFP/GETTY))

LIBRARY OF CONGRESS CONTROL NUMBER: 2020919618

ISBN: 978-0-87124-278-5

Bonus article:
Changing demographics in the world
by Joseph Chamie 5

1 Outer space policy
by Eric Berger... 17

2 The renewed climate change agenda
by Ronald J. Bee..29

3 Putin's Russia
by Allen Lynch.. 41

4 Myanmar's neverending crisis
by Hunter Marston 53

5 Xi's China takes on the Quad
by Kevin Rudd.. 63

6 No end in sight: a century of drug wars
by Mónica Serrano 73

7 Foreign policy, economic power, and U.S. industrial policy
by Jonathan Chanis.. 85

8 Biden foreign policy in an age of strategic competition
by G. John Ikenberry 95

World Map.................................... following page 32

About the Opinion Ballots................................. 105

Global discussion questions.............................. 107

Researched as of November 17, 2021.

The authors are responsible for factual accuracy and for the views expressed.

FPA itself takes no position on issues of U.S. foreign policy.

GREAT DECISIONS MASTER CLASS

This year's edition of the *Great Decisions* DVD features the *Great Decisions* Master Class format. This format will feature 20-30 minute long lectures on the nine topics from this current issue.

Master class lectures are presented by Jeffrey S. Morton, the Pierrepont Comfort Chair in Political Science at Florida Atlantic University and a Fellow at the Foreign Policy Association. He holds a Ph.D. in International Relations from the University of South Carolina and an M.A. from Rutgers University. Dr. Morton has delivered the *Great Decisions* program to live audiences since 1999.

FOREIGN
POLICY
ASSOCIATION
★★★★★ 1918 ★★★★★

FPA: Taking Stock and Looking Ahead

In 1918, President Woodrow Wilson imagined a world in which "conquest and aggrandizement" would be relegated to the dustbin of history. This new world order would be ushered in by a "general association of nations" that would offer "mutual guarantees of political independence and territorial integrity to great and small states alike."

That same year, concerned citizens from all walks of life came together in New York City with a clear mission: to win public support for Wilson's vision for this new world order. Having witnessed the horrors of the First World War, they believed that the League of Nations could become the bulwark for world peace.

The citizen effort that would come to be known as the Foreign Policy Association persevered. And, in 1944, in a major address to the Foreign Policy Association at The Waldorf Astoria in New York City, President Franklin D. Roosevelt would set out his vision for the United Nations:

> *Now, there are some who hope to see a structure of peace completely set up immediately, with all the apartments assigned to everybody's satisfaction, with the telephones in, and the plumbing complete – the heating system and the electric iceboxes all functioning perfectly, all furnished with linen and silver – and with the rent prepaid. The United Nations has not yet produced such a comfortable dwelling place. But we have achieved a very practical expression of a common purpose on the part of four great nations that are now united to wage this war, that they embark together after the war on a greater and more difficult enterprise, an enterprise of waging peace. We will embark on it with all the peace-loving nations of the world—large and small.*

The challenge of waging peace has been daunting. The "structure of peace" President Roosevelt envisioned remains unfinished. While the United Nations continues to champion conflict prevention, the list of global challenges has grown. From climate change to pandemics, the United Nations and its specialized agencies are immersed in the issues of the day.

The United Nations Climate Summit, the twenty-sixth Conference of the Parties (COP26) held in Glasgow, Scotland in November 2021 was not just another UN mega-conference. Under the presidency of the United Kingdom in

Photograph of President Franklin D. Roosevelt and FPA President Major General Frank R. McCoy during President Roosevelt's 1944 address to the Foreign Policy Association at The Waldorf Astoria in New York City. (Photo by George Skadding/The LIFE Picture Collection/Getty Images)

partnership with Italy, COP26 has succeeded in obtaining net-zero commitments from governments covering four-fifths of global emissions. In addition to ambitious climate policies by governments, the private sector, including financial services, has embarked on aggressive climate actions. The prospects for public/private collaborations coming out of COP26 are encouraging.

Less encouraging is the global governance on immunization against Covid-19. Robert D. Hormats has aptly characterized the global Covid-19 pandemic as World War III:

> *It was not what strategists had imagined decades ago. No nuclear weapons. No missiles or destructive cyber technology. But massively lethal and devastating to economies and the lives of hundreds of millions of people, nonetheless. And countries are not fighting one another but a small, unseen and unpredictable virus that poses a threat to virtually all nations regardless of the nature of their governments or political philosophies.*

The rapid development of vaccines for Covid-19 is a remarkable accomplishment. A full-court press should be mounted to immunize the planet's 7.8 billion people. We have the compelling precedent of the eradication of smallpox when global cooperation prevails. Morality and self-interest are conflated in such initiatives. Likewise, overcoming the Covid-19 pandemic and meeting the pressing challenges of climate change are in the interest of every nation.

Global cooperation will become more compelling over time as new technologies and transnational issues dominate national agendas. Such cooperation gives credence to what the anthropologist Robert Boyd describes as "cumulative cultural evolution." Boyd argues: "We humans would not be an exceptional species if we did not adapt culturally." Among our most important cultural traits is the ability to cooperate across diverse backgrounds. From what we know of human fallibility, there has never been a greater need for intensive and continuous cooperation than in the nuclear age. An inadvertent action could set off a train of events that could destroy civilization as we know it. A culture of global cooperation for peace and conflict prevention is our best hope.

Cumulative cultural evolution teaches us that challenging situations are resolved by leadership. And that our common humanity and the triumph of the human spirit over adversity are what bind us on this small, fragile planet.

At FPA, we are inspired by this vision. Our mission is anchored in the enduring value of inclusion. Never has it been more important for Americans from all walks of life to be knowledgeable about world affairs. Speaking to FPA members, David Skorton, Secretary of the Smithsonian Institution, observed: "We cannot begin to navigate the global economy without understanding world events."

In this our one hundred and fourth year, FPA, notwithstanding the pandemic, is committed to a process of renewal. FPA's programming is on the record and available to all. Indeed, FPA's mission is one in furtherance of access and transparency, a mission of imagination and voice. Through balanced, nonpartisan outreach initiatives, such as Great Decisions, FPA encourages the public to participate in the foreign policy process. Throughout its long and honorable history, FPA has served as a catalyst for developing awareness of and informed opinion on global issues. Hence FPA's motto, "An informed public is an engaged public."

Millions of Americans have engaged with FPA through the years to seek a more profound understanding of global challenges; to gather the facts that underpin effective policies. The purpose bringing us together has not been to impose a particular view but to consider and weigh many views.

At the heart of this citizen effort lies the conviction that America must continue to frame its policies by the processes of democracy. At FPA, we do not believe that global challenges are too complex for the public to understand when clearly briefed. Not to a limited circle, therefore, but to all, FPA extends an invitation to join an open dialogue on our collective future in an interdependent world.

Noel V. Lateef
President and Chief Executive Officer
Foreign Policy Association

Changing demographics in the world
by Joseph Chamie

Lagos residents, despite social distancing order, cluster at Oke-Odo Market, Lagos Nigeria on March 30, 2020, for last minute shopping. According to some projections, by 2100 Nigeria could have one of the largest populations on earth. (ADEKUNLE AJAYI/NURPHOTO/GETTY IMAGES)

The world experienced extraordinary demographic changes during the 20th century that are continuing to play out through the 21st century. In addition to unprecedented rapid rates of growth, the population of the world and virtually every country's population went through remarkable transformations in the three key demographic components, i.e., mortality, fertility, and migration, as well as major changes in their distributions across regions and within countries.

The demographic transformations and changes, which are continuing across the planet, have resulted in significant and far reaching social, economic, political, environmental and climate consequences for nations in every region of the world. Those consequences are in turn creating mounting critical challenges to demographic well-being, development efforts, international relations, security, climate, the environment and the sustainability of human populations.

To effectively consider likely future population trends and challenges, it is useful to examine past demographic trends particularly the unprecedented changes that took place during the 20th century. An understanding of population trends of the recent past, including the extraordinary changes in the key demographic components, provides instructive insights

JOSEPH CHAMIE *is a consulting demographer, a former director of the United Nations Population Division, who worked at the UN on population issues for more than a quarter century. He has written numerous population studies for the United Nations – as well as under his own name – on growth, fertility, mortality, estimates and projections, international migration and population and development policy.*

that can help guide sound policymaking, equitable socio-economic development, and environmental concerns, including addressing the devastating consequences of climate change.

WORLD POPULATION GROWTH

For most of human history, the world's population grew very slowly. By the close of the 15th century, for example, world population had increased to about a half a billion. The one billion milestone for world population was reached around the start of the 19th century (Table 1).

The reason for the slow growth of world population up to the one billion mark was due to high mortality rates largely the result of famine, disease, and war. Daily life was harsh, difficult, and limited for virtually all men, women, and children; the only exceptions were the wealthy and powerful few. Infant mortality and child deaths were common, maternal mortality was high, and few people reached the old age of 60 years.

While it took thousands of years for world population to reach one billion in 1804, the two billion mark was reached in 1927, approximately 123 years later. After that demographic milestone, the growth of world population accelerated (Figure 1). It took 33 additional years for world population to reach three billion in 1960 and another 14 years to reach the four-billion mark. The most rapid growth for world population to gain a billion people was from five billion in 1987 to six billion in 1998, a record-breaking span of only 11 years. In 2021, world population has grown to 7.9 billion and is expected to reach 8 billion by 2023.

During the 20th century, the world's population grew at a record-breaking pace, nearly quadrupling in size from 1.6 billion to 6.1 billion. The large part of this growth—some 80%—occurred during the second half of the 20th century.

In addition, the world's most rapid rate of population growth and largest annual increase also occurred during the second half of the 20th century. The global growth rate peaked at around 2% in the late 1960s and by the century's end had declined to about 1.3%. The peak annual increase in world population occurred in the late 1980s with the addition of approximately 93 million. Today the annual increase to world population is about 80 million.

Although its growth rate and annual increase are on the decline, world population is expected to continue growing throughout the 21st century. According to the United Nations' medium variant projection, world population is expected to add nearly 5 billion more people during the current century, reaching close to 11 billion in 2100.

The population projection variants show a wide range of possible population outcomes by the end of the 21st century. The constant variant, which assumes the current fertility rates of countries remain unchanged, has world population nearly tripling to close to 22 billion by 2100. If national fertility rates fall faster than assumed in me-

TABLE 1

Past and Projected World Population

Population	Year	Years to add one billion
1 billion	1804	from the dawn of humanity
2 billion	1927	123 years later
3 billion	1960	33 years later
4 billion	1974	14 years later
5 billion	1987	13 years later
6 billion	1998	11 years later
7 billion	2011	13 years later
8 billion	2023	12 years later
9 billion	2037	14 years later
10 billion	2056	19 years later

SOURCE: UNITED NATIONS

Before you read, download the companion **Glossary** that includes definitions, a guide to acronyms and abbreviations used in the article, and other material. Go to **www.fpa.org/great_decisions** and select a topic in the Resources section. (Top right)

FIGURE 1

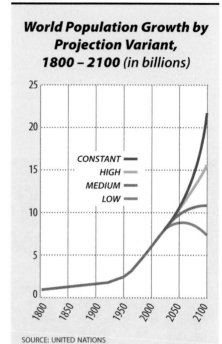

World Population Growth by Projection Variant, 1800 – 2100 (in billions)

CONSTANT
HIGH
MEDIUM
LOW

SOURCE: UNITED NATIONS

dium projection variant, world population by the end of the century would be slightly more than 7 billion, or approximately a half billion less than today. Alternatively, if country fertility rates remain slightly higher than assumed in the medium projection variant, world population by 2100 would be nearly 16 billion, or about double the size of today's world population.

DISTRIBUTION

In addition to the unprecedented rapid rate of world population growth during the past century, world population's distribution across the planet has changed markedly. Besides notable demographic changes at the regional and national levels, the distributions of populations within countries have also been transformed.

During the 20th century the relative demographic standing of Europe changed significantly. Whereas Europe represented about one-quarter of the world's population in 1900, its percentage declined to about 12% by the close of the 20th century. Today Europe's population of 748 million is slightly less than 10% of the world's population and is projected to decline to 712 million by 2050, or 7% of world population (Table 2).

Of the nearly 3 billion increase in world population expected by the close of the century, most of it, 2.9 billion or 97%, will take place in Africa. Africa is followed by Northern America, which increases by 120 million, or 4% of the projected increase. Europe's population, in contrast, is projected to decrease by 118 million, or a decline of 4%, over the next eight decades (Figure 2.)

Close to 50 European countries are expected to experience population decline over the next three decades. Among those countries whose populations are expected to decline by 10% or more are: Ukraine (19%), Hungary (12%), Poland (12%) and Italy (10%).

In contrast to Europe, the world's five other major regions experienced rapid growth during the 20th century that is continuing but at a slower pace in the 21st century. The populations of Africa and Latin America and the Caribbean increased six-fold and seven-fold, respectively, during the past century. Also, the populations of Asia, Northern America and Oceania increased approximately four-fold in the 20th century.

Particularly noteworthy is the growth of Africa's population, which increased from 8% of the world's population in 1900 to 17% today. That rapid demographic growth is expected to continue, with Africa's population projected to increase five-fold during the 21st century, reaching 4.3 billion or nearly 40% of the world's population by the close of the current century.

The future rapid growth of Africa is most evident in a dozen countries whose populations are expected to increase by more than 100% by mid-century. Especially rapid population growth is projected for Niger (161%), Angola (128%), Democratic Republic of the Congo (111%) and Tanzania (110%).

Nearly all the world's annual population growth by 2050—about 97%—is taking place in developing countries. By far, the developing country contributing most to world population growth during the next three decades is India at 17%. The next six contributing countries are: Nigeria (7%), China

(6%), Pakistan (5%), and Ethiopia, Indonesia, and Democratic Republic of Congo (all about 4%).

Among developed countries, the top contributing country to world population growth over the coming three decades is the United States at slightly more than 2%. After the U.S., and at considerably lower levels, the next five developed countries contributing to world population growth are: Canada (0.4%), United Kingdom (0.4%) Australia (0.4%), France (0.2%) and Germany (0.2%).

The population ranking of countries has changed remarkably during the past century and is expected to continue changing in the coming decades. In 1950 six of the ten most populous countries in the world were more developed countries, i.e., the United States, Russia, Japan, Germany, the United Kingdom, and Italy. By 2021 only the United States and Russia remain among the top ten.

Moreover, according to the United Nations medium variant population projection, the only more developed country among the top ten most populous by the end of the century is expected to be the United States in fourth place behind India, China, and Nigeria. However, according to the constant variant population projection, which assumes current fertility rates remain unchanged for the remainder

TABLE 2

World Population by Region and Percentage, 1900 – 2100

Population (in millions)

	1900	1950	2000	2021	2050	2100
WORLD	1,650	2,536	6,143	7,875	9,735	10,875
AFRICA	133	228	811	1,373	2,448	4,280
ASIA	947	1,405	3,741	4,680	5,285	4,720
EUROPE	408	549	726	748	712	630
LATIN AMERICA AND CARRIBEAN	74	169	522	660	761	680
NORTHERN AMERICA	82	173	312	371	424	491
OCEANA	6	13	31	43	57	75

Percent Distribution

	1900	1950	2000	2021	2050	2100
AFRICA	8.1%	9.0%	13.2%	17.4%	25.1%	39.4%
ASIA	57.4%	55.4%	60.9%	59.4%	54.3%	43.4%
EUROPE	24.7%	21.7%	11.8%	9.5%	7.3%	5.8%
LATIN AMERICA AND CARRIBEAN	4.5%	6.7%	8.5%	8.4%	7.8%	6.3%
NORTHERN AMERICA	5.0%	6.8%	5.1%	4.7%	4.4%	4.5%
OCEANA	0.4%	0.5%	0.5%	0.5%	0.6%	0.7%

SOURCE: UNITED NATIONS

FIGURE 2

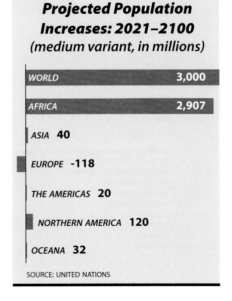

Projected Population Increases: 2021–2100
(medium variant, in millions)

WORLD	3,000
AFRICA	2,907
ASIA	40
EUROPE	-118
THE AMERICAS	20
NORTHERN AMERICA	120
OCEANA	32

SOURCE: UNITED NATIONS

of the century, not a single more developed country remains among the top ten most populous. In addition, in 2100 according to the constant projection variant, Nigeria's population at 2.3 billion takes the number one position, followed by India at 2.0 billion, Democratic Republic of the Congo at 1.6 billion and China at 1 billion. (Figure 3).

The distribution of the world's population has also changed markedly within countries. Prior to modern times populations largely lived in rural areas. At the start of the 20th century, for example, a minority of the world's population, 15%, lived in urban areas. That proportion doubled to 30% by 1950 and reached 47% at the century's close. Today most of the world's population, 56%, are urban dwellers and that proportion is projected to reach 60% by the end of the current decade.

In addition to urbanization, another striking demographic change that occurred within countries is the emergence of mega-cities, which are agglomerations of 10 million or more inhabitants. In 1950, there were two cities in this category: New York and Tokyo with 12 million and 11 inhabitants, respectively. Today there are 35 mega-cities and most of them, ap-

proximately 80%, are in less developed regions.

The world's largest mega-city is Tokyo with 37 million inhabitants, followed by Delhi with 30 million, Shanghai with 27 million, São Paulo and Mexico City with 22 million, Dhaka and Cairo with 21 million, and Beijing and Mumbai with 20 million. The number of mega-cities is expected to continue increasing, reaching 48 by 2035, with virtually all the increase taking place in less developed regions.

MORTALITY

Perhaps the most welcomed demographic change in world population during the recent past is the decline in mortality levels, including infant, child, and maternal death rates. The decline in mortality rates across every age group has resulted in increased life expectancies for men, women, and children throughout the world.

During the past 70 years, for example, the global infant mortality rate fell from approximately 140 to 40 infant deaths per 1,000 live births. Average life expectancy at birth for the world increased by 28 years, from 45 to 73 years.

Prior to the outbreak of the coronavirus pandemic, the improvements in

mortality levels were projected to continue throughout the 21st century, with world population's average life expectancy at birth projected to reach 77 years by 2050 and nearly 82 years by 2100. Some of the countries expected to have the highest life expectancy at birth of 88 years by midcentury are Italy, Japan, Singapore, Spain, and Switzerland.

Despite the impressive reductions in mortality rates, many countries, particularly those in sub-Saharan Africa, are lagging behind. The impact of diseases, epidemics and low levels of socio-economic development have resulted in life expectancies at birth of many African countries falling well below the world average of 73 years. For example, ten African countries, including Nigeria, Somalia, and South Sudan, have life expectancies at birth less than 60 years, the world average achieved a half century ago.

Before the arrival of the coronavirus pandemic, the five top causes of death were ischemic heart disease (16% of all deaths), stroke (11%), chronic obstructive lung disease (6%), lower respiratory infections (5%) and neonatal conditions (4%). Although the available data on mortality in 2020 are preliminary and believed to be seriously undercounted, the human toll due to the coronavirus pandemic has been substantial and has no doubt reduced life expectancies.

Since the beginning of 2020, Covid-19 has killed close to 5 million people worldwide, including more than 650 thousand in the United States; more than 580 thousand in Brazil; and close to 450,000 in India. Based on official reported statistics, Covid-19 has become the fourth leading cause of death globally, accounting for just under 1 in 20 deaths worldwide since the start of 2020.

However, recent estimates suggest that the total number of deaths could be more than twice as large as reported globally and many times greater than reported in some countries. Considering unreported deaths, the Covid-19 death toll could become the world's third leading cause of death after heart disease and stroke.

FIGURE 3

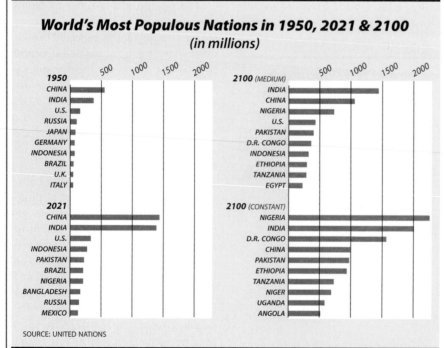

World's Most Populous Nations in 1950, 2021 & 2100
(in millions)

SOURCE: UNITED NATIONS

According to official statistics, Covid-19 was the leading cause of death in some countries, including France, Spain, and England. Also, when adjusted for undercounting, Covid-19 jumps from the second leading cause to the leading cause of death in some countries, such as Iran, Italy, and the United States.

Data for several hard-hit countries indicate that life expectancy at birth has declined because of the pandemic. In the United States, for the first half of 2020, life expectancy at birth declined by 1.2 years for males and 0.9 years for females.

Importantly, noteworthy differences in life expectancy declines were also observed across major U.S. socio-economic groups. The largest decline in life expectancy at birth was 3 years for non-Hispanic Black males and the smallest was 0.7 years for non-Hispanic white females.

Among the troubling concerns about the coronavirus pandemic in the near term is the emergence of more contagious and possibly more lethal variants of the coronavirus, which are challenging the effectiveness of current vaccines. For example, the Delta variant can generate roughly 1,000 times the viral load of its coronavirus predecessor and is undercutting the efforts of many countries to control its spread, with some worrying that vaccines may not be enough to stop the pandemic's spread.

Also, another unknown is the possibility for lingering consequences from Covid 19. Several variants of the SARS-CoV-2 coronavirus first detected in China have already been reported in Brazil, South Africa, the United Kingdom, and the United States.

Another major concern is the formidable challenge of ensuring global availability and access to Covid-19 vaccines. While more than three billion doses of vaccines had been administered by the middle of 2021, most of them have been in high-income countries. Also, the protections and immunity offered by current vaccines are increasingly believed to wane over time, consequently requiring a booster

Crowded wholesale market amid Covid-19 emergency in Kolkata, India, July, 14, 2021.
(INDRANIL ADITYA/NURPHOTO/GETTY IMAGES)

vaccine, especially for the elderly and most vulnerable.

Somewhat ironically, the refusal to take the Covid-19 vaccines has emerged as a major public health concern in both developed and developing countries. Based on more than a dozen country surveys, it is estimated that about a fifth of people across the world would refuse to be vaccinated. High levels of vaccine refusal threaten the goal of achieving herd immunity in many countries, resulting in increasing numbers of Covid-19 deaths.

In developing and developed alike, lines of men and women who have lost their employment stretch outside food pantries and distribution centers. Covid-19 has also killed many thousands of breadwinners, which has also contributed to higher levels of food insecurity, which is particularly bleak in Africa.

Numerous aspects of the coronavirus remain unclear, unresolved, and puzzling, including the implications for projection assumptions of mortality rates for the coming decades of the 21st century. One thing, however, appears certain for the second and third years of the pandemic: many more people will likely succumb to the Covid-19 and even more will be forced to deal with the consequences of those deaths and illnesses suffered by family members, friends and colleagues.

FERTILITY

Another remarkable transformation in world population that occurred during the 20th century and is continuing throughout the 21st century is the decline in fertility. For a variety of factors, including lower mortality, urbanization, education, improvements in the status of women, availability of modern contraceptives, delayed childbearing and increased costs of childrearing, global fertility has decreased significantly from an average of about 5 births per woman at mid-20th century to 2.5 births per woman today. According to the United Nations medium variant projection, the global fertility rate will fall below the replacement level near the close of the 21st century.

In 1950 less than a handful of countries had fertility rates below the replacement level of about 2 births per woman. Today approximately 80 countries, representing no less than half of the world's population, report fertility rates below replacement levels. According to the United Nations medium variant projection, by the close of the century, except for about 20 sub-Saharan African countries, all countries are projected to have fertility rates below replacement levels.

Future rebounds in fertility rates cannot be ruled out. However, once fertility rates fall below replacement levels, that trend typically endures. This pattern has been especially evident in the many countries where fertility has recently declined to 1.6 children or less per woman, including Canada, China, Germany, Hungary, Italy, Japan, South Korea, Russia, and the United States.

Aside from a global mortality catastrophe, the future size of the world's population is determined basically by the number of children women bear. If the average number of births per woman remains above the replacement level, as is assumed in the United Nations high and constant fertility projection variants, world population continues to increase. However, if women around the world have less than two births on average, as is assumed in the medium and low fertility projection variants, then world population eventually decreases.

In many of those countries, including Canada, Germany, Japan, Italy and the United Kingdom, fertility rates have remained below the replacement level for decades. As a result, governments are increasingly concerned about demographic decline, population aging, and the social, economic, and cultural consequences of very low fertility, with many adopting a variety of policy measures to encourage higher birth rates.

Nearly two out of three countries with below-replacement fertility, have adopted policies and established programs to raise birthrates, including most recently China with a fertility rate of 1.3 births per woman. In addition to public programs promoting marriage, childbearing, parenting and gender equality, governments try various incentives to raise fertility rates including baby bonuses, family allowances, maternal and paternal leave, tax breaks, flexible employment schedules and family-friendly work environments.

Pronatalist incentives may encourage some couples to have additional children or start families earlier than planned. Such measures by and large tend to be costly, the impact modest at best, and insufficient at raising fertility rates above replacement levels. Powerful forces overwhelm pronatalist policies, especially economic uncertainty related to automation and the decline of good jobs and the high costs of child rearing including higher education.

AGING

While rapid population growth for the world may be the defining feature of the 20th century, the hallmark of the 21st century is likely to be population aging. The consequences of population aging are reverberating across the globe, including challenging the existing world order and impacting virtually every aspect of society, including economic activity, investments, politics, taxation, education, housing, household/family structure, retirement, pensions, and healthcare services.

Due to the declines in fertility as well as mortality, the age structure of world population has aged markedly. For example, the median age of world population has increased by six years over the past seven decades, i.e., from 24 to 30 years. In addition, the elderly proportion aged 80 years or older has tripled over this time period, increasing from about 0.5% to 1.6%.

Throughout much of human history population age structures were comparatively young. In the past century, for example, the percentage of elderly, those aged 65 years and older, averaged around 5%. In striking contrast, the proportion of elderly will more than triple during the 21st century.

Nearly all the G20 countries, which together account for more than 80% of world GDP, 75% of global trade and 60% of world population, are expected to have no less than one-quarter of their populations aged 65 years and older by 2100. And eight of those countries, including China, Germany, Italy, and Japan, are projected to have one-third or more of their population elderly by the close of the century.

As a result of continuing low birth rates and increased longevity, population aging will be even more critical during the 21st century. In many countries, including Germany, Italy, Japan and Spain, the potential support ratio, which is the ratio of the working age population aged 15 to 64 years per one person 65 years or older, is projected to decline to less than two people in the working ages per one elderly person.

Due to the increasing elderly population coupled with the relative decline of workers paying taxes, many countries are confronting difficult choices concerning budgetary allocations, taxation levels and provision of social and health services. To avoid controversial budgetary reforms and unpopular tax increases, some governments are reducing expenditures and entitlements for the elderly and shifting more of the costs for support, care giving and health services to the individual and their families.

Another clear indicator of the unprecedented population aging underway worldwide is the Historic Reversal, or the demographic turning point when children (0 to 14 years) in a population become fewer than its elderly (65 years and older). The Historic Reversal first occurred in 1995 in Italy and today some 30 countries have experienced the Historic Reversal, including Canada, France, Germany, Greece, Japan, Spain, and the United Kingdom. In 2075, and for the first time in human history, the world's population is projected to go through the Historic Reversal with the elderly increasingly outnumbering children (Figure 4).

Housing and households are also

FIGURE 4

World Population of Children and the Elderly, 2000 – 2020

SOURCE: UNITED NATIONS

being affected by population aging. In the past and continuing today in some developing countries, elderly persons generally lived with adult children and grandchildren. With rising levels of urbanization, increasingly neither the elderly nor their adult children are choosing to live together but prefer separate households with proximity.

Population aging is certainly a significant human achievement, the result of smaller family sizes, lower mortality rates and increased longevity. However, this notable achievement comes with both challenges and opportunities for governments, businesses, organizations, and private citizens. Those able to recognize and adjust to the 21st century's demographic transformation of age structures are far more likely to benefit and prosper than those who ignore or dismiss the momentous consequences of population aging.

INTERNATIONAL MIGRATION

International migration has been a continuous and prominent characteristic of human populations and demographic change throughout the ages. During the recent past many millions of men, women, and children have crossed international borders to settle in another country, transforming international migration into a major modern global issue.

Following the Second World War, the number of international migrants grew rapidly during the second half of the 20th century from 77 million in 1960, or 2.1% of the world's population, to 173 million by the close of the twentieth century, 2.8% of the world's population.

In 2020, the number of people residing outside their country of birth reached 281 million, or 3.5% of world popula-

tion, nearly four times the number of migrants in 1960. If the current proportion of international migrants were to remain at its current level, the projected number of international migrants in 2050 would reach 343 million.

Most international migrants, approximately 60%, live in more developed regions. About 30% of international migrants live in Europe, slightly more than a fifth reside in North America, and 3% live in Oceania. Nearly a third of all migrants reside in Asia, with Africa at 10% and Latin America and the Caribbean at 4%.

Half of the world's migrants lived in ten countries. In 2020 the United States hosted the largest number of international migrants at 51 million, Germany had the second largest number at around 13 million each, Saudi Arabia, Russia and the United Kingdom followed with 13, 12 and 9 million, respectively.

People gathered at the Main Square to attend 'S.O.S. For the Border' protest in solidarity with refugees who got stuck or died at Polish-Belarusian border. Krakow, Poland on November 1st, 2021. Protestors demonstrated on All Saints' Day holding green lights and candles, a color that became a signal of help and shelter offered to refugees by locals living near the border. (BEATA ZAWRZEL/NURPHOTO/AP IMAGES)

Hiwot (left) with her baby Tarikua (six months) in a camp for internally displaced people. Tarikua was born in the local hospital that was one of the many buildings destroyed following an armed attack on the town of Ataye, Ethiopia, which destroyed more than 1,500 buildings and killed at least 100 people. Athough the Oromo Liberation Army (OLA), a rebel group that lawmakers designated a terrorist organisation in May 2021, are suspected to be responsible for the attack it is still not clear who was behind it. (PETTERIK WIGGERS/PANOS PICTURES/REDUX)

International migrants come from many sending countries. The top ten sending countries in 2020 accounted for slightly more than one-third of all international migrants. The leading countries of origin of international migrants were India with 18 million, followed by Mexico with 12 million, China with 11 million, Russia with 10 million, and Syria with 8.2 million.

In addition to the rapid growth of international migration, the remittances that migrants send home to assist their families have increased rapidly during the past half century. Annual remittances have increased from several billion U.S. dollars in 1970 to more than 700 billion US dollars today, far exceeding the level of overseas development assistance.

The coronavirus pandemic has largely brought human movement to a halt, an event that has been unprecedented in modern times. In addition to the global restrictions on international travel, billions of people have been negatively affected by the pandemic's far-reaching economic fallout.

Like the rapid increase in the numbers of international migrants, the numbers of refugees worldwide have also grown markedly during the recent past. The global number of refugees and asylum seekers at the end of 2020 was more than 26 million, an increase by approximately 11 million since 2010 and double the level in 2000.

About 21 million refugees are under the mandate of the UN High Commissioner for Refugees (UNHCR), and approximately 6 million Palestine refugees are registered with the UN Relief and Works Agency for Palestine Refugees (UNRWA). By the end of 2020, more than 4 million people were asylum seekers, including 850,000 Venezuelans. In addition to the civil war in Ethiopia that displaced more than a million people, close to five million people fled Venezuela to neighboring countries, the region's biggest exodus in recent history and one of the world's largest displacement crises.

Another major global migration challenge is illegal immigration. Millions of men, women, and children who have slim chances of immigrating legally are risking their lives to reach and settle in another country. While precise figures of migrants unlawfully resident are difficult to establish, the total number worldwide is estimated at no less than 50 million.

Often closely linked to illegal migration are smuggling and human trafficking. Due to the demands for cheap and compliant labor, sexual exploitation, and the low risks and high profits, criminal groups are increasingly involved in smuggling and human trafficking in virtually every region of the world. Growing numbers of men, women, and children are falling victim to deception and mistreatment, including debt bondage, torture, unlawful confinement, sexual abuse and rape, and threats and violence against them, their families, and their friends.

In recent years, international migration flows, especially illegal migration, have seriously challenged the capacities and finances of government authorities and intergovernmental organizations as well as public attitudes toward immigrants. Governments in virtually every region have adopted policies to limit international migration, including restricting levels and composition, reducing refugee flows, rejecting asylum seekers, repatriating those unlawfully resident, and redefining or denying citizenship to certain groups. Attempts by regional and international organizations to encourage acceptance of immigrants and growing numbers of refugees have encountered fierce political resistance, public opposition and nativistic policies.

EQUALITY OF WOMEN

Another noteworthy population trend during the recent past concerns the changes in the role and status of women. During the 20th century, significant social, economic, and political progress was achieved in women's equality.

Progress has been greatly facilitated by improvements in women's health, urbanization, delayed marriage and childbearing, and declines in family size. Among the more developed countries, and increasingly in the urban areas of less developed regions, the traditional stay-at-home mom is being replaced by the working mom. Also, growing numbers of women are seeking higher education, careers, and individual social identity.

At the same time, the powerful demographic changes taking place around the world are exerting pressure on governments to reexamine many of their policies and programs relating to the role and status accorded to women. In some instances, however, especially in African and Asian countries, conservative groups are resisting attempts to achieve gender equality in social, economic, and political spheres of society and are seeking to maintain traditional roles and lifestyles for men and women.

Son preference is one traditional gender belief that is of global concern, especially in the years ahead. With couples increasingly having one child in China and fewer children in India as well as other populous countries, and the growing use of prenatal ultrasound scanning, government authorities are facing difficulties enforcing laws and prohibitions against sex-selective abortion.

The biologically natural sex ratio at birth for human populations is typically around 105 males per 100 females, though it ranges from 103 to 107. Today, five countries with highly skewed sex ratios at birth show the highest numbers of missing girls, with a ratio of 113 males to 100 females in China and Azerbaijan, followed by Vietnam, Armenia, India at about 111 males per 100 females (Figure 14). Over time, those skewed sex ratios at birth produce abnormal gender imbalances in adulthood.

While the cultural belief that the family is incomplete or unbalanced without a son is evident in many parts of the world, this belief is especially widespread and strong in countries of East and South Asia. Among other things, couples desire a son to continue the family name and bloodline, earn money, look after the family, perform ritual functions, and take care of parents in old age. A daughter, in contrast, is often considered a liability as she is perceived as costly to marry off and once married, she is expected to move to her husband's household.

Gender imbalances related to missing girls have serious negative consequences for societies and individuals that are compounded over time. The gender imbalances at birth become especially problematic when children reach adulthood. Because of the relative shortages of marriageable women, growing numbers of men experience loneliness, encounter difficulties in finding wives and feel frustrated and saddened by being unable to establish families.

The progress achieved in women's equality during the 20th century is expected to continue during the 21st century. Worldwide women now outnumber men in both university attendance and graduation. Growing numbers of women are seeking higher education, employment, political office, and social identity. In addition, more women are entering professions that were traditionally the domain of men.

Although women's educational attainment exceeds that of men in most countries, women remain behind men in such areas as income, business ownership, research, and politics. Different fields of study and vocational training chosen by women and men may explain some disparities. However, the persistence of the female disadvantage suggests that societal expectations and cultural norms on the appropriate roles for women and men are limiting the achievement of gender equality.

Also, women continue to stay at home more than men. Across countries, even in those that actively promote the equality of the sexes, the labor force participation rates of women, while substantially higher than in the past, remain below those of men. Among OECD countries the average labor participation rates of women and men are 64% and 80%, respectively.

A leading factor influencing gender differences in labor participation involves childbearing and child rearing. By and large, a substantial proportion of mothers withdraw from formal employment after childbirth. In Germany and the United Kingdom, for example, one in four women leave the labor force following the birth of a child. In addition, the responsibilities for childrearing increase the levels of part-time work among mothers.

Gender differences in time devoted to unpaid care work also impact women's employment. In every region, women spend more than twice as much time than men on housework and family care. In addition to raising children and providing unpaid household work, caregiving responsibilities for the elderly, ill or needy family members typically fall on women's shoulders.

FAMILY COMPOSITION AND HOUSEHOLDS

The family consisting of a working father, stay-at-home mom, several children, and marriage "until death do us part" appears no longer to be the societal norm in many countries, especially more developed nations. In many countries, being married has become less of a necessity for financial survival, social interaction, and personal fulfillment.

Single-parent households have also increased markedly during the past several decades. In some regions such as Latin America, the proportions of births outside marriage are estimated at more than 60%. Also, in many European countries, most births occur outside marriage, with government assistance typically provided to single parents. Today, about 14% of the world's 2.3 billion children reside in a single-parent household, most often with only a mother.

A related global transformation in living arrangements with far-reaching consequences is the rise of one-person households, which increased rapidly during the 20th century, accelerating after 1950, especially among the more developed countries. Of the world's 2 billion households, about 15%—or 300 million—are estimated to be one-person households.

The proportion of people who live alone has grown steadily over the recent past. Since the 1960s, for example, one-person households in many countries have increased substantially. In many European countries, as well as in Australia, Canada, China, Japan, South Korea and the United States, the proportion of one-person households has more than doubled (Figure 15).

The highest rates of one-person households occur in Europe. Among European countries one-person households of 40% or more are reported in Denmark, Finland, Germany, Norway, and Sweden. Other European countries with high rates of one-person households include Austria (37%), Switzerland (37%) Netherlands (36%), France (35%) and Italy (33%). Moderately high levels of one-person households are also observed in countries outside Europe, such as Japan (32%), the United States (28%), Canada (28%), South Korea (27%), Australia (24%) and New Zealand (24%).

Developing countries generally have lower proportions of one-person households than developed countries. Some of the lowest rates of one-person households – less than 10%—are observed in China, India, Indonesia, Iran, Mexico, the Philippines, and Vietnam.

One-person households offer opportunities for men and women wishing to have privacy, solitude, introspection, and personal lifestyle choices. However, growing numbers of one-person households also pose challenges to the social and economic development of

TABLE 3

Major Population Trends in the 21st Century

1. Larger world population, billions added during 21st century
2. Future growth concentrated in less developed countries
3. Population declines in many countries by midcentury
4. Increased urbanization and larger cities
5. Lower mortality, higher life expectancies, with emerging risks
6. Lower fertility with below replacement level in many countries
7. Population aging and increased longevity
8. Increased international migration
9. Progress in women's equality
10. Changing family composition and household structure

urban centers and rural areas and the capacities of governments to provide services and care to those living alone, especially the elderly.

Also, the growth of one-person households has various societal and normative implications, including the well-being of the individuals residing on their own. One-person households tend to be more vulnerable and therefore potentially more costly to society than those having a partner or companion. With a single and often limited source of income, one-person households are more precarious with lower median household incomes and generally face more difficulties when dealing with unemployment, injury, illness, adversity, disability, social isolation, and loneliness.

In addition, the increase in one-person households has government policy implications. One-person households often mean smaller savings for retirement and therefore potentially greater financial aid and assistance needed for the elderly in the future.

CONCLUSIONS

The momentous demographic changes in the world's population that occurred in the 20th century and are continuing throughout the 21st century pose social, economic, political, environmental, and climate challenges and disquieting implications for the world's future. While many demographic changes are expected in the many countries across the globe, ten major world population changes in the coming decades stand out and should be highlighted (Table 3).

In brief, world population is expected to be adding billions more people during the remainder of the 21st century, with most of this future demographic growth concentrated in the growing urban areas of less developed countries. As noted earlier, population growth rates have declined relatively rapidly in virtually all regions of the world except sub-Saharan Africa. It is the last major region to go through the demographic transition from high rates of mortality and fertility to comparatively low rates.

Over the next three decades, African countries will contribute about 60% of world population growth of nearly 2 billion people, followed by Asian nations that will contribute about one-third of the world's growth. Some two dozen African countries are expected to have their current populations double by around midcentury. Increased efforts and assistance will be needed to expedite the demographic transition to low death and birth rates among sub-Saharan African countries.

At the same time of this rapid growth among sub-Saharan African countries, many other countries will be experiencing population decline due to fertility rates remaining below the replacement level and facing significantly older population age structures and increased longevity due to declining mortality rates. Also, migration, both legal and illegal, is expected to increase from the poorer less developed countries to the wealthier more developed countries. In addition, progress is expected in women's equality as well as significant changes in family composition and the structure of households.

It is widely recognized that the world's increased urbanization offers a large variety of social, economic, and cultural benefits, opportunities, and freedoms. In addition to employment and career development, urban residents have ready access to education, health care, social services, cultural institutions, recreation, information, and government agencies. However, urbanization places stresses on social services, infrastructure and the physical environment that can make urban living difficult, especially for low-income groups in developing countries.

More recently, many large cities are facing the devastating effects of climate change. In addition to flooding, rising sea levels, droughts, wildfires, and higher temperatures, many cities, especially those in Bangladesh, China, India, Indonesia, and Pakistan, are now confronting serious air pollution. In addition to the increased risks of morbidity and mortality, ambient air pollution has enormous economic and social costs, particularly for cities in low- and middle-income countries.

The coronavirus pandemic has also greatly impacted the demography of the world's population and sensitized global leaders to emerging health threats from contagious viruses and diseases. Preliminary data and trends point to a continuation of the pandemic's serious consequences on mortality, morbidity, fertility, and migration for the near future. Although long-term projections point to improvements in mortality levels in the coming decades, the coronavirus has certainly limited those improvements at least for the near term and will certainly require a rethinking of assumptions regarding mortality rates during the 21st century.

The failure to adequately meet the basic needs and aspirations of the world's growing population is having serious consequences, particularly in the less developed countries. In addition to rising poverty levels, shortages of water, food, and energy, and worsening environmental conditions, the serious consequences include social unrest, political instability, civil violence, and armed conflict.

Those consequences will not remain confined within national borders but will spill over into neighboring countries as well as distant regions. Among the likely repercussions are calls for increased development assistance, requests for emergency and humanitarian relief aid, rising numbers of internally displaced persons and asylum seekers, and substantially more men, women, and children seeking to migrate to wealthier nations by both legal and illegal means.

A variety of views have been offered regarding the major population trends expected in the 21st century. For example, it is widely acknowledged that slower population growth provides countries with more time to adjust to future population increases. This in turn increases the ability and prospects of those countries to improve the quality of life of their citizens and foster economic growth and development, while at the same time safeguarding the environment, natural resources, and the climate. In other words, slowing down rapid population growth would make it considerably easier for countries to build the foundations for future sustainable development.

Recognizing the benefits of slower rates of population growth, the 1994 United Nations International Conference on Population and Development recommended "... to facilitate the demographic transition as soon as possible in countries where there is an imbalance between demographic rates and social, economic and environmental goals, while fully respecting human rights."

However, others are concerned about the consequences of population declines and population aging for economic growth, the labor force, retirement, social security, and health-care systems. They would like to see a growing popu-

Nursing students show baby care skills during a capping ceremony on May 10, 2021, in Jinan, Shandong Province of China. (ZHANG YONG/CHINA NEWS SERVICE/GETTY IMAGES)

lation and labor force with fertility rates above the replacement level.

And still others view below replacement fertility and ensuing population decline as positive demographic changes resulting in numerous benefits, especially the conservation of resources and reduced stresses on the environment and climate. They see the growth of human populations seriously impacting earth's environment and contributing to climate change, which in turn are seriously imperiling human sustainability on the planet.

Thousands of scientists have unequivocally declared that the planet Earth is facing a climate emergency and continuing to experience serious environmental issues, including biodiversity loss, deforestation, drought, ecological degradation, natural resource depletion, crop yields, food production, pollution, and congestion. In particular, global warming is making things worse, with rising temperatures drying out soils and depleting mountain snowpack that normally supply water during the spring and summer.

A recently released landmark report on the hazards of climate change by the Intergovernmental Panel on Climate Change (IPCC) has predicted a devastating future for human populations. An essential part of efforts to address the many environmental and climate issues, according to the report is a rapid as possible transition to world population stabilization.

Finally, it is important to recognize the unprecedented growth of world population – the most rapid in human history—that tripled world population since the mid 20th century, adding nearly 5.5 billion more people. That extraordinary demographic growth continues to pose serious challenges for humanity.

The recent declines in world population growth provide some indication of future demographic stabilization or peaking, perhaps as early as the close of the 21st century. At that time, would population is projected to be nearly 11 billion by 2100, which is 3 billion more than today or nearly seven times as many people as were living on the planet at the start of the 20th century.

Demographic trends, particularly population growth, aging, urbanization, and international migration, are contributing to the many challenges facing humanity, including food production, water shortages, poverty, undernourishment, increased mortality, climate change, environmental degradation, reduced biodiversity. human rights, civil unrest, displacement, and armed conflict. Understanding and anticipating the consequences of those powerful demographic megatrends could stave off security, economic, social, and political crises and promote the development and wellbeing of countries worldwide.

(Additional charts for this topic can be accessed through the online glossary.)

discussion questions

1. What is more concerning, the boom in population growth and the negative impact this has on quality of life, or population decline and the negative impacts this has on the labor force, retirement, social security etc.?

2. How can developed countries such as the United States help combat the Covid-19 pandemic in other parts of the world?

3. How has the Covid-19 pandemic impacted some communities differently than others? What can be done to counter this?

4. Some countries have implemented pro-natalist campaigns to boost declining fertility levels. Should the government be involved with population control in this way?

5. International migration has increased over the past decades. How will this phenomenon impact the demographics in the United States? What are the potential benefits and consequences?

suggested readings

Harper, Sarah. *How Population Change Will Transform Our World.* Oxford University Press. 272 pgs. April 2019. Our next generations face challenges, especially women in poorer parts of the world; young people trying to find work in full labor markets; and governments balancing the needs of local and immigrant populations. But the future is not all bleak. Sarah Harper describes the opportunities open to us, and the important transformation our societies will need to make to grasp them.

Mackenzie, Debora. *COVID-19: The Pandemic That Never Should Have Happened and How to Stop the Next One.* Hachette Books. 304 pgs. July 2020. No one has yet brought together our knowledge of Covid-19 in a comprehensive, informative, and accessible way. But that story can already be told, and Debora MacKenzie's urgent telling is required reading for these times and beyond. It is too early to say where the Covid-19 pandemic will go, but it is past time to talk about what went wrong but rather how we can do better.

Winter, Jay and Teitelbaum, Michael. *The Global Spread of Fertility Decline: Population, Fear, and Uncertainty.* Yale University Press. 344 pgs. June 2013. This eye-opening book looks at demographic trends in Europe, North America, and Asia—areas that now have low fertility rates—and argues that there is an essential yet often neglected political dimension to a full assessment of these trends. Political decisions that promote or discourage marriage and child-bearing, facilitate or discourage contraception and abortion, and stimulate or restrain immigration all have played significant roles in recent trends.

Collier, Paul. *Exodus: How Migration Is Changing Our World.* Oxford University Press. 320 pgs. May 2015. In *Exodus,* Paul Collier, the world-renowned economist and bestselling author of *The Bottom Billion,* clearly and concisely lays out the effects of encouraging or restricting migration. Drawing on original research and case studies, he explores this volatile issue from three perspectives: that of the migrants themselves, that of the people they leave behind, and that of the host societies where they relocate.

Hartmann, Betsy. *Reproductive Rights and Wrongs: The Global Politics of Population Control.* Haymarket Books. 488 pgs. December 2016. Threaded throughout *Reproductive Rights and Wrongs* is the story of how international women's health activists fought to reform population control and promote a new agenda of sexual and reproductive health and rights for all people. While their efforts bore fruit, many obstacles remain.

United Nations (2019) "World Population Prospects: 2019." United Nations, Population Division. New York, NY.
(Report Highlights: https://population.un.org/wpp/Publications/Files/WPP2019_Highlights.pdf)
(Estimates & Projections: https://population.un.org/wpp/Download/Standard/Population/)

Don't forget to vote!

Download a copy of the ballot questions from the Resources page at www.fpa.org/great_decisions

To access web links to these readings, as well as links to additional, shorter readings and suggested web sites,
GO TO www.fpa.org/great_decisions
and click on the topic under Resources, on the right-hand side of the page.

Outer space policy
by Eric Berger

Technical personnel at the Beijing Aerospace Control Center celebrate after China's Tianwen-1 probe successfully landed on Mars, May 15, 2021. (XINHUA/JIN LIWANG/GETTY IMAGES)

The space domain has changed rapidly during the first two decades of the 21st century, with the rise of new national powers and the entry of commercial companies shaking up what had long been a static environment. China has begun accomplishing novel feats in space such as landing a rover on the far side of the Moon, and a private U.S. company, Space Exploration Technologies, built the world's largest rocket with its own funding, and now operates more satellites than any other country or company in the world. In this new era, China and SpaceX are but the exemplars of a range of new actors creating new opportunities and threats in space. Whereas the 20th century saw the dawn of the space age, the 21st century should see its maturity.

The launch of Sputnik 1 in October 1957 marked the beginning of the space era, with the first artificial satellite.

This set off a furious race between the two superpowers of the postwar era, the Soviet Union and the United States. The Soviets racked up a string of firsts, including launching the first human, Yuri Gagarin, into orbit in April 1961. The United States eventually pulled ahead with the Apollo

ERIC BERGER *is the senior space editor at Ars Technica, covering everything from astronomy, to private space, to wonky NASA policy. He is also the author of the book Lift-off, about the rise of SpaceX. Eric has an astronomy degree from the University of Texas and a master's in journalism from the University of Missouri. He previously worked at the Houston Chronicle for 17 years, where the paper was a Pulitzer Prize finalist in 2009 for his coverage of Hurricane Ike. A certified meteorologist, Eric founded Space City Weather and lives in Houston.*

In this undated file photo, Soviet cosmonaut Major Yuri Gagarin, first man to orbit the earth, is shown in his space suit. The successful one-orbit flight on April 12, 1961, made the 27-year-old Gagarin a national hero and cemented Soviet supremacy in space until the United States put a man on the moon more than eight years later. (AP IMAGES)

Program, landing Neal Armstrong and Buzz Aldrin on the Moon in July 1969. This decade represented a period of tumultuous activity in space. NASA, for example, built three crewed vehicles—Mercury, Gemini, and Apollo—in less than a decade. In the more than 50 years since, NASA has developed and flown just a single human spacecraft since, the space shuttle. The Soviet program, the remnants of which are now operated by Russia, has been even more stagnant. The Soyuz crew spacecraft first flew in 1967, and it remains the backbone of the Russian space program today.

Geopolitical tensions drove the period of frenetic activity during the 1960s. In response to Soviet achievements, the United States sought to demonstrate the technological superiority of a free and open democracy. U.S. political leaders had good reason to worry. Even among U.S. allies, in 1960, there were

serious doubts about American leadership in science and technology. In 1960 the Gallup Organization asked people around the world whether the Soviets or Americans would lead in the field of science a decade later. Citizens in Great Britain, France, India, and elsewhere voted by about three-to-one in favor of the Soviets. Thus the Apollo Program is best seen as a successful geopolitical effort. By the 1970s, the U.S. space agency found itself increasingly less central to the strategic interests of the nation. Its funding was slashed from 4.5% of the total federal budget in the late 1960s to less than 1% five years later.

The three decades from 1981 to 2011 witnessed two basic trends in space exploration. With its space shuttle, NASA's human spaceflight program focused on low-Earth orbit. And with the International Space Station, NASA became a tool not of geopolitical competition, but of cooperation. The United States, Russia, and about a dozen other nations joined together to build a massive orbiting laboratory that remains both an engineering and diplomatic marvel.

During this period NASA did interesting things. It launched the Hubble Space Telescope that revealed the majesty of the universe, and it built and flew a succession of increasingly sophisticated probes to explore the Solar System, venturing to the gas giants, Pluto, and beyond. But the basic pattern remained: NASA led the world in space exploration, Russia sought to maintain its position, and with repetitive missions of the space shuttle and Soyuz vehicles, human space exploration remained in something of a rut.

Other nations first began to make inroads into the U.S.-Soviet hegemony during this timeframe. Until 1990 there were typically more than 100 orbital launches a year, with all but a handful conducted by the United States and the Soviet Union. After that time, however, the European Space Agency, China, India, and Japan started to launch rockets more often. Europe, with its Ariane 4 rocket, became the first provider of commercial launch services. If a company or country had a satellite and enough money, Europe would launch it into orbit. Serving both European and international customers, the Ariane 4 would capture about 60% of this commercial launch business as telecommunications companies such as DIRECTV sought to put large satellites into geostationary orbit.

U.S. rocket companies were not competitive during this era. The two main launch providers, Lockheed Martin and Boeing, received large contracts from the U.S. military to develop their Atlas and Delta rockets. Because they had guaranteed revenues from the launch of military communications and spy satellites, Lockheed and Boeing were not nimble enough to compete for commercial satellite launches. As these two companies struggled financially in the early 2000s, the U.S. military stepped in and forced them to merge their launch businesses into a single entity, the United Launch Alliance.

And so by the early 2000s the global space industry was ripe for disruption. The Americans and Russians were no longer particularly innovative in space exploration, and large aerospace com-

Before you read, download the companion **Glossary** that includes definitions, a guide to acronyms and abbreviations used in the article, and other material. Go to **www.fpa.org/great_decisions** and select a topic in the Resources section. (Top right)

panies in the United States had grown so complacent they were no longer competitive with institutional launch providers in Europe and Russia. This provided openings for a multiplicity of emerging nations and commercial space companies to compete with and, in some cases, supersede traditional players in space. This article will first discuss the two biggest change agents who took advantage of this opportunity, China and SpaceX, and the landscape this has wrought for the decade to come.

China

Much as the United States and the Soviet Union had geopolitical aims in the 1960s for space exploration, China has similar goals in seeking to become a space power of the 21st century. The country aspires to project soft power as a leader in civil spaceflight, and hard power through military space activity. In short, China sees space as a means to place itself on equal footing to the United States as the only other superpower in the world.

Before 2003 the country averaged fewer than five orbital launches a year, using space primarily to establish a network of observation and communications satellites. But that year represents a watershed moment for China as the country became only the third nation, after the United States and Russia, to launch a human into space. Since Yang Liwei's 21-hour mission in low-Earth orbit, China has continued to make deliberate progress in space. By 2011, the country had its first short-term space station. A decade later, China launched the core module of a full-fledged space station, named Tiangong, or "Heavenly Palace." Although Tiangong will be smaller than the International Space Station, it will be similar in its modular construction, and perform many of the same functions in terms of scientific research and international relationships. Already, China has invited European astronauts to learn Chinese, and train in Asia for future missions to the Tiangong laboratory.

There are other metrics by which to gauge China's success in space. Notably, its rate of orbital launches has increased by nearly a factor of 10. China now launches as many as 40 rockets annually, and in some years has led all other nations in this measure of spaceflight activity. China also took a major step forward in deep space exploration in 2021, with the soft landing of its Tianwen-1 mission on the surface of Mars. A few days after this landing—only NASA had ever successfully landed a spacecraft on Mars and had it survive for more than a few seconds— the Zhurong rover rolled away from the Chinese lander. The Soviet Union had sent several missions to Mars to attempt soft landings there, and so had the European Space Agency. None were successful. Now came China, on its very first mission to Mars, sending an orbiter to Mars, landing a spacecraft, and deploying a rover as if it were a walk in the park. China's deep space exploration program now trails only that of NASA.

But for all of its success with launches and Mars, China has made its biggest investment in lunar exploration. Both the United States and China see the Moon and its nearby environment, known as cislunar space, as the eighth continent and a potential sphere of contested activity. NASA may have won the race to the Moon in the 1960s, but it has done precious little there since. Both U.S. and Chinese space policy officials understand that the country which goes to the Moon, to stay, will have ultimate bragging rights and influence on the closest body to Earth.

Like many of its space activities, China's lunar program has been deliberate, with each mission building upon the next. The country launched its first lunar probe, Chang'e 1, in 2007. Named after the Chinese Moon goddess, Chang'e 1 orbited the Moon for more than a year, and was followed by another orbiting mission in 2010. Then, in December 2013, the Chang'e 3 spacecraft landed in a large crater on the near side of the Moon and deployed the small Yutu rover. A more ambitious mission, Chang'e 4 landed on the far side of the Moon in January 2019. This marked the first time any nation had ever soft landed on the side of the Moon opposite the Earth, and necessitated a relay spacecraft to send communications between Earth and the lander. More success followed in December 2020 when the Chang'e probe landed on the Moon, scooped up 3.81 pounds of lunar regolith (loose powdery rock and dust that sits on a layer of bedrock), and launched the sample back to Earth. While 3.81 pounds pales in comparison to the 842.17 pounds of Moon rocks

This picture released on January 11, 2019, by the China National Space Administration (CNSA) shows the Yutu-2 moon rover, photographed by the Chang'e-4 lunar probe, on the far side of the moon.

brought back by six Apollo missions, it is nearly eight times as much material as the Soviets returned with from their Luna 24 mission in 1976.

By the end of the 2010s, China had made steady progress across an array of spaceflight activities, from human habitation in low-Earth orbit, to bold robotic missions on the Moon and Mars. While the country remained behind NASA and the United States in key areas, China has firmly established itself as the number two spaceflight power in the world, and its trajectory remains upward. With its authoritarian leadership style, the country can afford to devote large amounts of funding toward spaceflight activities, and make plans that span a decade or longer. By contrast, NASA and other U.S. space actors are constrained by the limitations of annual Congressional budgeting cycles, and a presidency that may change as often as every four years.

China seeks to become an equal to the United States, and one day, to lead.

SpaceX

Around the same time that China launched its first human spaceflight, in 2003, a small company in southern California was struggling through the early phases of building a rocket engine. Internet entrepreneur Elon Musk had founded SpaceX a year earlier with the goal of reducing the cost of access to space. Musk had the grandest of visions. He sought nothing less than to build a fleet of massive rocket ships that could one day allow humans to settle Mars. Musk shared these visions with his earliest employees, who nodded along. They had more pressing problems. No private company had ever built a liquid-fueled orbital rocket before, and Musk's $100 million investment was finite.

Like other U.S. entrepreneurs, Musk had diagnosed the problems with the U.S. launch industry, recognizing the lack of innovation and competitiveness. Lockheed Martin's "state of the art" new rocket, the Atlas V, used engines that were manufactured in Russia. Boeing's Delta rockets used American-made engines, but they were prohibitively expensive for all but the most valuable national defense and NASA launches. With SpaceX, Musk intended to fill this void by providing a rocket manufactured entirely in the United States, at a cost low enough that it could compete for commercial satellite launch contracts with European and Russian providers.

Musk had started out in Silicon Valley, so he imported its ethos to SpaceX, where employees worked long hours and tackled seemingly impossible engineering problems. Unlike traditional aerospace companies, which used linear design methods that required a lot of up-front engineering, SpaceX opted for iterative design. SpaceX engineers and technicians would quickly build and assemble parts, and test them. Often, they failed. But the company learned from these failures and it led to a more rapid development of engines and rockets. Musk also insisted on vertical integra-

SpaceX Starship SN15 with its fins untied and open on May 4th, 2021, in Boca Chica, Texas, after a scrubbed launch attempt. (REGINALD MATHALONE/NURPHOTO/AP IMAGES)

tion wherever possible, to control costs. For example, when confronted with the problem of latches for lockers on the Dragon spacecraft, a SpaceX engineer knew the company would not accept buying the existing $10,000 space-rated latches from an aerospace supplier. He found inspiration from the latch in a bathroom stall at SpaceX's headquarters near Los Angeles, and the company built its own latches.

Thanks to its innovative ideas and approach to spaceflight, SpaceX accelerated like no previous space company after surviving three initial launch failures. In 2010, SpaceX had not even launched the Falcon 9 rocket. By the end of the decade, this booster had launched more times than any other U.S. rocket since the space shuttle, and had actually launched humans into space with the Crew Dragon vehicle. Thanks to this success the company garnered NASA contracts to send cargo to lunar orbit, and even land humans on the Moon. SpaceX no longer is just a potential NASA contractor, as it was a decade ago. Today it is NASA's most important contractor, and on the way to building a relationship that may one day lead to a bonafide humans-to-Mars program.

The success of SpaceX sparked a legion of follow-up companies that cashed in on the appetites of investors for space. During the first decade of the 2000s, there were about 40 privately funded space companies, which had raised about $2 billion from 2000 to 2010. In the second decade of this century, following the first Falcon 9 launch, the number of companies increased by a factor of 10, and the total fundraising reached $20 billion. In documenting this trend, the early-stage venture capital firm Space Angels characterized this past decade as the Entrepreneurial Space Age. "The modern space economy was built upon 60 years of technology development funded largely by the government," the firm reported. "Today, business model innovation is putting that technology into the hands of entrepreneurs, stimulating competition, and creating a dynamic marketplace."

The rise of SpaceX and other pri-

In this screen grab from NASA's feed, NASA astronauts Doug Hurley (R) and Bob Behnken (2R) join NASA astronaut Chris Cassidy (C) and Russian cosmonauts, Anatoly Ivanishin (L) and Ivan Vagner (2L) aboard the International Space Station after successfully docking SpaceX's Dragon capsule May 31, 2020. The docking occurred just 19 hours after a SpaceX Falcon 9 rocket blasted off from Kennedy Space Center, the nation's first astronaut launch to orbit from home soil in nearly a decade. (NASA/GETTY IMAGES)

vate rocket companies has lowered launch costs and helped lead to a rapid increase in the number of small satellites for Earth observation, communications, and more. Alongside falling launch costs, the satellites themselves have become more affordable to build. Satellites have gotten smaller as their electronics have been miniaturized. Therefore, they need less power and typically have more powerful observational capabilities. This innovation has led to expanding telecom capacity, significant increases in the resolution

of commercially available satellite imagery, and detailed observations across the spectrum.

A large majority of this startup activity and investment has taken place in the United States, and therefore this country has a far more advanced commercial space industry than the rest of the world. According to the space-analysis firm BryceTech, a total of 124 startup companies received investment in the year 2020, with 67% of the funding going to U.S.-based businesses. This trend has been consistent for much of

Chairman and Managing Director of NewSpace India Limited (NSIL), G. Narayan, addresses a press conference in Bangalore, India, on March 12, 2021. (MANJUNATH KIRAN/ AFP/GETTY IMAGES)

the past decade, and other countries have started to take note. The Chinese government, in particular, has sought to respond in kind, especially during the last five years. Even so, China remains a distant second. The Bryce report found that Chinese ventures received less than 10% of the total startup funding in 2020.

Stimulating this new space sector remains a priority, however. The Chinese State Council's 2016 white paper on "China's space activities" expressly declares that developing a commercial space industry should be a priority. "Nongovernmental capital and other so-cial sectors are encouraged to participate in space-related activities, including sci-entific research and production, space infrastructure, space information prod-ucts and services, and use of satellites to increase the level of commercialization of the space industry," the document states. To encourage this development, China began to license technology held by its state rocket corporations to entre-preneurs in 2016. Three years later there were nearly 100 Chinese new space startups, with new companies popping up every week or two.

Other countries are investing in commercial space as well. In 2019, the Indian space agency, ISRO, created the New Space India Limited entity to facilitate the transfer of technology to Indian startups and support public-private partnerships with industry. In Europe, too, where state-owned en-terprises have long launched rockets for member nations there have been nascent efforts to support a more com-mercial approach to spaceflight. In short, at the end of the 2020s, space is more commercial in nature than ever, and the trend toward private space ap-pears to be accelerating.

Military, civil, and commercial space

So far this paper has addressed the two major paradigm changes in spaceflight over the last two decades, the introduction of new nation states with space aspirations, and the in-creasingly prominent role played by commercial space companies in the competition for government con-tracts and technological innovation. Now the focus turns toward the three primary domains of space activities, military, civil, and commercial space-flight, analyzing both recent achieve-ments and identifying advancements in the near future. All of these areas have seen dynamic changes in recent years, and are likely to undergo more tumult in short order.

Military space

For military space, the modern age could be said to begin in 2007. On Jan-uary 11, 2007, China launched a two-stage, solid-fuel ballistic missile from the Xichang Satellite Launch Center. When used as a "direct ascent" missile, it can reach an altitude of about 621.37 miles. The missile followed a ballis-tic arc, carrying a kinetic warhead that struck a Chinese weather satellite at an altitude of 536.24 miles. Traveling at a relative speed of 20,132.43 miles per hour, the kinetic vehicle obliterated the aging satellite, creating a cloud of more than 3,000 pieces of debris in low-Earth orbit, the largest amount ever tracked. Scientists later estimated there were likely ten times as many pieces of debris that were unable to be tracked.

This was the first successful anti-satellite missile test since 1985, when the Soviet Union and the United States had demonstrated their capability dur-ing the Cold War era. It marked China's entry into the domain of military space, and helped provoke India to conduct its own such test, called Mission Shakti, in 2019.

The diplomatic reaction to these tests, particularly China's high-altitude test that created an enormous debris cloud, was a mixture of concern about the impact of debris on other satellites and a desire to use space for "peaceful purposes." But there is no international treaty that prohibits such activity. The Outer Space Treaty, to which China is one of the signatories, prevents the deployment of weapons of mass de-struction in space, but not conventional weapons.

The truth is space has been a military domain since the beginning of space-flight. The German V2 rockets regularly flew higher than 62.14 miles when they were used to attack Great Britain during World War II. And but for its capability to quickly launch arms control verifi-cation satellites, NASA's space shuttle program probably would have been can-celed during the 1970s. While the Cold War's end may have pushed the mili-tary aspect of space somewhat into the background, the Chinese anti-satellite test brought the issue very much back to the front burner.

China has continued to develop its direct ascent space weapons capa-bilities, and it has conducted multiple tests of rendezvous and proximity op-erations tests in low-Earth orbit and geostationary orbit. This appears to be leading up to the capability of using co-orbital satellites to harm other satel-lites. China also has developed signifi-cant electronic warfare counterspace capabilities, according to the Secure World Foundation's Global Counter-space Capabilities report published in 2021. The country has taken steps to integrate space, cyber, and electronic warfare capabilities under a single military command.

"Although official Chinese state-ments on space warfare and weapons have remained consistently aligned to the peaceful purposes of outer space, privately they have become more nu-anced," the Secure World Foundation report states. "China has recently des-ignated space as a military domain, and military writings state that the goal of space warfare and operations is to achieve space superiority using offen-sive and defensive means in connec-tion with their broader strategic focus on asymmetric cost imposition, access denial, and information dominance."

After China's entry into military space, Russia responded by renewing its efforts to remain competitive in the space military race. In recent years the country has demonstrated its new "Nudol" system, a modern anti-satellite missile capability. The country has also worked on a co-orbital satellite program called Burevestnik, which could be used both to snoop on nearby satellites operated by other countries, and potentially also for more aggressive purposes. Russia's primary goal in space remains staying on par with the United States when it comes to military operations. According to the Secure World Foundation, Russia seeks to mitigate the superiority of U.S. space assets by fielding a number of ground-, air-, and space-based offensive capabilities.

There are other players in the modern military space age, as well. In 2019, to protect its satellites in space, French Defense Minister Florence Parly outlined a new space weapons program that would allow the country to move from space surveillance to the active protection of its satellites. French officials, working with a budget about one-tenth of that which the United States spends on space programs, said they were studying the development of technologies that might include swarms of nano-satellites that would patrol a few kilometers around French satellites, a ground-based laser system to blind snooping satellites, and perhaps even machine guns on board some satellites. India, of course, demonstrated an anti-satellite capability in 2019. Japan has a capable space program, and while it has not previously developed offensive space capabilities, government officials are studying whether to do so. North Korea and Iran have less-advanced space capabilities, but both have shown an interest in developing space-based weapons.

Finally, there is the United States. Just 13 months after China's anti-satellite test, the USS Lake Erie, a missile cruiser, shot down a non-functioning spy satellite that had been operated by the U.S. National Reconnaissance Office. This test happened at a much lower altitude, so it did not create a similarly large debris field. Nevertheless the test sent its intended message, that the Americans would not stand by as China developed new space weapons. The United States possesses the most sophisticated space offensive

MIG-31k fighter jet, with Kinzhal missile system, performs during Victory Day in Red Square in Moscow, Russia, on June 24, 2020. Victory Day parades commemorate the anniversary of the Soviet victory in World War II. (SEFA KARACAN/ANADOLU AGENCY/GETTY IMAGES)

capabilities in the world, from anti-satellite weapons to electronic warfare capabilities such as satellite jamming and likely ground-based, high-energy lasers for counterspace applications.

After the election of President Donald Trump in 2016, the U.S. military sought to strengthen its national defense. This included a focus on space, and the eventual establishment of the U.S. Space Force as the sixth branch of the armed forces. Vice President Mike Pence declared that the United States had no choice but to militarize space in response to actions by its adversaries.

"China and Russia are aggressively developing and deploying capabilities—including anti-satellite weapons, airborne lasers, menacing "on-orbit" capabilities and evasive hypersonic missiles—that have transformed space into a war-fighting domain," the Vice President said in 2019.

After Joe Biden became president in 2021, his administration did not make substantial changes to this policy. Biden's White House supported the Space Force, and allowed the nation's military leadership to continue talking about space as a war-fighting domain. The United States has as its highest priority in space the protection of its own assets, including spy and communications satellites in low-Earth and geostationary orbits valued at more than $1 billion each.

There is evidence the United States may soon seek to make a public demonstration of its superiority. In August 2021, there were reports that senior military leaders, including Gen. John Hyten, the vice-chairman of the joint chiefs of staff, were discussing whether to reveal a secret space weapon by providing a showcase of its capabilities. The weapon system, the details of which remain obscure, was developed as a "Special Access Program," which is reserved for highly classified information. A decision to publicly demonstrate a weapon indicates that military chiefs have determined that the knowledge of its existence would deter foreign actors from attempting to disable satellites—because such attacks would be futile.

Thus, it seems likely that the recent global interest in the militarization of space will continue. Although it may not come to open warfare in outer space any time soon, the major developed nations of the world clearly have a willingness to show some of their cards, and make it plain that if a shooting war were to start in space, there might not be an end.

Civil space

On December 14, 1972, the Apollo 17 Lunar Module carrying Eugene Cernan and Harrison Schmitt lifted off from the surface of the Moon. The astronauts knew it was the final Apollo mission to the Moon, but they believed NASA and humanity would return before not too long, and soon follow up with missions to Mars. The next human step on the Moon would come, Cernan said before he climbed into the Lunar Module, "We believe not too long into the future." Cernan died in January 2017 at the age of 82. He maintained until his death that a great regret of his life was carrying the title of "Last Man on the Moon" to his grave.

Since Apollo 17 nearly 50 years ago, humans have not flown beyond low-Earth orbit, going no higher than about 341.75 miles above the planet. This is less than the distance from Chicago to Detroit. In some ways, this is profoundly disappointing, as it suggests NASA and other civil space agencies around the world have not made much progress in half a century. But it is also understandable. The Apollo Program comprised a significant part of the United States' national security interests in the 1960s, and had a budget to match. After the end of Apollo and

its outsized budget, NASA had to make do with lesser funding and ambitions.

The two main space powers found themselves increasingly working together in space, at least on the civil side of the ledger. By 1998 NASA and the Russian space corporation, Roscosmos, trusted each other enough to embark on a major construction project in low-Earth orbit, the International Space Station. NASA launched the majority of modules used to build the massive orbiting laboratory, but construction was halted in 2003 when space shuttle Columbia disintegrated during reentry into Earth's atmosphere. This shuttle tragedy, the second during the program's history, killed all seven astronauts on board the vehicle.

In the aftermath of this accident President George W. Bush directed NASA to both complete construction of the space station and then turn its focus back toward deep space exploration. While his father, George H.W. Bush, had briefly flirted with a humans-to-Mars exploration program

more than a decade earlier, the younger Bush's post-Columbia deep space ambitions would have more staying power. NASA and the White House came up with a two-pronged approach. They would fly the aging space shuttle for as long as it took to complete the space station, and then transition the use of NASA's human exploration budget toward a return to the Moon, and the eventual exploration of Mars. This was called the Constellation Program. The space shuttle did retire, in 2011, after completion of the station.

The Constellation Program would not survive long after Bush left office; the Obama administration formally canceled it in 2010. By this time, about four decades after the heyday of Apollo, NASA had grown into a large bureaucracy, with field centers across the country competing for budgetary resources, and U.S. Representatives and Senators eager to take up the fight for parochial funding. Starting and sustaining any new program was a challenge. Therefore, like most large NASA initiatives, Constellation quickly fell years behind schedule and ran billions of dollars over budget.

The significance of Constellation, however, is that every presidential administration since then has had the stated programmatic goal of sending humans back into deep space. President Obama established a plan for humans to eventually travel to Mars. Although this "Journey to Mars" was more fanciful than real in terms of budgets, it nonetheless signaled that U.S. space policy leaders believed it was time to move beyond low-Earth orbit. The Trump administration sought more tangible, near-term goals for human exploration and established a preliminary focus on the Moon. Notably, the Trump administration viewed the Moon through the lens of military, commercial, and civil space. To White House officials, the Moon represented the "high ground" in space warfare, and assets put in cislunar space would be less vulnerable to adversaries. The Trump administration was also eager to encourage economic activity in space, and nascent businesses had a better opportunity to engage in

Eugene Cernan using the Rover on the lunar surface, Apollo 17 mission, December 1972. U.S. astronauts Eugene Cernan and Harrison Schmitt collected samples and drove the Lunar Roving Vehicle at the Taurus-Littrow Landing Site on the Moon. Apollo 17 was the last Apollo Moon landing mission. (HERITAGE SPACE/HERITAGE IMAGES/GETTY IMAGES)

commercial activity on the Moon than the much more distant Mars. And finally, from a civil space vantage point, the Moon was close, and something that NASA might reasonably accomplish in the near term.

So in 2019 Vice President Mike Pence announced NASA was going back to the Moon, this time to stay. And Pence set an extraordinarily short deadline for the "first American woman and the next American man" to set foot on the Moon: 2024. It was no coincidence that this would be the final year of a second Trump presidential term, if he were to win reelection. Pence left the details to a former Republican Congressman and pilot, Jim Bridenstine, who served as administrator of the space agency. Bridenstine soon got to work, naming the Moon initiative the "Artemis Program" after the twin sister of Apollo and lobbying Congress for funding.

Since 2019 the Artemis Program has dominated NASA's civil space activities, and it seems likely to do so for the foreseeable future. In less than two years Bridenstine brought the agency's field centers and much of the space industry behind a plan to use NASA's large new rocket, the Space Launch System, to launch humans to the Moon, and a commercially procured lander to send astronauts down to the surface and back to lunar orbit. Although NASA never really had a chance to meet the arbitrary, and arguably political, deadline of 2024, it has nonetheless served to shake up the space agency bureaucracy and spurred its employees to move with more vigor. Artemis has endowed NASA with a sense of purpose, and its greatest sign of success so far is that within days of his arrival at the White House, President Biden endorsed the plan.

"Lunar exploration has broad and bicameral support in Congress, most recently detailed in the FY2021 omnibus spending bill, and certainly we support this effort and endeavor," Press Secretary Jen Psaki said on February 4, 2021, only two weeks into the new administration. Rarely, if ever, has an existing space exploration program

NASA administrator Jim Bridenstine (L) welcomes Advance space suit engineer, Kristine Davis (R), to the stage during a press conference displaying the next generation of space suits as parts of the Artemis program in Washington, DC, on October 15, 2019. (ANDREW CABALLERO-REYNOLDS/AFP/GETTY IMAGES)

been endorsed so emphatically by a new administration from a different political party.

Many challenges remain for the Artemis Program, and NASA. Certainly a lunar landing is unlikely before 2026 at the earliest. But the agency has a clear path before it. NASA also has begun to win international support for Artemis, signing accords with about a dozen countries. Canada, for example, will have one of its astronauts join a lunar flyby mission—Artemis II, which may launch as soon as late 2023. Japan is likely to fly one of its astronauts on one of the first lunar landing missions.

Artemis has also provoked a response from NASA's major international competitors. After two decades of partnership on the International Space Station, Russia has been making noises about being unhappy in the relationship. The Russian space leadership has talked openly about building its own, separate space station in the latter half of the 2020s. And the director of Roscosmos, Dmitry Rogozin, a close political ally of Vladmir Putin, said the country wants no part of the Artemis Program. The Russians see Artemis as a nationalistic American program. In March 2021 Russia signed a memorandum of understanding with China,

which called for the two countries to cooperate on creation of an "International Lunar Science Station."

The reality is that Russia is a fading force in civil spaceflight. The country has struggled to develop modern space hardware. From a budgetary standpoint, its industry has long been propped up by the United States. For two decades, United Launch Alliance bought a dozen or more RD-180 rocket engines a year to power the Atlas V rocket. But the last of these engines has been delivered, and United Launch Alliance will soon move its launches to the new Vulcan rocket. NASA, too, spent hundreds of millions of dollars annually after the space shuttle retirement in 2011 to get its astronauts to the International Space Station on Soyuz vehicles. That arrangement is no longer necessary, as NASA can now rely on SpaceX's Falcon 9 rocket and Crew Dragon spacecraft for such a service. As a result, Russia has less money to pay its aging workforce, and relies on decades-old technology. And unlike NASA, it has no vibrant commercial space industry to provide new energy, ideas, and funding. Russia's first half century of space exploration was marked by moments of brilliant glory. Its second 50 years will be much grim-

A SpaceX Falcon 9 rocket carrying South Korea's ANASIS-II military communications satellite launched from pad 40 at Cape Canaveral Air Force StationJuly 20, 2020. Built in France by Airbus, this is South Korea's first military satellite. (PAUL HENNESSY/SOPA IMAGES/LIGHTROCKET/GETTY IMAGES)

mer, likely playing a secondary role to Chinese ambitions in space.

In contrast to Russia, the Chinese civil space program is very much on the rise. Since its first human spaceflight in 2003, China has subsequently flown six more missions. With its Tiangong space station now in low-Earth orbit, the country will fly more frequently into space. The country is developing the kinds of heavy lift rockets needed for deep space exploration and has signaled its intent to build an "international lunar station" at the South Pole of the Moon, beginning with robotic missions and followed by short-term human missions in the early 2030s. The country plans to establish a long-term human presence at the lunar South Pole—which is believed to contain vast reserves of water ice—during the period of 2036 to 2045. It will compete with NASA for international partners as it does so, seeking to burnish its credentials as a world superpower in spaceflight, and attempting to one-up the Americans where it can.

Civil space has been a relatively muted affair since the end of Apollo, but there are now strong indications that will change within the next decade. Although the term "space race" is certainly a cliché, that may nonetheless be what NASA and its partners find themselves in with China and Russia when it comes to returning to the Moon during that time frame. We are finally going back into deep space.

Commercial space

As U.S. decisionmakers contemplate future civil space policy, their plans appear to be increasingly intertwined with that of commercial space. This trend began in the wake of the Columbia tragedy, when NASA began considering what its human exploration plans would look like after the shuttle retired. President George W. Bush's initiative led to the Commercial Orbital Transportation Service program, or COTS, which paid private companies to develop the capability to launch and deliver supplies to the International Space Station. This proved a resounding success, leading to two separate delivery services by SpaceX and Orbital Sciences that have combined to fly about three dozen missions. By NASA's own estimates, had it developed such rockets and spacecraft using traditional procurement processes, it would have cost 4 to 10 times more.

Each succeeding U.S. president has leaned more into commercial space. President Obama championed the development of "commercial crew" by which SpaceX and Boeing would fly U.S. and international partner astronauts to the space station. This program began to show success in May 2020, with SpaceX's first crewed flight, bringing astronauts Doug Hurley and Bob Behnken to the station. Two more successful missions have followed. Boeing's first crew flight may take place during the second half of 2022.

The Trump administration, with its pro-business stance, went even further. NASA Administrator Jim Bridenstine repeatedly said NASA should be "one of many" customers for spaceflight services, and sought to buy commercially whenever possible. The decision to buy services at a "fixed price" marked an important turn for NASA away from the traditional method of procurement, using "cost plus" contracts. Under cost-plus contracting, NASA pays a vendor all of their costs, plus a fee. If there are delays or cost overruns, NASA pays them. Naturally this incentivizes delays and overruns because these actually benefit a contractor. But NASA had long felt it was necessary to use cost-plus contracting for difficult engineering problems that required significant development work.

NASA took a huge step away from this in April 2021 however, when it awarded its first "Human Landing System" contract to SpaceX on a fixed-price basis. Building a deep space vehicle that can safely land on the Moon and then fly back into orbit is a tremendously challenging problem. Nevertheless, NASA selected SpaceX after Bridenstine had pushed for a fixed-price award process. It is too early to tell whether NASA and SpaceX will succeed with the Starship project, but the potential cost savings to NASA are tremendous. The space agency awarded SpaceX $2.89 billion for Starship development costs, one uncrewed demonstration test, and one crewed landing. In a report prepared before this award, NASA's inspector general estimated that NASA would spend $17.3 billion for lander development and the first human landing. So with its fixed-price award to SpaceX, NASA saved more than $14 billion in its projected costs for the Artemis landing. Effectively, this meant that NASA could squeeze a Moon program into its existing budget rather than needing billions of dollars more in annual budgets from Congress.

The U.S. Department of Defense has benefitted as well. During the 2010s it annually awarded United Launch Alliance a $1 billion "subsidy" to augment the company's launch services. This was on top of launch contracts awarded to the sole bidder, United Launch Alliance, on a "block buy" basis. With the rise of SpaceX, and eventually Blue Origin, the U.S. military has moved toward firm, fixed-price launch contracts as well. There is no more billion-dollar subsidy.

The promise of commercial space is not limited to reduced costs. It draws in private capital that supports significant, and potentially disruptive innovation. SpaceX's Starship vehicle provides the most noteworthy example of this. If successful, and the company still faces some stiff technical hurdles, Starship would be the world's first fully reusable heavy lift rocket. Because it will have the capacity for refueling in low-Earth orbit, Starship also would be the world's first truly interplanetary transport system. It could bring dozens of astronauts to the Moon, instead of two. And its cargo capacity is unparalleled. NASA never built a "cargo" version of the Apollo Lunar Module, but it studied the concept in the 1960s, and found that a spacecraft not carrying astronauts could deliver about 5 tons to the Moon. Starship, by contrast, could bring more than 200 tons to the lunar surface when set to a mode in which it does not return to earth. NASA has recognized this by selecting Starship for its lunar lander. The U.S. military, too, is studying the reusable vehicle's potential for rapid, point-to-point deployment of supplies and possibly even troops from the United States to anywhere in the world within 90 minutes.

Such a vehicle would not exist but for a billionaire with a vision, who is able to raise private capital to support that vision, and intends to build the vehicle first and then sell services to the U.S .government. This is the promise of commercial space in the mid-21st century.

Policy implications

In the realm of military space, the trend over the last 15 years has been one of increasingly jingoistic actions and language in space, punctuated by the creation of the U.S. Space Force and potential unveiling of a new space weapon. The question is whether this trend should continue, and if so where will it lead? A shooting war in space could render certain orbits around Earth unviable for satellites due to large amounts of debris. The United States and China could also eventually come into conflict on the surface of the Moon. It may yet be possible to temper military actions in space. One potential area of cooperation between the United States and its adversaries

The combination of the Tianzhou-2 cargo spacecraft and the Long March-7 Y3 carrier rocket moves to the launching area of the Wenchang Spacecraft Launch Site on May 16, 2021, in Wenchang, Hainan Province, China. (LUO YUNFEI/CHINA NEWS SERVICE/GETTY IMAGES)

comes in space situational awareness. Each nation has its own capacity for tracking debris and potential collisions, so that satellites can be moved out of harm's way. These efforts fall within the armed forces of each country. As there are more and more satellites, especially from commercial providers, it is in the interests of all spacefaring nations to limit debris. Perhaps sharing data and collaboration could be one basis of cooperation for adversaries when it comes to national security.

A similar question concerns civil space. At the outset of the 2020s, the United States and China are poised to compete for international partners as both countries eye human exploration and potential outposts on the lunar surface. Presently, NASA is blocked by U.S. law from cooperating with China in space. But during the 1960s, the United States and the Soviet Union were similarly deadlocked in a competition to fly humans to the Moon, and win international hearts and minds. At a moment when the U.S.-China relationship is a minefield, it seems as though an opportunity might emerge for the two countries to find common ground by working toward international exploration goals in space. After all, fewer than three years after Eugene Cernan left the Moon, NASA and Soviet astronauts met one another in low-Earth orbit as Apollo and Soyuz vehicles docked. Space

could serve to ease tensions on Earth.

Finally, there is the question of commercial space. It is undoubtedly the most vibrant aspect of U.S. spaceflight today. But whereas U.S. presidents have embraced the innovation and lower costs of commercial space, members of Congress have been far more critical, preferring to protect jobs at NASA field centers and traditional contractors. For three years after NASA selected Boeing and SpaceX in 2014 to provide commercial crew services, Congress provided only about half of the funding NASA needed. And if one of these companies were to have a spaceflight tragedy, Congress would have the excuse it needed to significantly dampen NASA's efforts to "buy" services rather than owning them.

This would be unfortunate. Over the next decade of spaceflight NASA and China will be evenly matched in some regards. NASA has the advantage of facilities, institutional knowledge, and a decades-long head start. China has a clear plan, and because of its authoritative government can deliberately execute it without the fear of changing political priorities from election to election. If the United States has a clear edge in the future battle for space supremacy, therefore, it will likely come from the dynamism of the commercial space industry.

discussion questions

1. The current tension in space between the United States and China mirrors that of which we saw between the United States and the Soviet Union during the 1960's. How is the current dynamic similar and different from the original space race? How should the United States be addressing China's increased presence in space?

2. The rise of Space X showcases the growth of the commercial space industry in the United States. Other countries, particularly China, have taken notice and have taken measures to stimulate their own commercial space industry. What advantages does China have to undertake this task that the United States does not have?

3. Increased militarization in space provoked the creation of the "U.S. Space Force" under the Trump administration. Is it likely that space could become a war fighting zone? Should the United States maintain the space force program in the event that a shooting war breaks out?

4. In 1998 the international space station was launched, a joint U.S. and Russia venture. Does the presence of this international project in space indicate the possibility of positive diplomatic relations in space, or will it be more competitive?

suggested readings

Bizony, Piers. *Starman: The Truth Behind the Legend of Yuri Gagarin.* Bloomsbury Publishing. 256 pgs. May 2011. Starman tells the story of Gagarin's odyssey from peasant to international icon, and all the exceptional people behind his dramatic space flight.

Kramer, Barbara. *Neil Armstrong: The First Man on the Moon.* Enslow Pub Inc. 112 pgs. September 1997. Kramer explores the life and accomplishments of astronaut Neil Armstrong, from growing up in Ohio, to his years at NASA and his famous moon landing.

Gorn, Michael. *NASA: The Complete Illustrated History.* Merrell Publishers. 304 pgs. September 2005. This book tells the remarkable story of space exploration from the early twentieth century to the present, with compelling coverage--including a wealth of illustrations--of every US space mission ever undertaken, including those of projects Mercury, Gemini, and Apollo, and the development of the Space Shuttle.

Harvey, Brian. *China in Space: The Great Leap Forward.* Springer Nature. 552 pgs. October 2019. Harvey walks the reader through all of the advancements that China has made in outer space, from sending men and women into orbit, building a space laboratory (Tiangong), to sending probes to the Moon and asteroids.

Berger, Eric. *Liftoff: Elon Musk and the Desperate Early Days That Launched SpaceX.* HarperCollins Publishers. 288 pgs. March 2021. The dramatic story of the first historic flights that launched SpaceX and Musk from a small startup to the world's leading rocket company.

Dawson, Linda. *War In Space: The Science and Technology Behind Our Next Theater of Conflict.* Springer. 215 pgs. January 2019. Dawson describes to us how nations could utilize the technology that they have to initiate war in the theater of outer space.

Don't forget to vote!

Download a copy of the ballot questions from the Resources page at www.fpa.org/great_decisions

To access web links to these readings, as well as links to additional, shorter readings and suggested web sites,

GO TO www.fpa.org/great_decisions

and click on the topic under Resources, on the right-hand side of the page.

The renewed climate change agenda
by Ronald J. Bee

Firefighters spray down flames on the side of Interstate 210 in Sylmar, California, on January 19, 2021. Dozens of fires ignited as high winds and low humidity spread throughout the state. (JOSH EDELSON/AFP/GETTY IMAGES)

The challenges of addressing global climate change in the 21st century remain essentially the same as in the 20th: how should or can we reduce human-made greenhouse gas emissions worldwide to prevent damaging the planet upon which we live and depend? In 1957, Doctors Roger Revelle and Charles David Keeling of the Scripps Institution of Oceanography began measuring median global carbon dioxide (CO_2) levels, the most prevalent of greenhouse gases, at the Mauna Loa Observatory in Hawaii. That ongoing tracking, now maintained by Keeling's son, Ralph F. Keeling, shows that median global temperatures continue to rise, mirroring the increasing levels of CO_2 in our atmosphere. The original scientific measurements informed, if not jump-started, the 1992 Rio Earth Summit, which created the UN Framework Convention on Climate Change (UNFCCC) to prevent "dangerous" interference in the climate system.

In 2020, however, the world came to a forced standstill due to the Covid-19 pandemic. This outbreak also temporar-ily lowered world greenhouse gas emissions. According to the journal Nature, which analyzed data from the Global Carbon Project, emissions decreased by 6.4% in 2020. The United States accounted for 13% of that total mostly because of the decline in cars and trucks on the road, ships at sea, and planes in the air. Aviation, in fact, proved the most affected by lockdowns and travel restrictions. Emissions in that sector fell by 48% when compared to 2019.

Why does this matter? Covid-19's drastic effect on

RONALD J. BEE lectures in international relations, American foreign policy, and national security at the Oxford Study Abroad Program in the UK. He has also served as the co-director of the University of California Roger Revelle Program on Climate Science and Policy. He is an award-winning author (New York Times Notable Book of the Year, Christopher Award-recipient) and a founding director of the Hansen Leadership Institute at the University of San Diego.

the economic growth of nation-states made the air cleaner but created more unemployment—always a source of instability for both democratic and authoritarian governments. The pandemic serves as a bell-weather for the global challenge of mitigating human-made greenhouse gas emissions. As more individuals received the vaccine and went back to work, economies have begun to bounce back—along with increasing emission levels.

The long goodbye of the pandemic's effects points to the difficulties of squaring shorter-term economic needs with longer-term environmental protection. Fossil fuels have both enabled economies to prosper and increased greenhouse gas levels in the 20th and 21st centuries. Creative entrepreneurs like Bill Gates, Elon Musk, and others have visions for ways to square the circle with greener technologies. Politicians know that plentiful jobs, low interest rates, and low inflation rates prove key to winning elections. To achieve that, each candidate usually relies on their own political party platforms as guideposts. Democrats and Republicans have fundamentally disagreed on basic approaches to climate change, with extremes in both parties ranging from dismantling the fossil fuel economy immediately or else the world ends within a decade, to underscoring the remaining uncertainties of climate change science, calling them a collective hoax promoted by socialists to overthrow capitalism. Each side has slipped into their respective trenches, tossing epithets across a no-man's land of reconciliation. One has either become a "Climate Denier" or a "Socialist."

The ideological divide has almost taken on the doomsday vs. "don't worry be happy" dimensions of the threat of nuclear war during the Cold War (1947–62). Those who argued for dis-

Before you read, download the companion **Glossary** that includes definitions, a guide to acronyms and abbreviations used in the article, and other material. Go to **www.fpa.org/great_decisions** and select a topic in the Resources section. (Top right)

armament to prevent nuclear Armageddon then squared off with counterparts in government who embraced nuclear deterrence as the only way to prevent the same outcome. One can argue that we have seen a certain cross-over effect in terms of the climate debate. The Bulletin of the Atomic Scientists, while still maintaining the nuclear doomsday clock (now at 100 seconds to midnight), has devoted more and more of its articles to addressing the threats of global climate change. For example, most of the Bulletin's articles in its July 2021 issue focused on recent incidents mandating more focused climate action: from the June record-high temperatures of 111°F in Seattle, Washington, and 112°F in Portland, Oregon, (40% above normal) to implicating rising seas in the Surfside, Florida, apartment building collapse. Is the issue of climate change an "existential threat" like global thermonuclear war (which has not happened) or can we take reasonable measures over time to mitigate the negative consequences for life on earth? In life, science, and politics, however, the word "reasonable" remains open to interpretation.

If extreme political differences have stymied progress, extreme weather events at both ends of the thermometer have kept us focused. Summers have become warmer and winters colder. The California fires of 2020—nearly 10,000 of them—torched more than 4.2 million acres of forest and killed 33 people, the worst year in California's history. The fires in the golden state have continued in July and August 2021. South Lake Tahoe went under mandatory evacuation as the Caldor fire approached, filling the resort with choking smoke. Governor Gavin Newsome declared a state of emergency when the Dixie and Fly fires in Butte and Plumas counties combined, having destroyed over 700,000 acres by the end of August. Sixteen thousand people went under evacuation orders. To the north, the Bootleg fire in southern Oregon burned over 400,000 acres, an area the size of Portland, Seattle, Sacramento, and New York City combined.

The fires have not limited them-

selves to North America. In Russia's northeastern Siberia, 200 fires have defied firefighters, floating smoke that has drifted to Alaska. A heatwave across Greece in early August brought unprecedented fires and threatened to shut down the electrical grid. At the same time, 100 fires burned in Turkey as its president declared parts of five provinces "disaster areas." Italy had to remove tourists from beaches via helicopter as flames trapped them with the Mediterranean Sea at their backs.

As CNN has reported, "Wildfires are becoming larger and more intense, and they are happening in places that aren't used to them." What science can help explain this higher number of more intense infernos? According to the National Oceanic and Atmospheric Administration (NOAA), 2020 proved the second hottest year on earth in the past 140 years. Nineteen of the warmest years on record have occurred since 2000. NOAA also tracks droughts across the United States. Not surprisingly, where extreme drought occurs on its map, wildfires usually follow. According to the July 20, 2021, Drought Monitor, much of the Western United States finds itself in either "extreme drought" (D-3) or "exceptional drought" (D-4).

On the other extreme, an unprecedented three-week "Great Texas Freeze of February 2021" threw Texans accustomed to much warmer weather into chaos. Dallas-Fort Worth had a low of 4°F, with a 14°F high, causing the National Weather service to advise avoiding outside activities if possible. Nearly 4 million homes and businesses lost power due to rolling blackouts and utility outages. Power outages normally occur in the hot summer months, like they did during the 2020–21 fires in California due to overuse of air-conditioning, or in this case, the utility, Pacific Gas and Electric Company (PG&E), worried about limiting the liabilities of downed power lines (PG&E filed for bankruptcy due to lawsuits over fire-causing accidents and poor maintenance). How could this happen in the case of Texas during the winter? Rising global temperatures do not always generate heat. Sometimes one sees the exact opposite effect due to abrupt changes in atmospheric pressure which can change normal air flow patterns. The Texan deep freeze also shut down over 3 million barrels a day of oil refining which supplies more than 60% of the East coast oil supply. Gas prices skyrocketed as supplies went dead.

In early 2021, changes in the polar vortex, large areas of low pressure normally found around the earth's poles, sent waves of freezing Arctic air across several continents, with the following Texas-like international results:

■ In Asia, spot prices for liquid natural gas (LNG) rose 1,700% from the 2020 lows, which in turn increased European gas prices to 12-year highs

■ The United Kingdom's national grid issued emergency appeals for generator use as wholesale electricity prices rose to $1,367 per megawatt hour

■ China experienced the lowest temperatures since 1966, which spiked consumer demand for electric heat, as well as disrupted LNG delivery due to frigid weather

■ Japanese utilities asked consumers to cut back on power consumption

■ Sweden had the largest single-day snowfall since 2012, leaving grids disabled and customers without power. The Swedish government made utility companies pay for hotel rooms so that Swedes would not freeze to death.

■ In Iran and Pakistan, natural gas shortages triggered rolling blackouts in the face of frigid temperatures.

Germany and Belgium faced "floods of death" in the torrential downpours of July 2021, with over 100 dead and 1,300 missing. In any extreme weather event, and in particular floods, vulnerable citizens and those with disabilities face extreme dangers. On the banks of the Rhine River, in the German town of Sinzig, 12 residents in a disability care facility drowned when they became trapped overnight. As the heavy rains and flash floods spread to Northern France, the United Kingdom, the Netherlands, Luxembourg, and Switzerland, Western Europeans learned about "Bernd," a low-pressure vortex

This photo taken on July 26, 2021, shows rescuers searching inside the subway, which was flooded following heavy rains in Zhengzhou, in China's central Henan province.
(AFP/GETTY IMAGES)

that remained stagnant, continuously circling over Europe. Scientists from the World Weather Attribution group studied the rainfall data and concluded that rising global temperatures made the deadly German floods "up to nine times more likely."

On July 12, 2021, a month's full of rain fell on London, paralyzing many streets and shutting down sections of its Underground rail system. Deadly mudslides have occurred in India, and massive flooding has drenched New Zealand, Nigeria, and Iran. On July 22, in Zhengzhou, Central China, panicked passengers in subways clung to ceiling handrails as a flash flood rose to their necks, in what Chinese officials have called rainfall volumes as occurring "once in a thousand years."

On August 21, 2021, in Waverly, Tennessee, emergency crews searched through shattered homes, floating cars, and tangled debris looking for about a dozen people missing from a record-breaking torrential downpour that unleashed floods killing 22 people or more. Seventeen inches of rain fell in a 24-hour period, taking out roads, cellphone towers, and telephone lines.

Why have these unprecedented deadly inundations happened? One can resort to basic 17th-century science, and in particular, the laws of gravity,

to provide a plausible answer. "What goes up must come down," a phrase coined by Sir Isaac Newton at Cambridge University, also relates to rainfall. As the polar ice caps and glaciers melt, as many scientists have noted, that water flows back into the oceans. Higher atmospheric temperatures create more evaporation. As global median temperatures rise, this process not only produces more clouds, but also more intense storm systems. The more the ice melts, the higher sea-levels will rise. The more the atmosphere heats up, we see more evaporation of the oceans. As fires destroy trees, also known as "carbon sinks," because they store carbon from the atmosphere, less carbon gets absorbed. This cycle and process has repeated itself in a way whereby dryer climates have become dryer, and wetter climates even wetter. In the case of Bernd, the German Weather Service (Deutscher Wetterdienst) concluded the rainfall became so bad because "Bernd was surrounded by high pressure systems and was therefore unable to move on."

Regarding glaciers, one has worried scientists more than others: the ice shelf that keeps West Antarctica's Pine Island Glacier intact. This huge river of ice has started to melt and break up faster than anticipated. "The floating ice shelf," reports the journal Science Advances, "acts like a cork in the bottle for the fast-melting glacier and prevents its much larger ice mass from flowing into the ocean. That ice shelf has retreated by 12 miles between 2017 and 2020." The 160-mile river of ice, should it melt, "holds enough water to raise global sea-levels by more than 19 inches."

While scientists remain uncertain if warmer ocean temperatures, sea-level rise, and increased storm activity will lead to more hurricanes, they have concluded that recent hurricanes have shifted poleward and have become more intense. According to the Center for Climate and Energy Solutions, "The changing patterns of tropical storms (a shift northwards in the Atlantic) could put much more property and human lives at risk…. [M]ore recent work shows a trade-off between intensity and frequency—that as warmer temperatures bolster hurricane intensity, fewer storms form.

For those in these stronger hurricane's paths, massive flooding has created devastating conditions. Hurricane Harvey (August 2017), Irma (September 7, 2017) and Maria (September 20, 2017) caused over $300 billion in damage to Texas, Louisiana, and Puerto Rico alone. According to the RAND Corporation Homeland Security Operation Analysis Center, Hurricanes Irma and Maria (Category 5 and 4) destroyed 100% of Puerto Rico's grid, 95% of its cellular sites, 43% of its wastewater plants, and caused 40,000 landslides, making 97% of the roads impassable. Moreover, Puerto Rico has suffered a series of earthquakes in 2019–20 as well as the Corona Virus-19 pandemic of 2020–21.

Hurricane Florence (Category 4, September 2018) created 35 inches of rain in North Carolina and flooded 5,100 homes. In 2019, damaging slow-moving storms included Hurricane Barry (Category 1, Louisiana, $600 million in damage), Dorian (Category 5, Bahamas, Southeast United States, and Canada, $4.6 billion in damage), and Tropical Storm Imelda (Texas and Louisiana, $2 billion in damage). The 2019 Atlantic hurricane season proved the

fourth above-average damaging season since 2016. To date, Hurricane Katrina (2005, Category 5, Louisiana) remains the most expensive in terms of property damage ($168 billion). On August 29, 2021, the 16th anniversary of Katrina, Hurricane Ida struck the Gulf Coast. Over a million citizens lost power in New Orleans. Ida tied with Hurricane Laura from last year, and the Last Island Hurricane of 1856 as Louisiana's most powerful storm ever recorded. The damage continued as the storm traveled inland to the Northeast, ravaging New Jersey and New York. On September 7, President Biden surveyed the damage which left at least 67 hurricane-related deaths across eight states, warning that we have reached "code red" on addressing climate change.

The winds of political change on climate in the United States

The United States has witnessed a sea-change in Presidential politics, and with it, a renewed focus on addressing the threats of climate change. In 2016, the election of Donald J. Trump brought with him a basic executive branch belief that the climate change movement proved fundamentally counter-productive to "Making America Great Again." President Trump's first appointment as Secretary of State, Rex Tillerson, the former CEO of ExxonMobil, signaled to the world America had pivoted toward national energy independence based upon "Making Oil, Gas, and Coal Great Again." Tillerson's replacement, Mike Pompeo, carried forward the same strategy for the rest of Trump's term. This required withdrawing from the Obama-era Paris Climate Agreement of 2015, which Trump announced on June 1, 2017. During the Trump era, the United States became the leading world exporter of oil and gas.

In that vein, Mr. Trump supported the development of two major big oil initiatives:

■ The Canadian-U.S. Keystone pipeline is designed to bring up to 35 million gallons of oil daily some 1,200 miles from the oil sands of Western Canada to Steele City Nebraska. Once there, the crude would travel southwards through other pipelines to reach American refineries on the Gulf Coast; and

■ The auctioning of oil and gas leases for drilling rights to the Alaskan Arctic National Wildlife Refuge. In early January of 2021, before Joe Biden's inauguration, the Trump administration sold the rights to just over 550,000 acres on 11 tracks of land, netting $14.4 million dollars. A 2017 law authorized the government to sell the rights to another several hundred thousand acres by 2024.

The November 3, 2020, presidential election of Joe Biden brought with it a promise to rejoin the Paris Agreement of 2015, and stop both the building of the Keystone pipeline as well as any proposed drilling in the Artic National Wildlife Refuge. As these stances suggest, President Biden has distinctly different—if not polar opposite—views on climate compared to former President Trump (see box).

Where do Americans stand on climate change? According to an April 2021 Morning Consult poll, half of American voters now believe "the climate threat is critical," up 10 percentage points from 2017 and up 6 points from 2019. The share of Democrats who view the threat this way, the study shows, "increased most substantially since 2017, jumping 16 points to 75%." Three in five voters expressed that the United States should be in the Paris Agreement; about one out of five said it should not. Mr. Biden took advantage of these growing numbers of the climate-concerned electorate to win his election, and now has set up an ambitious array of climate-related initiatives to help bring greenhouse emissions under control.

According to Jennifer Marlon at the Yale School of the Environment, we are more likely to interpret weather events through political lenses than scientific ones. "The signal of climate change is difficult for people to notice against the noisy background of day-to-day and seasonal changes in weather…. We do not simply use our senses to record information and our surroundings and daily events—we interpret those events and filter them through our emotions, memories, culture, and in the case of weather and climate, our politics." What this may simply mean is that democratic presidents—from Bill Clinton to Barack Obama to Joe Biden—have seen climate action as more key to their political constituencies than Republican ones—George H.W. Bush, George W. Bush, and Donald Trump. Towing the party line for politicians also means speaking to what their constituents see as priorities. Professor Marlon further notes that only 22% of Republicans agree that they have experienced global warming compared to 60% of Democrats.

Worldwide, according to the Pew Research Center, "majorities in most surveyed countries say global climate change is a major threat to their nation." About 20% believe climate change represents a minor threat to no threat at all. Moreover, most citizens in advanced economies say they would change the way they live and work to combat the effects of global warming.

The Media and Climate Change Observatory (MeCCO), a consortium based at the University of Colorado, monitors 127 sources across television, radio, and newspapers in 59 countries and seven worldwide regions. They produce monthly newsletters relaying the incidence of weather and climate-related stories. In 2021, there have been 40% more stories worldwide on extreme weather events compared to 2020. MeCCO's June 2021 summary reported a New York Times essay by Michael Mann and Susan Joy Hassol: "In the old days we would escape the summer by heading north—to the Adirondacks in the East or to the cool, forested Pacific Northwest in the West. But this is not your grandparents' climate." With fires ablaze in the United States and Canada—300 fires in British Columbia, and another 130 in North-

Presidents Trump vs. Biden on Climate Change		
Issue:	**President Trump**	**President Biden**
The Climate Change Threat	It's a hoax	It's a national emergency
The Paris Agreement of 2015	Withdrew in 2017	Rejoined in 2021
New Pipelines and Arctic Drilling	Suported both	Stopped both
Energy Priorities	More U.S. coal, oil, and gas	No carbon in the power grid by 2035
Housing and Climate	No change	Weatherize 2 million homes; Build 1.5 million green homes; subsidize poor
Transportation Priorities	Improve roads, airports	$2 trillion for R&D to get to zero emmissions (net zero) by 2050; Increase numbers of electric cars

western Ontario—what used to serve as a holiday refuge from the heat have become flaming no-go zones. Numerous countries and regions have noticed the trend and have devised specific policy initiatives which they hope will help mitigate these negative effects of climate change.

Biden climate initiatives

On January 27, 2021, President Biden signed executive orders to "tackle the climate crisis at home and abroad while creating good-paying union jobs and equitable clean energy future, building modern and sustainable infrastructure, restoring scientific integrity, and evidence-based policy-making across the federal government." Therein, the president committed to center the climate crisis squarely within U.S. foreign policy and national security considerations. The executive order affirmed the intention of implementing—and building upon—the Paris Agreement of 2015, which first means delivering upon shorter-term global greenhouse gas emission reductions to enable the goal of attaining a net-zero by 2050.

President Biden further instructed the Director of National Intelligence (DNI) to prepare a National Intelligence Estimate (NIE)—the American intelligence community's most authori-

tative and dedicated written assessment of national security issues—on climate change. The president further tasked the U.S. Department of State (DoS) and all related agencies "to develop strategies for integrating climate considerations into their international work."

Domestically, the order calls for the creation of jobs "in construction, manufacturing, engineering, and the skilled trades" so that every federal investment in infrastructure reduces climate pollution, accelerates clean energy, and will tie the permitting process directly to these goals. The president directed that conservation of at least 30% of American lands and oceans by 2030 be accompanied with a process of "stakeholder engagement." To that end, Mr. Biden announced the establishment of a Civilian Climate Corps initiative to "put a new generation of Americans to work restoring public lands and waters, increasing reforestation, increasing carbon sequestration in the agricultural sector, protecting biodiversity, and improving access to recreation." A new Whitehouse Environmental Justice Interagency Council will help coordinate a government-wide mandate "to develop programs, policies and activities to address the disproportionate health, environmental, economic, and climate impacts on disadvantaged

The Paris climate agreement: key points

Temperatures 2100

- Keep warming "well below 2 degrees Celsius"
- Continue efforts to limit the rise in temperatures to 1.5 degrees Celsius"

Financing 2020-2025

- Rich countries must provide 100 billion dollars from 2020, as a "floor"
- Amount to be updated by 2025

Specialisation

- Developed countries must continue to "take the lead" in the reduction of greenhouse gases
- Developing nations are encouraged to "enhance their efforts" and move over time to cuts

Emissions goals 2050

- Aim for greenhouse gases emissions to peak "as soon as possible"
- From 2050: rapid reductions to achieve a balance between emissions from human activity and the amount that can be captured by "sinks"

Burden sharing

- Developed countries must provide financial resources to help developing countries
- Other countries are invited to provide support on a voluntary basis

Review mechanism 2025

- A review every five years. First mandatory world review: 2025
- Each review will show an improvement compared with the previous period

Climate-related losses

- Vulnerable countries have won recognition of the need for "averting, minimising and addressing" losses suffered due to climate change

AFP●

communities." Moreover, the executive order calls for a "Justice40 Initiative," which aims to deliver 40% of the federal government's investment to disadvantaged communities while tracking performance through an Environmental Justice Scorecard.

On Earth Day, April 22, 2021, President Biden convened a two-day virtual leader's summit on climate. The summit convened leaders of 17 of the world's leading economies and greenhouse gas emitters. The President revealed the U.S. intention to keep the median rise of global temperature to 1.5°C by 2030. Mr. Biden, Vice President Kamala Harris, Special Envoy for Climate John Kerry, and National Climate Adviser Gina McCarthy represented the United States. In his opening remarks, Biden reiterated his intent to create green jobs to clean up oil, gas, and coal plants, to build more electric cars and a network of 500,000 miles of electric fueling stations as part of America's "nationally determined contribution" (NDC) to upholding the Paris Agreement of 2015. Yet Biden underscored that the United States represents only 15% of the world's GHG emissions. "All of us, all of us—and particularly those who represent the world's largest economies—we have to step up."

With a view toward the November 2021 26th annual meeting of the UN Framework Convention on Climate Change (UNFCCC, Conference of the Parties, COP 26) in Glasgow, the virtual meeting meant to send several signals: the gathering fulfilled a campaign promise to elevate American leadership on climate, it revealed America's NDC (50% from 2005 levels by 2030), and encouraged others to work with the United States to embrace innovation and investment in new, greener technologies to mitigate human-made GHG emissions.

■ Chinese President Xi Jinping restated China intended to peak its emissions by 2030 and would reach carbon neutrality by 2060.

■ Canadian Prime Minister Trudeau pledged to reduce Canada's GHG emissions 40-45% by 2030.

■ Japanese Prime Minister Yoshihide Suga shared that Japan will cut emissions 46% below 2013 levels by 2030.

■ The launch of a Net Producers Forum between the energy ministries of the United States, Canada, Norway, Qatar, and Saudi Arabia.

■ A Greening Government Initiative co-chaired by the United States and Canada to review and implement green procurement strategies net-zero supply chains for government buildings and vehicle fleets.

■ A bilateral United States-India Clean Energy Agenda 2030 Partnership intended to build upon similar agreements to review the best ways to finance climate initiatives with Japan and Australia to form a Quad Climate Working Group.

■ The United States and the United Arab Emirates (UAE) will create an Agricultural Innovation Mission for Climate to enhance low-carbon growth food security.

■ A Global Climate-Smart Infrastructure Program led by the U.S. Trade and Development Agency (USTDA) connecting American industry to energy and transportation infrastructure in emerging markets.

A major challenge to meet the ambitious international goals will involve both public and private financing and investment. Especially with the global economic downturn created by Covid-19 and its variants, how much deficit spending can national economies—let alone the global economy—afford, especially one reliant on fossil fuels which has in general provided cheaper energy than its renewable alternatives? Or are we being penny-wise and pound foolish? Can we sustain a global economy that relies less—or not at all--on oil, gas, and coal? Do we really have a choice as the incidence of fires, the freezes and the floods continue to accelerate in intensity? The Biden administration has made a commitment to invest in a greener future, but it cannot happen overnight, it cannot happen alone, and the envisioned retooling of industry, infrastructure, and transportation will prove very painful for many.

On the financial side, the U.S. government has released an International Climate Finance Plan wherein the U.S.

Agency for International Development (USAID) will play a key role. The U.S. International Development Finance Corporation (DFC) aims to set aside at least one-third of all new investments in climate-linked activities. Over the next five years, the Millennium Challenge Corporation (MCC) will provide 50% of its program funding to reducing GHGs. The Treasury Department will seek to mobilize World Bank and other regional development bank funding for the same purpose. By 2024, the Biden administration aims to have the U.S. Congress authorize double the annual climate finance expenditure to developing countries that was spent during the second half of the Obama era (2013–16).

The U.S. Green New Deal

On February 7, 2019, a group of Democratic Congressmen and Congresswomen led by Ms. Alexandria Ocasio-Cortez (D-NY) of the House and Mr. Ed Markey (D-MA) of the Senate introduced a non-binding resolution (H.Res.109) entitled, "Recognizing the duty of the Federal Government to create a Green New Deal. (GND)" The GND aims, in its essence, due to the immediate climate threats to health and safety: to unravel and replace the fossil fuel economy in the United States; to guarantee "a family-sustaining wage to everyone"; and provide all Americans with "high quality health-care, housing, economic security, clean water, clean air, and healthy food, while addressing social systemic exclusion and injustice."

According to the Council on Foreign Relations, the GND represents "a broad and sometimes vague aspiration to rapidly mobilize American government, society, and industry to create a sustainable low-carbon future. For supporters, such an effort represents a last chance to avoid the worst consequences of catastrophic climate change. For detractors, it's a financially profligate proposal concerned more with traditional left-wing economic policies than environmental necessity."

President Biden, by his early executive actions, has embraced the "green" portion of the H. Res. 109 regarding the

threat of climate change representing "a direct threat to the national security of the United States." The other half of the "New Deal," which aims to redistribute national wealth, remains more politically divisive—let alone expensive—in the wake of post-Covid-19 public spending to provide vaccines, pay-out unemployment and stimulus checks, and rebuild the American economy with grants to small and large businesses. The American Action Forum initially estimated the total cost of GNP to be between 53 and 92 trillion dollars. Mr. Biden may decide to slay one dragon at a time and begin by tackling the climate change beast that has set the Western United States and the Mediterranean on fire. Alternatively, when Democrats introduce a Green New Deal budget, the president does have a "climate change first" green-only fall-

back option when that high figure runs into rough waters with Republicans.

By November of 2021, through hard-fought negotiations, Congress reduced an initial $3.5 trillion budget resolution to $1.75 trillion for the Biden "Build Back Better" domestic blueprint. The new budget still represents the largest U.S. investment in addressing climate change in U.S. history. The bill sets aside $555 billion dollars to cut carbon emissions by including tax credits for businesses and consumers. The legislation will make it easier to buy electric cars, install solar panels, retrofit buildings, and manufacture wind-turbines and other energy-efficient equipment. As a nod to Republican objections, however, the bill does not specifically target reforming the energy sector—including the coal, oil and gas industries.

Issues and challenges for the UN COP26 meeting in autumn 2021

The UN's Inter-Governmental Panel on Climate Change (IPCC), in its August 2021 report, set an urgent tone. The report concluded unequivocally that the current climate crisis stems directly from human activities. Hundreds of the world's top scientists have coldly and clearly made the anthropogenic link to our warming planet

and its dire consequences. The report spells out that carbon dioxide levels in the atmosphere have reached their highest level in two million years. The last time we saw heating this fast—"at least 2,000 years ago, and probably 100,000 years ago." It will require, "immediate, rapid and large-scale reductions" in emissions to prevent

Justice and Peace artist Greg Mitchell completes his climate-crisis themed mural that depicts the Earth on fire and reads 'While you were talking,' on the side of St John's Church on Princes Street, Edinburgh, to coincide with Cop26 in Glasgow. (JANE BARLOW/PA IMAGES/GETTY IMAGES)

worsening effects. Thus far, 90% of the world's regions have been affected by drought, heatwaves, and flooding. Professor David Reay, at the University of Edinburgh, put it this way, "It's clear that every extra ton of CO_2 emitted today is pushing us into a minefield of effects tomorrow."

The Paris Agreement has called for commitments to keep warming well below 2.0 degrees Celsius, with a global target of 1.5°C. According to Scientific American, in an opinion by Rebecca M. Peters, "Temperatures have already risen 1.2°C since pre-industrial levels, resulting in devastating floods, fires and droughts reflected in distressing daily headlines. Every increment of warming beyond 1.5°C will result in increasingly destructive and costly repercussions, particularly for the most vulnerable communities and countries in low-income and small island states." Ms. Peters argues that "The International Energy Agency (IEA) needs to make that goal [of keeping below 1.5°C] the centerpiece of its World Energy Outlook." The IEA, a Paris-based autonomous inter-governmental organization formed in the wake of the 1973–74 oil crisis, currently has a mission of "shaping a secure and sustainable energy future for all."

At the Glasgow COP 26 summit, concluded on November 13, 2021, world leaders made the following agreements:

■ A first-time compromise agreement on "drawing down" the use of coal. India argued for this language instead of "phasing out" this widely used fossil fuel. No specific targets, however, were reached. Many nations, including the United States, subsidize the drilling for and mining of fossil fuels, as these industries create national wealth and jobs. To counter the effects of climate change, activists argue such government subsidies must stop. Strong language to that effect, however, did not enter into the final documents of Glasgow.

■ The nearly 200 countries present agreed to come back in a year to announce their national commitments to reducing greenhouse gases. This indicates a nervousness about the rapid increase in emissions, and will keep the biggest emitters on notice. Before, countries would have had five years to divulge their plan. No agreement was reached, however, on how to verify member-state reductions, let alone create an enforcement mechanism to ensure compliance.

■ On September 28, 2021, the United States and the EU announced a joint initiative to reduce methane gases, which constitute up to 30% of all greenhouse gases (CO2 being the prominent of GHGs). Leaders in Glasgow signed onto the pledge which aims to reduce global methane emissions by 30% to 2020 levels by 2030. Considered the "low-hanging fruit" of emissions, this assumes everyone will voluntarily meet these targets. It is worth noting that neither Russia nor China, two of the world's top methane emitters, attended COP26. Moreover, the high-hanging fruit of CO2 emissions did not get addressed in a way that either youth activists—who protested in the streets of Glasgow—or concerned scientists—who wrote the IPCC warnings—would consider satisfactory to address the threat.

Speaking of trees, British Prime Minister Boris Johnson and Prince Charles led an initiative at Glasgow whereby 100 nations agreed to stop destruction of the world's forests. Deforestation takes away key plants that take carbon out of the atmosphere and store it. Without trees, carbon is released back into the atmosphere. While a noble goal, a country widely known for deforestation of the Amazon, Brasil, did not even show up at COP26.

Developing nations did not receive specific assurances on how they will be compensated for the climate damage created by the industrialized countries, let alone monies to help them adapt to future climate damages.

All told, keeping below 1.5°C will not prove easy to meet by 2030, let alone achieving net zero by 2050. If we look at how Covid-19 and the global lockdown affected GHG emissions— only slightly lower due to less transportation use—the challenge becomes apparent. And as economies began to recover from Covid-19, emissions rose again. Transportation, according to the Environmental Protection Agency (EPA), remains the largest source of GHG (29%). The other sources include electricity production (25%), industry (23%), commercial and residential (13%), and agriculture (10%). For decarbonization to have any chance to work, all sources of emissions require mitigation.

Moreover, the global pandemic made it harder to coordinate international climate efforts. The UN parties to the Climate Convention had not met since December 2019 in Madrid. Virtual meetings took place during the last three weeks in the Spanish capital. Technical and logistical glitches, however, marred progress and as did political differences. The UNFCCC postponed the 2020 Conference of the Parties (COP) until Glasgow 2021 to accommodate dealing with Covid-19 as well as use the time to mend fences between differing factions. As a result, COP 26 made progress on some issues noted above, but fell short of the necessary international political will needed to reach the Paris Agreement goals.

Achieving decarbonization

If, as IPCC scientists recommend, we must immediately make rapid and large-scale reductions in greenhouse gas emissions, this will collectively require using all the tools and innovations at our disposal to transform our current fossil-fuel economy into a more renewal one. The Biden initiatives provide funding for new technologies at home and abroad. Foreign Policy Analytics, an independent research division of *Foreign Policy* magazine, has produced a series of reports on the status of key technologies for deep decarbonization of the grid.

Wind and Solar Power: Seventy-six percent of greenhouse gas emissions derive from the energy sector, and eighty-four per cent of energy production still comes from coal, oil, and gas. Wind and solar power, however, have made great strides over the past decade. In 2019, for example, these two renewable sources of energy accounted for 80% of new capacity installed worldwide. Yet, according to the IEA, wind and solar power combined only to account for 10% of today's global entire energy mix. New capacity is not supplying current demand fast enough. For this to happen, according to the journal, Joule, governments must focus on providing more carbon-free electrical power. "Pushing to near-zero emissions requires replacing the vast majority of fossil-fueled power plants or equipping them with carbon capture and storage (CCS)." Lithium-ion batteries, with flexible demand, can smooth out the daily variability of wind and solar power, but they to date cannot store enough power to meet overall longer-term demand. New battery technologies and chemistries show some promise but remain unproven.

Hydrogen: According to the Center for Climate and Energy Solutions, hydrogen holds the promise to fulfill both low-carbon energy and transportation needs. "It can be burned to generate heat or passed through a fuel cell to create electricity in a chemical conversion process." Three car companies—Toyota, Honda, and Hyundai—

Photovoltaic solar panels and wind turbines, San Gorgonio Pass Wind Farm, Palm Springs, California. (IMAGE SOURCE/ALAMY)

each produce a hydrogen fuel vehicle. Pathways to produce hydrogen include higher and lower carbon alternatives. Hydrogen only exists in compounds. The primary method for making hydrogen involves the heating of natural gas, which produces methane, a significant greenhouse gas byproduct. Yet if one combines this process with carbon capture technology, emissions diminish. Electrolysis, another lower-emission method, uses electricity to make pure streams of hydrogen and oxygen from water. This process, however, currently costs double that of the primary method of making hydrogen. As production capacity and improved technologies develop, experts believe that the cost of electrolysis will go down by as much as 70%.

Nuclear Power: The current generation of nuclear power plants have encountered four main problems: storage of nuclear waste, nuclear melt-down accidents, high cost, and long construction times. Long memories of nuclear power plant disasters in Chernobyl, Ukraine, (1986) and Fukushima, Japan, (2011) have made many countries wary to rely on nuclear energy at all. Yet France has successfully used their nuclear power to provide 75% of its national energy needs. Nuclear power does not generate greenhouse gases. Most proponents have argued that a fourth generation of nuclear power plants can both avoid the four main headaches connected to current reactors while helping decarbonize the planet.

Small modular reactors (SMR) use multiple small reactors with a passive cooling system to create the same power as a large reactor at less cost and no chance of meltdown. SMRs still use uranium, however, and the disposal of nuclear waste remains an issue. Molten salt reactors (MSR) use liquid salt as a coolant and have 30% more efficiency than water-cooled plants—yet they, too, generate nuclear waste. Travelling wave reactors (TWR) use depleted Uranium-238, thus producing 80% less radioactive waste. Moreover, this technology aims to use a "once-through fuel cycle" that eliminates safety issues as well as proliferation concerns connected to the reprocessing of spent fuel. Bill Gates has invested "several hundred million dollars" into developing this approach in a new venture called TerraPower. In Gate's book, *How to Avoid Climate Disaster,* he argues that "The only solution I could imagine was to make clean energy so cheap that every country would choose it over fossil fuels."

China and Canada have invested in developing reactors that use thorium instead of uranium as fuel. Thorium, more plentiful than uranium, also has the added benefit that it can't be split or reprocessed to create nuclear chain reactions—which cause safety and nuclear waste issues in reactors and can facilitate nuclear explosions in military weapons. Jim Hansen, a former NASA scientist and climate change guru, has concluded, "The time has come for those who take the threat of global warming seriously to embrace the development and deployment of safer nuclear power systems."

Transportation: Cars, buses, trucks, trains, ships, and airplanes have traditionally relied upon the gas-fueled combustion-engine to propel us to our destinations. Natural gas, biofuels and fuel-efficiency standards have helped reduce GHGs slightly. To reach zero-emissions by 2050, however, will require a total transformation of the transportation industry and the fossils fuels they rely upon worldwide. Whether or not we reach that goal, some entrepreneurs have tried to help. One successful innovator, Elon Musk, has created three companies—SpaceX, Tesla, and Solar City (now Tesla Energy)—with his vision to reduce global warming through sustainable energy production and consumption, and mitigating the risk of human extinction by creating a colony on Mars. Musk has also proposed a high-speed train system called the Hyperloop for both passenger and freight transport that could travel at airline speeds.

Hal Harvey, Robbie Orvis, and Jeffrey Rissman, in their book, *Designing Climate Solutions: A Policy Guide for Low-Carbon Energy,* note that "vehicle electrification policies can contribute at least 1% of cumulative emission reductions to meet a two-degree target through 2050. Although 1% does not seem like much, electric vehicles (EVs) have other benefits: they prove three-times more efficient than gasoline cars—59% to 62% of the energy converts into power to turn the wheels compared to gas cars' 17% to 21%. This efficiency means they cost less to operate—one dollar buys 43 miles, about one-fourth the cost of powering a 2016 gas-powered passenger car. EVs have far fewer moving parts (typically without a radiator or transmission) so they need less maintenance. On the downside, EVs still cost more than gas or diesel vehicles, and they need access to recharging stations—not always easy for families that lack access to electricity in a garage or on the street. And when faced with providing food on the table, and struggling in a post-covid economic turndown, buying a more expensive car won't be in the cards. Buses, trucks, and motorbikes can all be electrified—again, if communities and states want to invest in expanding charging station access. For developing countries

like China and India, among the largest emitters, the biggest concern about EVs remains their cost.

Forty-five states and the District of Columbia provide tax breaks and other incentives for buying either hybrid or electric vehicles. These as well as federal incentives also exist for installing solar panels on our homes. Subsidies, rebates, and carbon taxes/fees altogether encourage EV ownership by businesses and consumers. Officials have tried reducing bridge tolls and providing free electricity to recharge your EV at public charging stations. For example, the San Francisco-Oakland Bay Bridge toll is $6.00 during commute hours for most cars but EVs and carpools cost only $2.50—providing a $900 a year savings. One can ask if such measures profoundly matter or merely chip away at the periphery of a much larger, rolling boulder. Can and will they collectively make enough of a difference to counter the negative effects of climate change on a global level?

The heat of the moment: humanity's challenge

In a 1931 address to students at the California Institute of Technology, Nobel Laureate Albert Einstein advised, "It is not enough that you should understand about applied science in order that your work may increase man's blessings. Concern for man himself and his fate must always form the chief interest of all technical endeavors…in order that the creations of our mind shall be a blessing and not a curse to mankind. Never forget this in the midst of your diagrams and equations." Ninety years after this speech, scientists have signaled an alarm to warn humankind about the dangers of a warming planet for our collective fate.

Their measured scientific opinions have sought to inform and prompt global political will to act. To reverse the effects of climate change—let alone prevent future ones—will prove hard among a host of competing day-to-day and longer-term priorities. Covid-19 generated a second front of environmental war—requiring immense resources for vaccines and creating strains on our emergency medical services infrastructure. Those most vulnerable suffered the worst outcomes. So, too, have extreme weather events affected the frail with higher mortality rates in the wake of heat, cold, and torrential downpours. We will have to battle on both fronts, but can we find the technical equivalent of a global vaccine for climate change?

As the evidence mounts through

fires and floods, winter freezes, intensified hurricanes and heatwaves, our changing climate has become for many, a higher matter of national security, and even a critical matter of public health. More than 200 medical journals—including the *New England Journal of Medicine* and the *British Medical Journal*—recently made an unprecedented joint statement urging world leaders to cut emissions to avoid "catastrophic harm to health that will be impossible to reverse." The statement, building on the August 2021 IPCC report's conclusions, provides more ammo to international negotiators to put climate change at the top of the global agenda.

"In the past 20 years," the statement reads, "heat-related mortality among people over 65 years of age has increased by more than 50%." Climate change requires "the same kind of funding and focus that the Covid-19 pandemic received." Dr. Eric Rubin, editor in chief of the New England Journal of Medicine, described the document as "more of a call to action than an obituary for the planet."

Are we up to the task? Can we hedge our international bets to improve our environment for current and future generations? According to Foreign Policy Analytics, about 70% of today's emissions belong to countries that have made net-zero commitments under the 2015 Paris Agreement. The recent report, however, signaled that "tangible policy actions to those ends continue to fall short." An article in *Foreign Affairs* by Alice Hill entitled "The United States Isn't Ready for the New Phase of Climate Change," goes even further to argue our national strategy to adapt to extreme weather has fallen short. Focusing on emissions alone will not repair the damage already done today, let alone those likely to occur tomorrow from future fires, freezes, and floods. If the most advanced economy in the world has not prepared properly, with 15% of global emissions, what about the remaining countries responsible for 85% of the world's greenhouse gases?

For two years, in the late 1990s, this author served as a co-director of the University of California Roger Revelle Program on Climate Science and Policy. We brought distinguished climate scientists to the UNFCCC Conference of the Parties meetings to discuss their research. The group included world-renowned researchers from the Scripps Institution of Oceanography at UC San Diego, from other campuses of the University of California, Woods Hole, Massachusetts, and several distinguished British and German institutions. The scientists quickly realized that the questions coming their way after public presentations always had more to do with politics than science, more with political will than scientific measurements of CO2, melting glaciers and sea-rise, climate modeling, air quality, and the effects of a global median rise in temperature for ocean chemistry, biodiversity, and public health.

To this day, the term "climate change" has become such a heated political term in the United States and elsewhere that it has stymied progress, funding, and ultimately practical solutions to improving the environment. One approach in conflict resolution involves reframing the debate to identify common stakes in the game. Most everyone across the political aisle agrees that air pollution and bad water affects human health negatively and that the government must play a major role in reducing both threats. The Air Pollution Control Act of 1955 provided the first federal legislation to conduct research on bad air quality. The Clean Air

Demonstrators join the Fridays For Future march on November 05, 2021, in Glasgow, Scotland. Day Six of the 2021 climate summit in Glasgow focused on youth and public empowerment. (JEFF J MITCHELL/GETTY IMAGES)

Acts of 1963 and 1970 provided laws on controlling it. Congress has amended the Clean Air Act many times to address new circumstances. The U.S. Environmental Protection Agency (EPA) opened its doors in December 1970 to implement the legislation. Can we acknowledge that global conditions now affect national air quality to the point that we must address it?

Concern about water quality in the United States prompted even earlier legislation. In 1948, Congress passed the Federal Water Pollution Control Act. Later this led to sweeping amendments in 1972 which gave the EPA authority to regulate the pollutants released into our waters by industry while setting water quality standards. This law also delegated the EPA to deal with "nonpoint source pollution," meaning excess fertilizers, herbicides, insecticides from residential areas, toxic chemicals like oil, grease and runoff chemicals from energy production, salt from irrigation practices and acid drainage from abandoned mines. Do we now not face a global nonpoint source pollution that affects national water quality which we must redress?

Constant fires threaten our nation's air quality. Persistent flooding jeopardizes our water purity. The two together, whether they originate from state-wide, nationwide, or global sources,

require our collective attention if we want to secure a healthier future for our sons, daughters, and their families. We must acknowledge that fossil fuels have helped create the wealth and prosperity we have enjoyed thus far. We must also face the fact that non-renewable energy has, according to many of our best scientists, created a sharpening dual-edged sword. We should look to leverage real events in the air and on the ground to transform how we do and fuel our daily business. It does not have to happen overnight, but we can use the recent climate events as impetus to hedge our bets soon. As Stephen Hawking, the brilliant British author, cosmologist, and theoretical physicist once said, "Intelligence is the ability to adapt to change."

In the heat of the moment, if we don't adapt to climate change, we may soon face more uncomfortable perils. The Economist, in its July 2, 2021, issue poignantly editorialized that we will soon have "no safe place" in a 3°C future. The cover hosts a graphic of two penguins sitting on a wingback chair floating in the ocean, watching a TV depicting the world ablaze. Alternatively, we can all—7.8 billion of us—start making reservations on Elon Musk's space shuttle to Mars. He's likely to need a bigger spaceship. All aboard?

discussion questions

1. According to an April 2021 poll, the number of Americans concerned about climate change has increased in recent years. What can we attribute this rise in concern to?

2. Democratic presidents are much likelier to make combating climate change part of their platform than Republican presidents are. Why is the issue of climate change more of a political issue than a scientific one?

3. How has President Biden incorporated tackling climate change into his foreign policy agenda?

4. The transition to green energy will be economically difficult for many. How can this transition be made so as to avoid massive job loss and economic hardship?

5. There are multiple decarbonization options that are present, such as wind power, solar power, and hydrogen to name a few. Which of these is the best option to pursue?

6. To what extent does cost remain the biggest factor in the way of combatting climate change? How can this be countered?

suggested readings

David Remnick and Henry Finder, eds., *The Fragile Earth: Writing from the New Yorker on Climate Change*, 541 pp. New York: HarperCollins Publishers, 2020. With an introduction by Elizabeth Kolbert, this anthology of writings from the popular magazine addresses three topics: "A Crack in the Ice: How We Got Here," "Hell and High Water: Where We Are," and "Changing the Weather: What We Can Do Now."

Bill Gates, *How to Avoid a Climate Disaster: The Solutions We Have and the Breakthroughs We Need,* 257 pp. New York: Alfred A. Knopf, 2021. Gates, a technologist, business leader and philanthropist, argues that every country must change its ways because virtually every activity in modern life involves the release of greenhouse gases. His new venture TerraPower aims to produce a fourth-generation nuclear power plant to provide cheap energy while reducing emissions.

Ashlee Vance, Elon Musk: *Tesla, SpaceX, and the Quest for a Fantastic Future,* 402 pp. New York: HarperCollins Publishers, 2015. A bestselling biography of the man and entrepreneur who would go to Mars, just in case we cannot turn the negative effects of climate change around. He is also responsible for producing the popular Tesla electric cars.

Marc Shaus, *Our Livable World: Creating the Clean Earth of Tomorrow,* 310 pp. New York: Diversion Books, 2020. A cogent summary of the challenges and opportunities before us to tackle climate change, including the related implications of Covid-19. He proposes bold solutions such as solar cells capable of storing energy, smart highways that charge electric vehicles, indoor farming, bioluminescent vines to replace streetlights, and jet fuel created from landfill trash.

Greta Thunberg, *No One is Too Small to Make a Difference,* 106 pp. New York: Penguin Books, 2019. A collection of speeches made by a young woman who as a 15-year-old decided not to go to school to protest the climate crisis, inspiring millions of other students to go on strike to do the same. Her impassioned speech at the 2019 UN Climate Summit and her follow-up street protests at COP26 in Glasgow admonished the older generation for handing hers a global environmental disaster.

Alex Epstein, Fossil Future: *Why Global Human Flourishing Requires More Coal, Oil, and Natural Gas—Not Less,* 480 pp., Portfolio Press, 2022. The best-selling author of *The Moral Case for Fossil Fuels,* Goldstein throws cold water on the effects of a warming planet by arguing that the benefits of fossil fuels will continue to outweigh their side-effects—including climate impacts—for generations to come.

Don't forget to vote!

Download a copy of the ballot questions from the Resources page at www.fpa.org/great_decisions

To access web links to these readings, as well as links to additional, shorter readings and suggested web sites,

GO TO www.fpa.org/great_decisions

and click on the topic under Resources, on the right-hand side of the page.

Putin's Russia
by Allen C. Lynch

Russian President Vladimir Putin attends an annual televised phone-in with the country's citizens "Direct Line with Vladimir Putin" at Moscow's World Trade Center studio in Moscow on June 30, 2021. (SERGEI SAVOSTYANOV/SPUTNIK/AFP/GETTY IMAGES)

On New Year's Eve 2021, Vladimir V. Putin will have completed his 22nd year as Russia's undisputed ruler, giving him a longer tenure than any Kremlin leader in the past century save Joseph Stalin (ruled 1927–53). In that time, Putin has presided over the economic recovery of Russia (1999–2008) from a decade-long depression that started in the Gorbachev period (1985–91); the survival of his state-oriented, fossil-fuels dependent model of political economy after the collapse in world oil prices in 2008 and 2014; won a war in 1999-2000 against the secessionist province of Chechnya that his predecessor Boris N. Yeltsin had lost in 1994–96; enforced a "red line" against further NATO expansion eastward through a successful five-day war against post-Soviet Georgia in August 2008 and the

annexation of Crimea from Ukraine in March 2014; and ordered an air- and naval-intervention in Syria in the fall of 2015 that achieved its goal of keeping Damascus's dictator Bashar al-Assad in power at reasonable cost to Russia. Putin has also built a personalist political machine that has

ALLEN C. LYNCH *is a Professor of politics at the University of Virginia and Senior Research Associate at the Center for Russian Studies at East China Normal University, Shanghai. He is author of numerous works on Russian foreign and domestic policy, including* Vladimir Putin and Russian Statecraft *(Potomac Books, 2011). His scholarship has also been published in Russian, Chinese, French, and German. Professor Lynch has been writing for the Foreign Policy Association since 1992.*

respected the quadrennial timetable of national parliamentary and presidential elections while ensuring that such elections cannot be the means of removing Putin and his network from power. Such accomplishments, among others, help explain why independent Russian polling agencies have registered popular support for Putin in the range of 60-80% throughout nearly the entirety of his tenure in office.

Under Putin's tenure, Russian-American relations—after a brief alliance to defeat al-Qaeda and the Taliban in Afghanistan in the fall of 2001—deteriorated to the point where in 2015–16 Russian internet agents and intelligence operatives intervened in the U.S. Presidential election through a combination of hacking of computer systems and networks, disingenuous Facebook and other social media posts, etc. Putin and his network evidently concluded that Russia had so little to hope for from the bilateral relationship with Washington that the inevitable costs of such interference would be tolerable. In fact, the political fallout in the United States was so great that

Congress passed veto-proof legislation preventing President Trump from lifting economic sanctions against Russia, imposed after Russia's seizure of Crimea, without Congress's prior approval.

U.S., and especially European Union, economic sanctions against Russia, in place since 2014, have reinforced a marked economic stagnation in Russia that was apparent before their imposition. The Russian economy, which grew on average about 7% per year during Putin's first two terms as President (2000–08), recovered to just half that after the rebound from the world recession of 2008–09 and by 2013—before the onset of Western economic sanctions and while the price of Russia's most important export oil was at a historically high average of $100 per barrel—Russian economic growth was tending toward zero. Once again, while the Russian economy survived the twin shocks of historically low oil prices and economic sanctions, the country struggled to grow much beyond 1–2% per year, even as oil prices recovered from lows of approx. $30

per barrel in 2014 to over $80 at time of writing. This suggests that Putin's economic model of a state-dominated natural resource (especially fossil fuels) economy may have reached the limits of its capacity for development.

To the extent that this is true, this economic impasse (not yet a crisis) intersects with a political challenge that bedevils every authoritarian regime: how to arrange for a succession that preserves the leader's legacy without undermining his authority in the interim? From this perspective, a central strength of Putin's political system—the intense personal loyalty toward him of the network of military, paramilitary, intelligence and others—could serve to work against the future political stability of Russia were Putin no longer in the picture: authoritarian government is not necessarily the same thing as well-institutionalized governance. The analogies with the Soviet Union in the late Brezhnev period, when the government continually deferred hard choices until there were no longer any good ones, are highly suggestive.

The Putin political machine

When Putin was appointed prime minister by then President Yeltsin in August 1999, Russia was in many respects teetering on the verge of becoming a failed state: national political and economic institutions barely functioned and where they did, they were often captured by small networks of well-financed private banking interests exploiting the state for their own purposes. As already noted, the government had lost the war of secession against Chechnya between 1994–96. The Russian state was precariously dependent on foreign creditors, including the strongly U.S.-influenced International Monetary Fund; by the late

1990s, the cost of servicing Russia's external public debt was approaching 80-90% of government revenues. Not surprisingly under these circumstances, in August 1998 the Russian Treasury defaulted on its domestic and foreign debt obligations. Barter exchange had replaced cash payment throughout much of the economy and the government was frequently unable to pay the budgeted salaries of military officers, police, and border troops, not to mention teachers, doctors, and millions of ordinary workers still dependent on the state for employment. Amidst this widespread social and economic dislocation, suicides and divorces skyrocketed, births plummeted, and male life expectancy declined into the high 50s, where it remained throughout the decade. The Russian military-industrial base survived principally due to sales abroad, especially to China, as the Russian government was in no condition to

pay for the weaponry produced in local factories. In foreign policy, NATO had begun to admit former Soviet satellite allies Poland, Hungary, and the Czech Republic while almost at the same moment (March 1999) NATO launched a three-month air war against Russian historical ally Serbia; Russia protested without effect as NATO bombers (99% of which were U.S.) devastated the Serbian economy. From Moscow's vantage point, there seemed to be no limit to NATO's future expansion and Russia's geopolitical retreat.

A significant, though now waning, source of Putin's popularity in Russia stems from the comparison that most Russians make with life and policy under his rule with the Russia of the late Gorbachev period and 1990s. The establishment of economic and financial stability at home and the assertion of Russian interests abroad in the Putin years are seen as a major improvement

! Before you read, download the companion **Glossary** that includes definitions, a guide to acronyms and abbreviations used in the article, and other material. Go to **www.fpa.org/great_decisions** and select a topic in the Resources section. (Top right)

over the Gorbachev and Yeltsin years. Indirect confirmation may be found in a September 2021 poll conducted by the independent Levada Center that found that a plurality of Russians nostalgically prefers the economic, social, and even political security—real and imagined—of the Soviet system, even in its later, declining years, to alternatives associated with the liberal West. In addition, specific policy decisions taken by Putin as well as his demonstrated capacity for crisis management in key instances have reinforced his hold on Russian opinion. For instance, early in his tenure, Putin imposed a 90% charge on oil exports earned by Russian firms above the price of $28 per barrel. Enough of those funds were directed into state-managed accounts so that by 2006, Russia had fully paid off its foreign sovereign debt; and in 2008–09, when a truly existential crisis struck the Russian economy in the form of the collapse of global oil prices, Putin could exploit a $600 billion reserve fund of dollars and euros to act as a financial shock absorber and avoid the collapse that Gorbachev and Yeltsin experienced under comparable circumstances in 1986 and 1998, respectively. To the present day, Russia's public finances and trade balances are remarkably healthy by international standards: that $600 billion financial reserve has been periodically replenished; Russia's public debt as a percentage of GDP (less than 20%) is a small fraction of that of more developed economies such as the United States (more than 100%), Japan (nearly 250%), and Germany (more than 80%); and the country runs significant foreign trade surpluses year in, year out. Moreover, in 2018, after his overwhelming reelection as president, Putin pushed through parliament a controversial bill reforming the country's social security system, progressively raising the eligibility age for men and women by five years. Though Putin's popularity took a short-term hit (down to about 60% approval), the measure solidified the long-term financing of the Russian public pension system. In sum, while Putin's Russia faces major challenges

Gas pipes at the Comprehensive Gas Treatment Unit No.3 at the Gazprom PJSC Chayandinskoye oil, gas, and condensate field, a resource base for the Power of Siberia gas pipeline, in the Lensk district of the Sakha Republic, Russia, on Oct. 11, 2021. Amid record daily swings of as much as 40% in European gas prices, Russian President Vladimir Putin made a calculated intervention to cool the market by saying Gazprom can boost supplies to help ease shortages. (ANDREY RUDAKOV/BLOOMBERG/GETTY IMAGES.)

in modernizing its economy to be less dependent on fossil fuels, his economic team has managed the country's assets with a degree of prudence that reflects the impact of the twin shocks of the financial collapses of the late 1980s and late 1990s. By all evidence, a significant majority of Russians appreciate the relative economic and social stability that this has made possible.

Putin and his network have also built a political machine that, while authoritarian in its essence, has succeeded in attracting impressive levels of popular support over two decades. The cultivation of public opinion takes various forms.

First, Putin's upper leadership team—drawn disproportionately from military and paramilitary circles (Putin himself was a career intelligence officer in the KGB)—have exploited a favorable vacuum in Russian national politics in order to present Putin and those loyal to him (such as in the United Russia party) as the only plausible choice before the country. Russia's liberals were discredited by the disaster that befell the country in the "liberalizing" 1990s and have remained uncompetitive for national office since. In addi-

tion, the anti-liberal Russian Communist Party is commonly seen a party of nostalgia, one without a true program for what remains a post-communist Russia. Communist participation in national elections thus gives them the appearance of competition without the substance: in the last several presidential elections, Communist candidates have struggled to reach the 20% mark. With both liberal and communist alternatives being non-competitive, it has been simpler for Putin to present his national-patriotic program and persona as the only viable one for Russia.

Second, what Russian scholar Olga Kryshtanovskaya has termed Putin's "militocracy" has taken no chances. Electoral laws have been changed scores of times in the Putin era. These include: prohibiting foreign non-governmental organizations (NGO's) from monitoring Russian elections; changing the threshold of votes needed for parties to be represented in parliament as parties' fortunes waxed and waned; raising the membership minimums for parties to be legally registered; alternating between direct and proportional representation in parliament; prohibiting electoral alliances among parties;

Russian Cyber and Information Measures

The Russian interference in the 2016 U.S. presidential election was conducted by methods and agencies characteristic of earlier such interventions in European politics. It is based on the assumptions that: (a) a series of efforts to "reset" Russian-U.S. relations have failed and that there are no prospects for a revival of ties in the foreseeable future; (b) that Russia is now on its own and involved in a zero-sum competition with the United States and European Union for influence along Russia's historical borderlands, including inside Russia itself; and (c) that as the inferior power Russia must resort to every effort short of open war to defend its interests. This includes the use of relatively cheap electronic measures targeting the internet and computer systems of influential Western leaders, the exploitation of social media networks to spread information and disinformation unfavorable to the U.S. and most EU governments, as well as the targeting of vulnerable infrastructure systems. Non-governmental as well as official governmental organizations participate in these. A dramatic recent example was the ransomware cyberattack launched by DarkSide, a Russia-based but unofficial criminal organization that targeted the Colonial Pipeline gasoline distribution system covering much of the American southeast, disabling it and causing serious gasoline shortages for most of a week in May 2021. President Biden brought this issue up with Putin in his meeting with him in mid-June 2021 in Geneva and apparently made it a priority item with the Russian leader, who knows that the U.S. government has penetrated the Russian electricity grid with potentially disabling malware. DarkSide quickly ceased its operations.

Russia thus employs unofficial, including openly criminal organizations, as well as official government departments in conducting its cyber operations abroad. This assists in providing the Kremlin with "plausible deniability" when faced with accusations of interference by Western governments. No doubt, some of these operations are rogue in nature; but there is also no doubt, based on the nature of Putin's political regime, that he can put a stop to them when he has determined that they have gone too far and are harming Russia's international interests. This seems to have been the case with the DarkSide intervention just mentioned.

According to Andrew Bowen of the Congressional Research Service, the principal Russian government agencies involved in these cyber activities include:

The Main Directorate of the General Staff (GRU in Russian), which is responsible for Russian military intelligence. GRU used cyberattacks to great effect during the Five-day Russia-Georgia War of August 2008 but it also is in charge of a number of agencies conducting foreign political operations. The U.S. government has identified one such unit as the hacker of Democratic Party sites in the 2016 U.S. presidential election and another as the principal coordinator of hacked computer operating systems and e-mail accounts in that campaign.

The Foreign Intelligence Service (SVR in Russian), which is Russia's counterpart to the CIA and National Security Agency. While mainly concerned with the collection of intelligence on Russia's external adversaries, SVR has also been charged by the U.S. government with hacking activities during the 2016 U.S. presidential race.

The Federal Security Service (FSB in Russian), akin to the FBI. Once headed by Putin before he became President, FSB works with a network of unofficial and even criminal cyber experts, according to U.S. Department of Justice indictments of Russian cyber agents. These unofficial cyber units are often given leeway to conduct profit-making ransomware operations abroad in exchange for providing their technical expertise to FSB, so long as they do not negatively affect Russian international interests. DarkSide's attack on the Colonial Pipeline gasoline distribution system in May 2021 fits this profile.

The Internet Research Agency is technically a private, non-governmental organization but is headed by Yevgeny Prigozhin, a former high-level chef and caterer with close ties to Putin. Specializing in troll-type disinformation efforts and propaganda, Prigozhin's agency and officials working for it have been indicted by the U.S. government for disseminating anti-Clinton and generally inflammatory disinformation during the 2016 U.S. presidential election. The Agency also played a significant role in trying to reinforce the pro-"Brexit" movement during the 2016 referendum in Great Britain.

alternating between appointment and election of regional governors; introducing a constitutional amendment extending the presidential term from four to six years (2011); holding a national referendum allowing Putin to remain president until 2036 (2020); etc. Putin's regime has long supplemented such legal changes with other measures designed to suppress votes for opposition candidates. For instance, several candidates with identical or similar names (and even looks) are often registered to run in a district where an opposition candidate might have a serious chance of winning; in the September 2021 national parliamentary elections, such candidates appeared in fully 10% of all individual races. During that same campaign, the Putin-controlled Central Election Commission disqualified more than 90% out of 174 candidates for parliament running as independents. New but fake opposition parties and candidates appear from time to time to siphon off votes from genuine opposition slates (this practice was first tried on a major scale in 1996, when the Yeltsin government sponsored the presidential candidacy of General Aleksandr Lebed, who attracted enough votes from otherwise communist voters to assure Yeltsin's victory in the first round of the presidential vote that year). In another practice dating back to the 1990s, key constituencies such as soldiers, pensioners, and families with school-age children receive cash payments from the national government on the eve of balloting. Direct (through ownership) and indirect (through appointment of board members) government control of national television, radio stations, and other media companies has allowed Putin's government to maximize positive coverage of Putin while restricting routine access of critics to a national audience. In addition, closing opposition websites, selective arrests, harassment, imprisonment, and apparently even the poisoning of prominent critics of the regime—such as the social media–savvy critic Aleksei Navalny--reinforce the message that you "can't fight the Kremlin."

Navalny, an active Kremlin critic since he played a crucial role in organizing election protests in December 2011, has found it difficult to expand his political appeal beyond a core base of mainly urban, younger, well-educated Russians. He has his finger on the one issue—corruption—that Putin's Kremlin evidently fears could potentially escalate into a crisis for the regime. Yet even after Navalny disseminated on social media seemingly devastating videos detailing the opulence and malfeasance of Putin's circle, including former President and Prime Minister Dmitri Medvedev, as well as Putin himself in early 2021, the overwhelming majority of Russians reacted with indifference, as recorded in polling done by the independent Russian polling agency The Levada Center: fully 77% of Russians polled, evidently seeing corruption as an endemic condition of national life and fearful of change after two decades of relative stability under Putin, had not changed their predominantly positive view of Putin in light of such material. In June 2021, Levada registered approval for Navalny

Russian opposition activist and blogger Alexei Navalny holds a poster reading "I'm against repression and torture" during his lone protest in Moscow on October 27, 2012. About 200 people gathered near the headquarters of Russia's Federal Security Service (FSB) to protest the latest wave of arrests and allegations that one opposition leader was tortured into making a confession. (ANDREY SMIRNOV/AFP/GETTY IMAGES)

at 14% and disapproval at 62%, nearly the inverse of opinion on Putin.

The world-famous "Pussy Riot" case from 2012 likewise revealed the enormous gap between Western (and Russian liberals') perceptions of Putin and his regime and those of the Russian "silent majority." In that instance, five young women clad in balaclavas danced, suggestively in the minds of some worshipers, in front of the altar inside The Church of Christ the Savior in Moscow, chanting anti-regime slogans. Arrested for "inciting religious hatred" and "hooliganism," two of the women served out the two-year prison terms meted out and confirmed by Russian courts. "Pussy Riot" became a cause célèbre among liberals in Western Europe and the United States; the prosecution of the women involved was decried as persecution and a violation of core civil rights. Yet when polled on the subject, again by the independent Levada Center, 78% of Russians—many of whom regarded the incident as an act of sacrilege--either agreed with the sentence or thought that it was too short.

In this case, Putin benefited from

his close and considered identification with the Russian Orthodox Church, and more broadly with Russian traditionalism. In May 2007, he brokered the reunification of the domestic and foreign branches of the Church, rent asunder by the Russian Revolution and ensuing Civil War (1918–20). Since becoming president in 2000, he has taken great pains to be seen wearing the baptismal crucifix that his mother had him bless in Jerusalem in the 1990s. Since about 80% of Russians identify culturally (if not religiously) with Russian Orthodoxy, Putin's embrace of the Church reinforces a legitimacy that is based significantly on the conceit of Putin as the restorer of continuity in Russian history: his embrace of selective Soviet motifs such as victory in World War II and triumphs in outer space as well as non-Soviet motifs (given the persecution of the Church by the Communists) allows Putin to make a broad appeal to at least those Russians not very interested in politics. (This is in almost every society, including the United States, a significant majority of the population.)

Putin has thus combined a degree of charismatic legitimacy with a record in power that enough Russians have found defensible, certainly in comparison to perceived likely alternatives. Combined with the efforts of the Putin Machine, which includes the Central Electoral Commission, to limit the competitiveness of political challengers, a series of multi-candidate national elections held since 2000 reveals the scope of Putin's appeal to the Russian public. Putin's performance in these elections may be summarized as follows:

> 2000: 53.4%
> 2004: 71.9%
> 2012: 63.4%
> 2018: 76.7%

Moreover, in the 2008 presidential election, Putin's hand-picked candidate and protégé Dmitri Medvedev garnered 71.2% of the votes, which were cast in full knowledge that Putin would remain the power behind the scenes as Medvedev's publicly announced, to-be-appointed prime minister. This was in fact a maneuver to avoid violating the Constitution's two four-year presidential term limit; in 2011, the government moved a constitutional amendment to extend that term to six years' each. In 2020, Putin moved another amendment to extend his term limit potentially to 2036: it received 76.1% approval in a national referendum. These levels of support correspond closely to the degrees of popular support for Putin that the independent Levada Center has recorded over the past two decades, underscoring the success of Putin's machine in capturing the public as well as the state.

Elections for the Russian Duma, or parliament that were held on September 17–19, 2021, reflected Putin's grip on the Russian political system. Most true opposition candidates had been disqualified by the Putin-controlled Central Election Commission in the months leading up to the vote. The most prominent opposition figure, Aleksei Navalny, was in jail. In what he termed "smart voting," Navalny urged his supporters to vote for the strongest party outside of United Russia in the given electoral district by exploiting on-line apps available on Google and Apple systems; in this way, a semblance of a protest vote might be engineered. On the eve of the elections, under tremendous pressure from the Russian government, the two U.S.-based internet companies dropped those apps from their Russian stores. Finally, mysterious delays in tabulating votes from the new on-line voting system saw dramatic improvements in United Russia's standing. The results? Putin's United Russia party, which consistently polled at just under 30% approval by both independent and government pollsters, registered 50% of the vote (with 52% voter participation) and won 198 out of 225 parliamentary seats determined by races by individual candidates. Combined with proportional distribution of votes by party for the other 225 seats, United Russia retained a two-thirds supermajority in the Russian national legislature, allowing it to pass any constitutional amendments that may be desired by the government. The Putin machine had managed to preserve the Russian legislature as a de facto extension of the presidential administration. And unlike during the aftermath of the comparable December 2011 elections, there were few large-scale public protests.

Putin's foreign policy

Russian soldiers prepare to attack a Chechen military post just outside of Chechnya's capital Grozny on October 20, 1999. A Russian rocket strike in a crowded market area of Grozny on October 21 killed and wounded scores of people. Russian forces said they had targeted an "arms bazaar." (WOJTEK LASKI/GETTY IMAGES)

Putin's popular support is reinforced by the widespread Russian perception that he has asserted Russian influence in the outside world prudently and effectively.

Even before Putin came to power in 2000, the post-communist government of Boris N. Yeltsin had striven, mainly unsuccessfully, to combine a relationship of partnership with the United States with Washington's recognition of a Russian sphere of influence throughout former Soviet territories. Moscow termed the latter policy Monrovskaya doktrina, or Monroe Doctrine Russian-style, in an attempt to legitimize it in U.S. eyes. On the eve of Putin's appointment as prime minister in August 1999, while he was head of the Russian National Security Council, the U.S.-led NATO military alliance had begun its expansion eastward toward Russia's borderlands and waged a three-month air war against Serbia against strong Russian opposition. That war was a catalytic moment in Russian politics and public opinion: Russia's liberals were discredited because of their identification with the United States while Russian opinion, encouraged by the government and the media under its influence, rallied to an anti-American consensus.

In the fall of 1999, as Putin had begun to wage all-out war in order to recover the lost province of Chechnya, the Clinton administration began to criticize the Russian government and military for its conduct of the conflict in ways that it had not done when Putin's predecessor Yeltsin waged (and lost) the first stage of the war between 1994–96. In the event, Putin's policy of total war galvanized Russian opinion and cemented his relationship with the Russian military. By early 2000, the capacity of Chechen rebels to conduct large-scale, organized combat operations against Russia had been broken; this, more than any single factor, catapulted Putin to the Russian Presidency in the March 2000 election. As far as Putin and his national security team were concerned as they assessed U.S. policy, Russia was on its own.

It is all the more remarkable, then, that after the 9/11 terror attacks in the United States, Putin rejected the consensus advice of his advisers and allied Russia with the United States in the war against al-Qaeda and the Taliban in Afghanistan. Ironically, it was the presence of Russian troops outside of Russia, in Tajikistan along the Afghan border, that allowed Russia to reinforce anti-Taliban rebels in the north of Afghanistan quickly and effectively: it was these Russian-supplied troops that captured Kabul in November 2001.

Putin quickly discovered that Washington was uninterested in his agenda of a broader partnership. Against Putin's preferences, the United States maintained military bases in post-Soviet Uzbekistan and Kyrgyzstan years after the initial intense combat phase of the Afghan war was over in late 2001. The U.S.-led invasion of Iraq in March 2003 was only the most dramatic in-

U.S. President George W. Bush and Georgian President Mikheil Saakashvili (R) wave to the crowd May 10, 2005, at Freedom Square in the Georgian capital Tbilisi. The peaceful resolution of separatist conflicts on its territory is "essential" for Georgia to be integrated into the West, President Bush said in an open-air speech to tens of thousands of locals in this strategic ex-Soviet republic. (AFP/GETTY IMAGES)

stance of Washington ignoring Moscow's (and Paris's and Berlin's, among others) interests. By 2004, the United States was supporting Ukrainian presidential candidate Viktor Yushchenko against Putin's choice, Viktor Yanukovich, in a contested election that eventually saw the defeat of Moscow's candidate. At the same time, Bush administration officials were encouraging the new Georgian President Mikheil Saakashvili in the latter's effort for Georgia to join NATO as rapidly as possible. At NATO's summit meeting in Bucharest, Romania, in April 2008, U.S. pressure induced NATO to issue a communiqué to the effect that both Georgia and Ukraine would one day join the trans-Atlantic alliance. In the meantime, NATO continued to expand eastward to include Estonia, Latvia, and Lithuania, all part of the Soviet Union between 1940–91, as well as ex-Warsaw Pact members Bulgaria and Romania.

This is the political context for the five-day Russia-Georgia War of August 2008. Twice, Putin had offered to withdraw Russian troops from Georgia's border provinces of Abkhazia and South Ossetia, where they had been

stationed since the early 1990s, in exchange for a treaty in which Georgia would renounce NATO membership for 40 years. Twice had Saakashvili's government refused. When Saakashvili recklessly sent ground troops into South Ossetia in early August 2008 in the hope of eliciting U.S. support before Putin could react, Putin ordered the Russian Army across the border and in five days the Georgian army was defeated decisively. Fortunately, there was no contact between the Russian army and several hundred U.S. soldiers in Georgia training and equipping the Georgian army. Russian troops were suddenly withdrawn from Georgia proper but the message had been sent: Georgian (as well as Ukrainian) admission for NATO was a red line for the Kremlin that it was prepared to police by force. Putin had managed to assert Russian interests forcefully and without provoking a military confrontation with the United States or NATO. Russian opinion overwhelmingly supported this move.

In 2009, the Obama administration proposed a "reset" of relations with Moscow, based in part on the belief that the Bush Administration had overreached in its foreign policy in general and its approach toward Russia's borderlands in particular. Yet in spite of a number of impressive accomplishments—including a new nuclear arms control agreement, the expansion of Russian land and air space to assist NATO operations in Afghanistan, U.S. commitment to accelerate Russia's admission to the World Trade Organization (WTO), and even Russian restraint in arms sales to Iran pending the conclusion of a nuclear materials deal—the reset began to unravel in less than two years. This reflected in part the continuing enormous disparity in power between the two countries in favor of the United States and American unwillingness to grant Moscow the status of substantive equality; but it was also the result of deep policy differences over the international status of Russia's borderlands and the increasingly deep-rooted animosity in the bodies politic of Russia and the United States toward each other.

In March 2011, the Russian government had assented to UN Security Council Resolution 1973, which granted NATO the authority to engage in "humanitarian" intervention in the Libyan Civil War, in particular to prevent what was believed to be an impending genocide of Qaddafi's opponents in Benghazi. The Obama administration assured then Russian President Medvedev that such authority would not be used for purposes of regime change. By the summer, however, Libyan dictator Muammar al-Qaddafi's regime had indeed been overthrown by an opposition strengthened by the presence of NATO air power and Qaddafi himself had been killed. Putin, nominally prime minister but still the power behind the throne, was outraged, concluding that the Kremlin had been lied to by Washington and that Russia—with its veto on the UN Security Council—would never allow such authorization of NATO power again. The progressive destabilization of Libya, with consequent massive refugee flows outside the country, informed Putin's determination to prevent such intervention in the subsequent civil war in Syria, much closer to Russia. It was a simple mat-

ter for the Russian media machine to use video of the anarchy in Libya to persuade most Russians of the justice of this policy and of the danger allegedly posed by NATO (French and British warplanes, with U.S. logistical support, had flown most of the sorties over Libya.)

A few months later, in December 2011, protests broke out in several Russian cities against the apparent manipulation of parliamentary election results in favor of Putin's United Russia party. It was then that Aleksei Navalny emerged as a talented exploiter of social media to encourage and organize crowds against the Kremlin. The Obama Administration, led by Secretary of State Hillary Clinton and the newly appointed Ambassador Michael McFaul, quickly and publicly sided with the protestors against Putin's government. In the end, such remonstrances had no effect on those elections or on Putin's election once again as president just four months later but they reinforced the conviction in the Kremlin that the United States was bent not just on rolling back Russian power abroad but on undermining Putin's power from within.

The unraveling of the Obama-Russia reset was also driven by domestic-level factors in the United States beyond the control of the White House. In the fall of 2012, a major goal of the reset was achieved when Russia entered the WTO. One consequence of this was that cold-war era human rights legislation still on the books, namely the Jackson-Vanik Amendment to the 1972 U.S.-Soviet Trade Act that tied trade levels to Soviet emigration practices, was illegal under WTO rules. In order to protect U.S. companies from likely legal action, the U.S. Congress not only abrogated Jackson-Vanik (favored by the Obama administration) but substituted new human rights legislation in the form of the Magnitsky Act (opposed by the White House). This bill targeted individual Russian officials that the Congress deemed responsible for the death of the eponymous Russian lawyer of a U.S.-born businessman who died in a Russian jail after

abusive medical neglect: their assets in the United States could be seized, visas denied, etc. Almost immediately, Putin pushed through the Russian parliament a bill that prevented Americans from adopting Russian orphans: predictably, the law passed almost unanimously. Shortly before, Putin's government had expelled the U.S. Agency for International Development from Russia, fearing that it was encouraging Russians to organize civically and politically against Putin's regime.

By summer 2013, the bottom was falling out of the bilateral relationship. U.S. intelligence defector Edward Snowden wound up in Moscow and Putin refused to extradite him to the United States. In reply, President Obama cancelled a summit meeting with Putin scheduled for September 2013. Thus, even before the outbreak of the Ukraine crisis in late fall 2013, U.S.-Russia relations lay in tattered shreds.

That crisis revealed that Moscow and Washington were engaged in a "zero-sum" game for influence in Ukraine, whose international status Moscow regarded as a vital Russian national interest. In late November 2013, Putin had rewarded Ukrainian leader Viktor Yanukovich with an immediate $15 billion credit and assurances of continued low prices for the import of Russian natural gas for not signing an Association Agreement with the European Union. Subsequent protests throughout Ukraine were met with force, entailing deaths of demonstrators shot by police in early December; this triggered a massive escalation of protests and the effective loss of control over much of Ukraine's territory by Yanukovich's government. For the next two months, the national government in Kiev was paralyzed and Yanukovich, who retained Putin's support, seemed politically isolated. In mid-February, U.S. Undersecretary of State Victoria Nuland was recorded, no doubt by Russian intelligence, on an open cell phone call in Kiev with U.S. Ambassador to Ukraine Geoffrey Pyatt, reviewing the acceptability to the United States of candidates to run a post-Yanukovich Ukrainian government, one that all observers were convinced would pursue a strongly anti-Russian and pro-NATO policy once in power. In late February, an EU-brokered deal for accelerated national elections collapsed when street protestors, many well-armed, refused to support any deal that had Yanukovich remain as President, even provisionally. Yanukovich, whose taste for lavish corruption was well known, suddenly fled Ukraine to find protection under Russian jurisdiction and a new, pro-American government took power. This was the immediate context for the Russian seizure of Crimea in March 2014, the subsequent instigation of armed resistance in eastern Ukrainian regions bordering Russia, and the imposition of trade and financial sanctions by the United States and the European Union that remain in force to the present day.

Since that time, Putin's government has pursued a foreign policy based on the premise that Russia's core interests cannot be achieved through collaboration with the United States. In turn, a bipartisan U.S. consensus has emerged to the effect that Washington cannot maintain good relations with Moscow so long as Putin rules the Kremlin. Economic sanctions by the United States and the EU, most of whose members also belong to NATO, have induced Putin's government to find ways to counteract the overwhelming economic superiority that the Western states collectively have over Russia, on the order of 20:1 in terms of dollarized GDP. These ways include, but are not limited to, the cultivation of privileged bilateral relationships with key European countries, above all Germany; financing of nationalist and anti-EU parties throughout the EU; as well as intervention in electoral campaigns, including the 2016 U.S. presidential race between Donald Trump and Hillary Clinton. Russia has also sought to diversify its foreign policy, for instance, by intensifying its relationship with China in order to reduce the impact of growing economic isolation from the trans-Atlantic world. And, as Russia's Syrian intervention has shown, Putin is prepared to directly assert Russian

LUCIDITY INFORMATION DESIGN, LLC

military power abroad, regardless of U.S. and EU opposition.

The EU as a bloc is Russia's most important trading partner, although the Russian economy is much more dependent on the EU than vice versa. At the same time, many EU countries, above all Germany, import a significant percentage of their oil and natural gas from Russia (about 40% for Germany). Such imports are so important to EU states that the economic and financial sanc-

tions that Brussels imposed on Moscow in 2014 over Moscow's interference in Ukrainian affairs do not extend to Russian fossil fuels exports. Moreover, much of that fuel transited Ukraine and Poland on its way from Siberian producers to West European consumers, a legacy of Soviet-era infrastructure practice. This has meant that disputes between Kiev and Moscow allowed Ukraine a certain leverage over Russia, as Ukrainian governments have from

Russian President Vladimir Putin (R) shakes hands with Hungarian Prime Minister Viktor Orban during their meeting at the Kremlin in Moscow, Russia, September,18, 2018. (MIKHAIL SVETLOV/GETTY IMAGES)

time to time blocked or siphoned off Russian deliveries to Western Europe (those customers pay the highest prices of all of Russia's energy clients). In response, and well before the outbreak of the 2013–14 Ukraine crisis, Russia concluded a bilateral agreement with Germany for the construction of two natural gas pipelines under the Baltic Sea that directly connect Russia and Germany, bypassing Ukraine and the rest of Eastern Europe. In this way, Russia hopes that it can isolate its relations with Ukraine from those with the EU, where Germany remains the leading power. Russian pressure on Ukraine would thus no longer lead to a significant cut in fuels deliveries to key European customers, thereby reducing the incentives for the EU to intervene in disputes between Moscow and Kiev. In summer 2021, as the second pipeline was being completed, the Biden Administration effectively dropped its opposition to the project, implicitly acknowledging that it could not influence Germany on a question of such obvious economic importance to Berlin. Putin, himself an energy expert, had thereby established a balance between Moscow and the EU that Russia's macro-level economic dependence on the EU would not otherwise justify.

At the same time, Russia has cultivated relations with EU nationalist and populist parties and leaders in an effort to sow division and weaken the Union's capacity to act en bloc against Russia. These include the Hungarian populist leader Victor Orban, who has met at least annually with Putin since 2017 and has taken a number of initiatives on Russia that place him outside of the EU mainstream. These include: calling for an easing of EU sanctions against Russia; approving a contract with Russia (signed on September 27, 2021) for a natural gas pipeline that would bypass Ukraine by moving fuel under the Black Sea and thence through the Balkans to Hungary, a major consumer of Russian fuels; and approving for use in Hungary Chinese and Russian Covid-19 vaccines before they were approved by the EU. In this case, Putin is mainly reacting to an opportunity that Orban's own assault on EU influence in Hungary has presented but it underscores Moscow's preference for bilateralism versus multilateralism in relations with Europe. In Western Europe, official Russian institutions as well as internet agents with often murky ties to Russian intelligence have embraced far right parties advancing anti-EU agendas. The most prominent such case involved France's extreme right wing National Rally (at the time National Front) party, led by Marine Le Pen. Le Pen's party, openly

anti-immigration and anti-EU, could not obtain financing for its political operations within France or the EU in spite of approaching a dozen banks; in 2014, it was eventually able to obtain a $11.7 million dollar loan at 6% interest from the First Czech Moscow Bank, which is under the supervision of the Kremlin controlled Central Bank of Moscow. Le Pen's father Jean-Marie, founder of the party, secured a $2.5 million personal loan from a Russian-controlled holding company based in Cyprus belonging to an ex-KGB agent. In effect, Moscow is committed to supporting forces that weaken the EU and thus the bloc's potential to act as a unified whole against Russian interests in Europe, East and West.

Putin has also reinforced Russia's relationship with China in the face of growing hostility with the EU and the United States. In spring 2014, at the height of the crisis over Russia's seizure of Crimea from Ukraine, Russia signed a 20-year, $400 billion energy deal with China, guaranteeing China essential supplies of fuel for its booming industrial economy while affording Russia financing from China that was now unattainable on global capital markets dominated by the United States and European Union countries. Russia-China bilateral trade, which includes major Russian arms exports to China, now approaches $100 billion annually, up dramatically from less than $10 billion per year in the 1990s. In recent years, Russia has conducted regular naval maneuvers with the Chinese navy in the Sea of Japan and consults closely with China on matters related to Central Asian security through the Shanghai Cooperation Council. The two countries tend to vote in unison on the UN Security Council in opposing U.S. and/or EU countries' resolutions condemning human rights abuses by governments in situations like the Syrian Civil War and are determined that the UN not be made an instrument of Western military pressure against "sovereign" states. While far from a formal security alliance, Moscow's relations with Beijing have acted as an economic, diplomatic, and security shock absorber in the wake of Russia's semi-isolation from the West since 2014.

Along Russia's western border, EU and U.S. sanctions against the Belarusian regime of Aleksandr G. Lukashenko—over election fraud and the apparent hijacking of a commercial airliner in May 2021 to arrest a Belarusian dissident--have driven Minsk ever closer to Moscow. In September 2021, Russia pledged $630 million in new loans to Lukashenko's government and the continuation of deliveries of natural gas from Russia at prices well below those on the world market. In light of the end of immigration controls between the two countries and regular, large-scale joint military exercises, Belarus now clearly falls within an exclusive Russian sphere of influence.

U.S. President Joe Biden (2L) and Russian President Vladimir Putin shake hands as Swiss President Guy Parmelin (R) looks on during the U.S.-Russia summit at Villa La Grange on June 16, 2021, in Geneva, Switzerland. Biden is meeting his Russian counterpart, Putin, for the first time as president. (PETER KLAUNZER/POOL/KEYSTONE/GETTY IMAGES)

Concluding reflections

The collapse of the Obama-Russia reset that began in 2011 was the third failure to stabilize bilateral relations since the onset of the post-Soviet period in U.S.-Russian relations. By 1999, the Clinton-Yeltsin attempt to establish a comprehensive partnership died in consequence of Russia's socio-economic collapse, NATO expansion, and NATO's air war against Serbia. The U.S.-Russia alliance on Afghanistan after the 9/11 terror attacks imploded shortly after the overthrow of the Taliban in November 2001. In all three cases, the imbalance of power between Moscow and Washington in favor of the latter combined with irreconcilable objectives about the international status of Russia's historical borderlands undermined leaders' efforts to build a stable and mutually beneficial relationship. By October 2014, in the aftermath of the Russian annexation of Crimea from Ukraine, President Obama stated that the United States faced three principal threats: from the Ebola virus, from the ISIS terrorist group, and from Russia. His former Secretary of State Hillary Clinton, in running for president in 2016, implicitly made the case that in voting for her one would be voting for Obama's third term. The personal rancor between Putin and Clinton,

stemming from her public criticism of the 2011 Russian parliamentary elections, was intensified by Clinton later publicly comparing Putin's policies to those of Hitler. By all evidence, Clinton would be the handy winner of the 2016 presidential election against Donald Trump and be inaugurated in January 2017, just 14 months before Putin was to stand for yet another reelection. In sum, prospects for Russian-American relations seemed bleak; Putin had little to hope for and much to fear from a Clinton presidency.

This is the political context for assessing Russia's interference in that election. That Russian agents, both official and non-official, sought and in some cases succeeded in penetrating confidential and politically charged electronic accounts connected with the Democratic National Committee, is not in doubt. That these agents then sought to exploit such information to the embarrassment of the Hillary Clinton campaign is also well established. The scale and scope of such efforts, however, are not easily compatible with the thesis that their objective was to help elect Donald Trump President. How was the self-styled realist Vladimir Putin to believe that Trump had a serious chance of being elected when virtually every U.S. electoral expert held this to

be virtually impossible? Rather, taken in the context of the collapse in Russian-American relations since at least 2013, Putin sought to sow embarrassment about the U.S. political process in the expectation that Clinton would be elected. In this way, he sought to hinder a future President Clinton's ability to launch an anti-Putin campaign of political pressure based on allegedly superior U.S. political values precisely at the time when he was preparing his own campaign for reelection (March 2018). Ironically, had Clinton in fact been elected, Putin's efforts could be judged effective. But with Trump elected, and the poorly disguised Russian interference becoming a matter of common knowledge, the bipartisan political backlash in the U.S. Congress led to veto-proof legislation that prevented now President Trump from lifting economic sanctions against Russia without prior Congressional approval. Trump was thus powerless to offer Putin concessions on the single-most important item on the bilateral agenda. An otherwise polarized American political establishment now agreed that there could be no significant improvement in ties between Washington and Moscow so long as Putin remains in power. Russian-American relations have remained barren since.

discussion questions

1. Why has Putin enjoyed such high levels of popularity? Does he deserve this admiration?

2. Both Aleksei Navalny and Pussy Riot received low levels of support in response to their acts of resistance. Despite this, should they and other dissidents continue to challenge Putin's regime? Is it worth doing so?

3. Obama's "reset" of relations with Russia began to unravel only two years after it was established. This is in part due to the U.S. unwillingness to see Russia as its equal. Should the U.S. reconsider this perception of Russia in order to improve relations with Putin?

4. Should the United States be seeking influence in Ukraine? Is it important for American foreign policy to be supporting an anti-Russian government in that country?

5. Is there hope for a better relationship between Russia and the United States? Why or why not?

suggested readings

Timothy Frye, *Weak Strongman. The Limits of Power in Putin's Russia* (Princeton: Princeton University Press, 2021). Frye introduces the reader to the Russia which is often overlooked. By answering such questions as: "How popular is Putin?", and "Why are relations with the West so fraught?", Frye offers a new reassessment of Russian politics that provides a detailed examination of this modern autocracy.

Richard Rose, William Mishler, and Neil Munro, *Popular Support for an Undemocratic Regime: The Changing Views of Russians* (Cambridge, UK: Cambridge University Press, 2011). Rose, Mishler, and Munro use a series of surveys from 1992 to 2009 to show how popular support for the Russian regime has increased over the years, despite becoming more undemocratic. They explore why this phenomenon has occurred.

Andrei Tsygankov, *Russia and America. The Asymmetric Rivalry* (UK: Polity Press, 2019). Tsygankov argues that Russia, being the weaker power, exploits its relations with non-Western allies to defend and promote its interests and avoid yielding to U.S. pressures.

Richard Sakwa, Henry Hale and Stephen White, eds. *Development in Russian Politics 9* (Durham, NC: Duke University Press, 2019). Sakwa, Hale, and White explain recent developments in Russian politics including such topics as: executive leadership, political parties, and elections.

Angela Stent, *Putin's World. Russia against the West and with the Rest* (New York: Twelve Books, 2019). Stent examines Russia's turbulent past, its influence on Putin, Russian's understanding of their position on the global stage, and their belief that the West has denied them a seat at the table of great powers.

https://www.levada.ru (a bilingual website of the independent Russian polling agency The Levada Center with data and analysis of Russian public opinion going back to the 1990s).

Don't forget to vote!

Download a copy of the ballot questions from the Resources page at www.fpa.org/great_decisions

To access web links to these readings, as well as links to additional, shorter readings and suggested web sites,

GO TO www.fpa.org/great_decisions

and click on the topic under Resources, on the right-hand side of the page.

Myanmar's neverending crisis
by Hunter Marston

Protestors and local residents defend their makeshift barrier as military and police joint security forces attempt to clear the road blocks in Bayintnaung junction across the river from Hlaingtharyar. On February2, 2021 the Maynmar military, known as the Tatmadaw, seized power from the civilian government of Aung San Suu Kyi. (PANOS PICTURES/REDUX)

The latest coup in Myanmar which took place in early February 2021, has plunged the country into chaos and brought on the return of military rule, putting an end to nascent democratic institutions and a hard-fought peace process with numerous ethnic armed groups.

Myanmar is a country of more than 54 million people, representing a diverse patchwork of different ethnic groups, religions, languages, and cultures. After securing independence from British colonialism in 1948, the country soon found itself plagued by separatist forces, ethnic political grievances, and multiple communist insurgencies. The armed forces, under General Ne Win, seized power in a legally finessed coup in 1958 and held power for two years under a caretaker government before handing it back in 1960. However, the military soon found pretext for a coup d'état in 1962 and would hold power continuously for nearly five decades. Following a nationwide uprising in 1988, the regime refused to recognize the results of multiparty elections in 1990, which pro-democracy political icon, Aung San Suu Kyi and her party National League for Democracy (NLD)

HUNTER MARSTON *is a PhD candidate in International Relations at the Australian National University in the Coral Bell School of Asia-Pacific Affairs, and nonresident WSD-Handa Fellow at the Pacific Forum in Honolulu. He was the recipient of a 2018–19 Robert J. Myers Fellows Fund from the Carnegie Council for Ethics in International Affairs. From 2015–19, he was a Senior Research Assistant for the Center for East Asia Policy Studies and The India Project at the Brookings Institution. He previously worked at the Center for Strategic & International Studies (CSIS) Southeast Asia program, and completed his Masters in Southeast Asia Studies and Masters in Public Administration at the University of Washington in Seattle in 2013.*

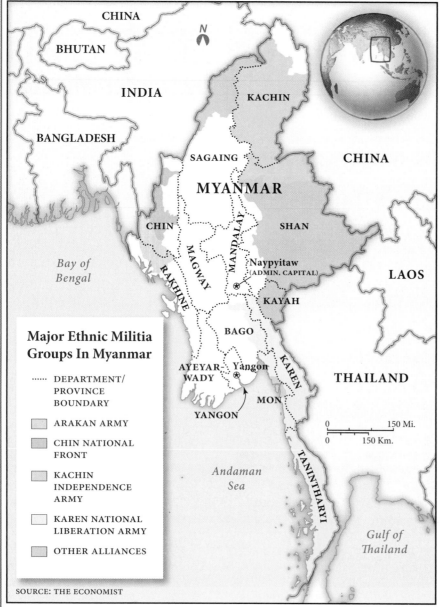

Major Ethnic Militia Groups In Myanmar

...... DEPARTMENT/ PROVINCE BOUNDARY

☐ ARAKAN ARMY

☐ CHIN NATIONAL FRONT

☐ KACHIN INDEPENDENCE ARMY

☐ KAREN NATIONAL LIBERATION ARMY

☐ OTHER ALLIANCES

SOURCE: THE ECONOMIST

LUCIDITY INFORMATION DESIGN, LLC

contested the 2015 national election, winning a majority of parliamentary seats and ushering in a fragile power sharing arrangement with Myanmar's armed forces.

Despite numbering more than 300,000 (a figure disputed by Myanmar scholars), the military has never managed to control the country's restive, mountainous frontiers. Ethnic minority armed groups have fought the military for decades, with some conflicts even dating back to independence from British colonial rule in 1948. However, the military, or Tatmadaw, as it is known in Myanmar, has prevented the emergence of a capable centralized government, while its economic mismanagement has kept the country mired in poverty, near the world's lowest development indicators, for decades. To stay in power, it has practiced divide-and-rule tactics by occasionally signing ceasefires with certain armed groups, while appealing to a potent form of Buddhist nationalism to sustain limited support from the country's powerful religious community. Given the successful holding of multiparty elections in 2015 and again in 2020, many Myanmar analysts were cautiously optimistic about the country's political future despite numerous problems. However, that democratic experiment ended suddenly when the armed forces staged the dramatic coup on the morning of February 1.

Background of the coup

Myanmar's democratic transition came to a sudden, unexpected halt on February 1, 2021, when the country's armed forces detained top civilian politicians and prominent civil society activists in an early morning raid. The military had clearly coordinated its round-up to occur before elected leaders were able to convene the Union Parliament that day to form a government based on the November 2020 election, which the NLD, led by Aung San Suu Kyi, won with a commanding majority. The military alleged "huge discrepancies" in the voters lists and declared the election results fraudulent. The generals announced a state of emergency for one year and promised to hold free

won. Instead, it clung to power and arrested thousands of political activists, including Suu Kyi whom they placed in house arrest where she would spend 15 years off and on until 2010. In 2008, the regime forced a military-drafted constitution through a controversial referendum under undemocratic conditions. The 2008 Constitution specifically enshrined the armed forces' control over

the country's most important political and economic institutions. In 2010, the military junta finally held multiparty elections under a tightly controlled process according to its constitution. Unsurprisingly, the Union Solidarity and Development Party (USDP), comprised mostly of retired officers and generals, won the election, which the NLD boycotted since Suu Kyi remained under house arrest. From 2011 to 2021, the Tatmadaw allowed a degree of civilian parliamentary politics and semi-competitive elections, despite wielding control over 25% of elected seats and several important government ministries. Aung San Suu Kyi's party

Before you read, download the companion **Glossary** that includes definitions, a guide to acronyms and abbreviations used in the article, and other material. Go to **www.fpa.org/great_decisions** and select a topic in the Resources section. (Top right)

and fair elections after that. In the interim, the Tatmadaw formed the State Administration Council (SAC) with commander-in-chief Min Aung Hlaing at the helm. Despite her arrest, detained leader Suu Kyi managed to release a statement on Facebook urging the people "not to accept the coup" and "resist" the military's efforts to take control from the elected government.

Peaceful protests ensued across the country, beginning with citizens banging pots and pans on rooftops in defiance of the coup. For the first several days, police and security forces merely looked on as protesters held demonstrations across the country, though the military also deployed armored vehicles to major cities. Days after the coup, a nationwide Civil Disobedience Movement (CDM) arose to protest against the military's seizure of power. Civil servants, bankers, and hospital staff across the country went on strike amid an already serious wave of Covid-19. The CDM spread its message effectively online and soon attracted a tremendous following and outflow of support on Facebook. The military junta cut off internet services and imposed curfews at night in a struggle to stem the tide of organized opposition to its power. When the military blocked Facebook, Myanmar users flocked to Twitter, and when the military cut off the internet and began targeting online activists, savvy internet users switched to the use of virtual private networks (VPNs) to hide their identity and circumvent the junta's control of their access to data and certain websites. The SAC has also raided NLD offices and arrested party leaders of all levels around the country. The military has filed at least 10 charges against State Counsellor Aung San Suu Kyi (a title she assumed after the 2012 election) and President Win Myint, ranging from corruption to violation of Covid-19 travel restrictions during the campaign period preceding the 2020 election.

On February 5, elected civilian politicians across different political parties formed the Committee Representing Pyidaungsu Hluttaw (Pyidaungsu Hluttaw is the Burmese term for the Union

A youth holds a sign of Gen. Aung San as demonstrators marched to protest the military coup in Yangon, Myanmar, Feb. 13, 2021. Feb. 13 is the birthday of the late Gen. Aung San, who is the father of Aung San Suu Kyi, and the founder of Myanmar's armed forces, and widely considered the father of the nation. (THE NEW YORK TIMES/REDUX)

Parliament) (CRPH). The CRPH retained Aung San Suu Kyi and Win Myint as State Counsellor and President, respectively, and included various members of parliament from a range of other parties, including the Kayah State Democratic Party, Ta'aung National Party, and Kachin State People's Party, though the majority came from the NLD, which had won 396 of 498 elected parliamentary seats in the 2020 national election. According to the

List of abbreviations:

NLD: National League for Democracy

USDP: Union Solidarity and Development Party

SAC: State Administration Council

CDM: Civil Disobediance Movement

CRPH: Committee Representing Pyidaungsu Hluttaw

NUG: National Unity Government

PDF: People's Defence Forces

EAO: Ethnic Armed Organizations

CDF: Chinland Defence Force

AA: Arakan Army

ASEAN: Association of Southeast Asian Nations

2008 Constitution, 25% of all parliamentary seats were reserved for active-duty military.

In mid-February, Mya Thwe Thwe Khine, a 20-year-old college student, became the first protester to die, after police in the capital Naypyidaw shot her in the head on February 9. At this point, violent protests erupted across the country, leading to well over a million people of Myanmar in the streets by some estimates. The Civil Disobedience Movement remained strong, though the junta threatened bank and hospital staff participating in CDM for refusing to return to work. In March police and military forces escalated lethal crackdowns against protesters, killing more than 38 on March 3. By mid-August, the death toll had surpassed 1,000, many of those having died in custody and showing signs of horrific torture. According to the Assistance Association for Political Prisoners, the junta has detained over 7,000 political prisoners, including children as young as four. In March, the CRPH designated the State Administration Council a terrorist group. The military likewise has referred to the CRPH as an unlawful and terrorist organization.

In early April, the CRPH announced a Federal Democracy Charter, annul-

Russian Defense Minister Sergei Shoigu, left, and Commander-in-Chief of Myanmar's armed forces, Senior General Min Aung Hlaing walk past the honor guard prior to their talks in Moscow, Russia, Tuesday, June 22, 2021. (VADIM SAVITSKIY/RUSSIAN DEFENSE MINISTRY PRESS SERVICE/AP IMAGES)

ling the 2008 military-drafted constitution and promising a new one to come. Weeks later, on April 16, the CRPH declared the formation of a National Unity Government, which in addition to Aung San Suu Kyi and Win Myint, who retained their positions in the new government, included Vice President Duwa Lashi La of the Kachin National Consultative Council and Zin Mar Aung as Minister of Foreign Affairs. The NUG's Minister for International Cooperation, Dr. Sasa, from Chin State, has emerged as a highly visible public figure speaking to numerous international conferences and liaising with foreign officials to promote the NUG's cause. The NUG is more diverse than the NLD and boasts a coalition of ethnic minorities, who make up roughly half of the cabinet, signaling the elected leadership's intent to bridge Myanmar's historic divides in order to challenge military rule.

The resistance movement began hinting at the creation of a federal army in March, which it hoped would bring together various ethnic groups and mobilize civilian resistance against military rule, but so far a true coalition force has yet to emerge. In its place, numerous local People's Defense Forces (PDF) have sprung up around the country, amounting to between 20,000 and 30,000 members

by some estimates. The Chinland Defense Force, one such example, has engaged in fierce combat with the Tatmadaw, reportedly killing 165 junta troops between April and June. Broad support for resistance to the coup and battlefield successes on the part of various PDFs and ethnic armed organizations (EAOs) have sapped the Myanmar military's morale, leading to increasing defections. According to the U.S.-ASEAN Business Council, the number of defections from the military doubled between August and September, bringing the total number to around 1,500. In June, roughly 800 troops reportedly abandoned ranks to join the Civil Disobedience Movement. The total number, including police, that have defected to the NUG's movement for a federal army is now thought to be around 2,000.

Commander-in-Chief Senior General Min Aung Hlaing and deputy commander-in-chief Soe Win have toured military facilities to try and boost morale. They have also used international diplomacy, including a trip to Moscow in June 2021 to meet with Defense Minister Sergei Shoigu to claim political legitimacy. In August, Min Aung Hlaing declared himself prime minister of an interim or "caretaker" government. A junta spokesperson insisted in a press conference at the end of August

that the military would not hold onto power for a long time, and reiterated its commitment to hold elections in August 2023. Many remain skeptical of these promises, since the Tatmadaw continues to indiscriminately kill civilians, arbitrarily detain families, and torture political prisoners, and it has recently burned down entire villages in rural upland states.

On top of the political crisis and overlapping armed conflicts, Myanmar has experienced a deadly third wave of Covid-19 since July 2021, exacerbated by the military's hoarding oxygen and refusing treatment (and testing) to prisoners exhibiting symptoms of Covid-19. As of mid-November, the official death toll from Covid-19 was nearing 19,000 with thousands of new cases every day. The pace of the junta's vaccination drive remained incredibly slow, while testing numbers and reports of a declining positivity rate aroused suspicion. The military has been quick to blame ethnic minorities for spreading the virus after returning across borders from Thailand or China. Somewhat surprisingly, the junta has administered vaccines to internally displaced Rohingya Muslims in Rakhine State. State media reported that over 3 million Rohingya have received two doses of the Covid-19 vaccine as of mid-September (just over six percent of Myanmar's total population), with 1.6 million having received one dose. The junta has repeatedly proclaimed its intention is to vaccinate half the population of Myanmar (upwards of 26 million) by the end of 2021, though this appears highly unlikely.

The junta has indicated its intent to dissolve the National League for Democracy based on its fraudulent claims of election irregularities in the voters list. The SAC has also pursued corruption charges against 45 different senior NLD leaders. The former mayor of Naypyidaw, former chief minister of Mandalay, Myanmar's second largest city, as well as a number of regional chief ministers all face trial for allegations of corruption filed by the SAC. The junta has also doled out criminal charges against journalists and activists of all stripes under Section 505(a) of the Penal Code, which carries a mandatory three-year jail term. The SAC has also used Section 505(b) of the Penal Code to arrest activists for protesting for alleged violations of Covid-19 restrictions. However, Beijing has reportedly pressured the regime not to eliminate the NLD, making clear that it still views Suu Kyi's party as integral to Myanmar's future.

Authoritarian resurgence

The military's return to power in Myanmar is emblematic of a larger trend in Southeast Asia of democratic erosion and authoritarian durability. Thomas Pepinsky, a Professor of Government at Cornell with a focus on Southeast Asia and the Muslim world, has written, "The real story of the state of democracy in Southeast Asia is not the threat of contemporary reversal—it is the strength of durable authoritarianism in the non-democracies." In fact, Southeast Asia has seen a gradual and discernible erosion of democracy over the past decade. According to Freedom House's 2021 rankings, only one country in the region fit the description of "free": Timor-Leste, which gained its independence from Indonesia in 2002. Four countries were partly free (Indonesia, Malaysia, the Philippines, and Singapore); and six were not free (Brunei, Cambodia, Laos, Myanmar, Thailand, and Vietnam). Freedom House downgraded Myanmar from partly free to not free in 2020 on account of escalating conflicts between the Tatmadaw and ethnic armed groups, which displaced thousands in Rakhine, Kachin and Shan states.

Despite the outbreak of Covid-19 in 2020, Myanmar went ahead with a general election in November, which was described as free and fair by election observers. Yet the NLD drew criticism for its perceived abuse of power, particularly due to restrictions on campaigning by smaller parties and the opposition Union Solidarity & Development Party (which held power from 2011–16 and is largely composed of retired military officers) as a result of the pandemic. Nonetheless, the NLD won handily with an overwhelming majority, though the USDP filed accusations of voter fraud and appealed to the military to intervene and force a recount. At first, few took these claims seriously. However, in the lead-up to the February 1 coup, talks between the military and representatives of the NLD broke down in late January, when Aung San Suu Kyi refused to concede to the military's demands for an investigation of the Union Election Commission's handling of the election. As a result, some analysts claim to have seen the writing on the wall in advance of the coup d'état.

The military's retaking political power and subsequent brutal crackdown on the opposition dashed many hopes for the country's ongoing transition to civilian parliamentary democracy. Others, however, had warned for years that Myanmar's transition was more fragile than hopeful analysts believed. As they pointed out, the military had never truly left Myanmar politics. The 2008 constitution, which underpinned the NLD's election victories, rested on a tenuous power-sharing arrangement that granted the Tatmadaw outsized control over political decision-making by reserving a quarter of all parliamentary seats for active-duty military officers as well as control of three powerful ministries: Home Affairs, Border Affairs, and Defense. The military also held the majority of seats on the shadowy National Defense and Security Council, on which both Suu Kyi and Min Aung Hlaing sat but which, notably, Suu Kyi had not convened for several years. The rift between Suu Kyi and Senior General Min Aung Hlaing deepened in recent years but reflected broader instability in the constitutional balance of power.

Under the NLD government, which was deposed on February 1, State Counsellor Suu Kyi had already displayed worrying authoritarian tendencies, consolidating political power and cracking down on critics in the media and civil society. After winning the 2015 election, upon coming to power in 2016 the NLD appointed chief ministers for each ethnic minority state from its own party even in those states where it had not won a majority of the vote. Rather than build trust with ethnic political parties that could have been useful in forming a stronger coalition to cement democratic precedent against the Tatmadaw's incursions into civilian affairs, the NLD thus isolated itself and therefore had few supporters from ethnic minority states. Min Aung Hlaing likely calculated that his coup would enjoy tacit support from those alienated by the NLD's centralizing tendencies. Secondly, the NLD (as well as the military) increasingly leveled defamation charges against critics of Aung San Suu Kyi and her policies for speaking out in seemingly innocuous ways through legal channels such as print media and peaceful demonstrations. Most infamously, in 2019 Suu Kyi traveled to The Hague to defend the military against charges of genocide against the Rohingya, which The Gambia had filed in the International Court of Justice. These anti-democratic leanings worried human rights proponents and fed into the military's narrative that the NLD was undermining national unity.

The Tatmadaw also likely judged that the general hollowing of democracy across the region offered a conducive environment for its political aims. Outside of Myanmar's own power struggle, Southeast Asia is rife with examples of autocratic rulers, providing an authoritarian handbook in how to dismantle democratic opposition and stay in power. In neighboring Thailand, a military coup in 2014 successfully brought Senior General Prayut Chan-o-Cha to power. He has since donned civilian clothes and named himself prime minister, putting in place a military-dominated senate. Next door in Cambodia, Hun Sen has ruled since coming to power in 1985 and, despite losing elections in 1993, managed to eliminate his rival Norodom Ranariddh in a military coup. Min Aung Hlaing may have also taken note of the Donald Trump administration's efforts to resuscitate U.S. alliances with authoritarian governments in Manila and Bangkok despite ongoing human rights abuses, thereby concluding that his seizure of power would not draw much criticism from Washington. At the same time, China's growing power and influence have given succor to autocrats in Southeast Asia who can benefit from emerging superpower competition by hedging between the two larger states.

Deteriorating human rights

The coup has gravely exacerbated numerous humanitarian crises in Myanmar. Since the coup, roughly 1.2 million people in Myanmar have lost their jobs, while the World Bank has estimated that the economy is set to contract by 18% in FY2021. According to Richard Horsey, Myanmar expert at the International Crisis Group, in April the country was "on the brink of state failure." The value of Myanmar's currency, the kyat, has dropped precipitously as millions have rushed to withdraw savings from banks and convert them to foreign currencies. Strikes by central bank employees who joined the Civil Disobedience Movement (CDM) also hampered the ability of banks to continue operating, while the Ministry of Electricity has suffered from taxpayers refusing to pay bills on top of striking civil servants not showing up for work. As mentioned above, the general state of emergency as a result of Covid-19

and the combined effect of the military coup have startled international investors and brought the economy to a crashing halt.

A general state of anarchy persists. Every week new reports emerge of local People's Defense Forces or vigilante actors confronting military units. For instance, in early September an attack targeted a military vehicle with an explosive in Mandalay, injuring two soldiers. Days before, PDF forces attacked Tatmadaw forces in eastern Naypyidaw, just miles from the capital. The junta denied these clashes took place, insisting they were propaganda, though local media corroborated the attacks with residents in the area. The Chinland Defence Force (CDF) claimed that it killed around 20 Tatmadaw troops in one attack on September 6 and more than 30 in another two weeks later. Similarly, PDF forces in Sagaing Region claimed to have killed 22 soldiers in two days of attacks in September. According to the NUG, PDF attacks caused 800 Tatmadaw casualties in 400 separate encounters in August alone. Resistance forces have also targeted local junta-appointed representatives, retired military officers, or members of the USDP, with assassinations panning out across the country. In a press conference in September the military charged that 933 individuals have died as a result of "terrorist attacks," a figure which includes 102 local administrators, 369 informants, and 140 security forces and other civil servants. According to USDP estimates, 253 members have died as a result of these targeted killings since February.

Junta opponents have also destroyed numerous telecommunication towers owned by MyTel, a corporation linked to the Myanmar military. In response, the junta has ordered widespread internet shutdowns.

Myanmar's security forces have responded to anti-junta violence and targeted assassinations with crackdowns on local PDF chapters, attacks on entire villages and townships, and arbitrary arrests, often detaining the family members of suspected NUG supporters. Villagers have come across mass graves revealing military massacres of civilian or PDF combatants, often with their hands tied behind their backs. Elsewhere military and police violence has been purely random, with numerous reports of security forces firing on unarmed bystanders or civilians on motorbikes. The combined result has been to instill absolute fear and uncertainty, as people are loath to trust police when family members are often reported to have died from unrelated illnesses after being detained.

For months the NUG had warned people to prepare for the announcement of "D-Day," a time when it would call upon the country to rise up against military rule. On September 7 that day came. Acting President Duwa Lashi La declared a "people's defensive war" against the Tatmadaw and urged citizens to resist the junta across the country. The announcement did not seem to have a discernible impact on day-to-day violence in the country, which has already been seized by ongoing conflict. However, the NUG no doubt hopes that the formal declaration of war will boost morale in the loose-knit movement against the military and possibly incentivize further defections from the armed forces and police.

A few EAOs, such as the Karen National Union (KNU) and Kachin Independence Army (KIA) have actively supported PDF forces and Bamar civilians fleeing central Myanmar to join the resistance. In late September the NUG claimed that a joint strike by KIA and PDF forces in Sagaing Region resulted in 40 Tatmadaw deaths. The coup and subsequent conflict has

The Rohingya

The Tatmadaw unleashed devastating "clearance operations" against the Rohingya in 2017 following limited strikes on police and border guard stations in western Rakhine State, leading more than 700,000 to flee across the border to Bangladesh for survival. The military has repressed Rohingya for generations and refused to acknowledge their claim to citizenship. The country's Buddhist majority generally opposes granting the Muslim Rohingya citizenship as well, and many Burmese insist that there is no such Rohingya group. Rather, they claim that Rohingya are illegal migrants from Bangladesh and a relic of British administrators' dissolution of the border with India under colonial rule. Myanmar's 2014 census refused to acknowledge the Rohingya's identity.

split KNU leadership, with different brigades responding divergently. A group of signatories to the 2015 Nationwide Ceasefire Agreement (NCA) have spoken out against the SAC and warned the Tatmadaw of retributions if it attacks civilians within the former's territory. As ceasefires break down, various subnational conflicts have merged into a tapestry of civil war across the country.

However, most ethnic minority groups have been reluctant to fully endorse the Burmese-led NUG and PDFs, while trust between ethnic minorities and the Burmese, or Bamar, remains limited. Despite the NUG's calls for a nationwide uprising against the junta, a handful of large ethnic armed organizations (EAOs) that have been in conflict with the Myanmar military for decades (some since independence in 1948) have remained on the sidelines, wary of taking sides. Some are reluctant to trust the NUG which they see as little different from the NLD that betrayed their cause for federalism and sided with the military in the violence committed against Rohingya in 2016–17. Others emphasize retaining fragile ceasefires signed with the military in 2015 before the NLD came to power. The majority of armed ethnic organizations either prioritize their own individual political autonomy or separatist territorial claims. The Arakan Army (AA) in particular proved a capable force in challenging the Tatmadaw on the battlefield in 2019. Since signing a ceasefire with the AA in 2020, the military has been careful not to aggravate it. Following the coup, the junta dropped criminal charges against a number of AA leaders as well as the leader of the Arakan National Party (ANP), Aye Maung, who served three years in prison for treason after vehemently criticizing Aung San Suu Kyi in 2018. As a result, the Tatmadaw has deliberately courted the Arakan Army in an effort to stave off a larger outbreak of armed conflict. If it were to turn against the junta now, the AA could lend significant momentum to the resistance movement.

Despite the incredibly bleak state of affairs currently, there are flickers of

hope of a more inclusive and democratic society as these previously isolated groups have joined causes and patched over historic divisions. For the first time, ethnic minorities have expressed sympathy with the struggle of majority Burmese fighting against the junta, and the Bamar say they finally understand the plight of ethnic minority groups, who have suffered under military rule for decades in their struggle for autonomy. Bamar Buddhists, who comprise roughly two thirds of Myanmar's population, have apologized to the Rohingya, whom the military has repeatedly targeted in attacks of ethnic cleansing over multiple decades, leading to refugee crises in the 1960s under General Ne Win and again in the 1990s, when hundreds of thousands fled Rakhine State to Bangladesh and were later partially repatriated. In the early days after the coup, one protester held a sign that read, "I Really regret about Rohingya crisis [sic]."

The Federal Democracy Charter, which the CRPH issued in April, calls for the "eradication of dictatorship and emergence of Federal Democracy Union," and furthermore promises that it will recognize the rights of "all ethnic nationalities" to live peacefully and exercise their right to self-determination. Notably, following skepticism from U.S. lawmakers, the NUG said that it will offer Rohingya citizenship, and in August it announced that it accepted the International Criminal Court's jurisdiction to "seek justice and account-

ability" for the military's crimes against Rohingya in 2016–17. The chief of the powerful Arakan Army, Major General Htun Mrat Naing, claims that his organization intends for "Muslims in Arakan State" to play a greater role in the administrative state and police force going forward. Interethnic and religious harmony between Muslims and Buddhists (Rohingya and Rakhine peoples respectively) could introduce a powerful antidote to the military's de facto partnership with the AA.

The fundamental challenge for the NUG now is to sustain opposition to junta rule, unite disparate armed groups under an overarching vision of federal democracy and ethnic harmony, and convince the international community that it is the legitimate representative of Myanmar. At present, it is uncertain whether the NUG enjoys sufficient international support to elicit stronger action from global powers to not only speak out against continued military rule, but to translate political will into collective pressure to force the military junta to abandon its current path of repression.

ASEAN adrift

The international community's response thus far has been painfully slow, heavy on rhetoric, and sadly lacking concrete action. Myanmar's democratic resistance has lost hope in the possibility for intervention by the United States or United Nations, both of whom it called upon in the early days of the coup to intervene and prevent the military's violent crackdown on civilian demonstrations. Hopes of international cooperation through the regional Association of Southeast Asian Nations (ASEAN) were similarly dashed when the multilateral group failed to mount an effective response or collectively denounce the coup. In fact, as mentioned above, several ASEAN states are themselves authoritarian dictatorships and therefore have been careful not to criticize the Tatmadaw and have even embraced coup leader Min Aung Hlaing. Several ASEAN countries have spoken out against the coup, namely Singapore, Indonesia, Malaysia, and the Philippines, but none have been able to compel the bloc to act with a unified voice or diplomatic response. The coup has exposed the deepening rift within ASEAN along the fault line of democracy and authoritarianism.

In early March, ASEAN convened an informal virtual meeting to discuss instability in Myanmar. The joint statement that emerged "expressed…concern on the situation in Myanmar and called on all parties to refrain from instigating further violence, and for all sides to exercise utmost restraint." It continued by urging "all parties concerned to seek a peaceful solution through constructive dialogue." However, it shied away from imposing any punitive actions or criticizing the military for instigating the coup in the first place. Furthermore, by emphasizing that "all parties" shared responsibility to deescalate, it seemed to cast equal blame on protesters and security forces alike, despite the fact that the Tatmadaw was to blame for the crisis. Finally, the virtual meeting included the military-appointed foreign minister, Wunna Maung Lwin, thus undermining opportunities for a frank and open discussion.

It took more than two months for ASEAN to hold a special summit on Myanmar in Jakarta in April, which Min Aung Hlaing attended in person. The NUG complained that it had not been invited to the summit, which it decried as lacking legitimacy because of its failure to include representatives from the ousted civilian government.

Nevertheless, the NUG welcomed the Five Point Consensus that emerged from the special summit and which even Min Aung Hlaing approved. The document called for:

■ "immediate cessation of violence N in Myanmar and [for] all parties [to] exercise utmost restraint";
■ "constructive dialogue among all parties concerned…to seek a peaceful solution in the interests of the people";
■ The nomination of "a special envoy of the ASEAN Chair" to "facilitate mediation of the dialogue process";
■ ASEAN to "provide humanitarian assistance through the AHA Centre";
■ "the special envoy and delegation shall visit Myanmar to meet with all parties concerned."

A subsequent ASEAN-U.S. Foreign Ministers' Meeting in July brought together ASEAN foreign ministers virtually and included the junta's representative Wunna Maung Lwin as well as U.S. Secretary of State Antony Blinken. This special summit was the first indirect interaction between an American official and the junta. Blinken expressed the Biden administration's "deep concerns" with developments in Myanmar and urged the junta to release all those "unjustly detained." Singaporean Foreign Minister Vivian Balakrishnan underscored his country's "full support" for the implementation of the five point consensus, but there was little substantive discussion of the crisis.

After months of waiting and internal division, ASEAN at last designated a special envoy for Myanmar, Brunei's Second Minister for Foreign Affairs, Erywan Yusof, on August 4. Erywan was largely perceived as a compromise choice after prolonged disagreement between alternate candidates put forward by Thailand and Indonesia. When the Bruneian minister traveled to Myanmar in June he was granted meetings with representatives of the junta but did not manage to access Aung San Suu Kyi or elected leaders. He later promised not to repeat this mistake on a forthcoming visit, which he said he hoped to make in late September. However, Yusof ultimately decided not to make the trip when it became clear that the junta was dou-

bling down on its refusal to grant access to Aung San Suu Kyi or representatives of the NUG. In late August, the 42nd ASEAN Inter Parliamentary Assembly convened, again including military representatives but none from the NUG. Yet as of late September, there has been no sign of progress for dialogue, and Erywan has failed to secure a meeting with representatives of the NUG. In a notable step, ASEAN made the unprecedented decision to bar Min Aung Hlaing from attending the annual ASEAN Summit and relevant meetings with dialogue partners, instead saying it would only permit a "non-political representative" to attend.

U.S. policy responses

The Biden administration was quick to condemn the coup and demand the restoration of Myanmar's democracy based on recognition of the 2020 election results. On the day that the coup occurred, the White House issued a statement from President Biden saying, "We will work with our partners throughout the region and the world to support the restoration of democracy and the rule of law, as well as to hold accountable those responsible for overturning Burma's democratic transition." The statement also declared the administration was reviewing existing sanctions policies, which would be "followed by appropriate action." On February 10, President Biden signed an executive order granting emergency powers to direct sanctions against the leaders of the coup. In a televised address, Biden said the United States was sanctioning senior members of the Myanmar military, their families, and business interests. The order also placed restrictions on the ability of U.S. companies to do business with corporations or individuals connected to the Myanmar military. The administration also froze $1 billion in assets tied to the Myanmar government, held at the Federal Reserve Bank of New York.

The U.S. government insisted development assistance would continue to flow to civil society and health care organizations operating in Myanmar. According to the State Department's website, the United States has provided nearly $1.5 billion in support for Myanmar's democratic transition since 2012, including funds for the country's peace process and assistance for economic reforms. The United States also provided $16.5 million in assistance to Myanmar's Covid-19 response in 2020. In March the U.S. Department of Homeland Security designated Myanmar nationals Temporary Protected Status, enabling those residing in the United States on visas to extend their stay up to 18 months due to political instability in their home country. In August, Washington directed an additional $50 million to nongovernment organizations assisting Myanmar's Covid-19 response during a devastating third wave.

The United States incrementally expanded targeted sanctions against the military junta and its business entities in the months after the coup. In March the Treasury Department announced sanctions on two light infantry divisions of the Myanmar military associated with ongoing human rights abuses and crackdowns on demonstrations. It also targeted two of the military's largest corporate networks, Myanmar Economic Holdings Limited (MEHL) and Myanmar Economic Corporation Ltd. (MEC). These groups are among the most profitable in the country and represent a significant revenue stream for the Tatmadaw. The European Union and United Kingdom announced similar targeted sanctions against MEC and MEHL. However, the United States has yet to direct sanctions against the Myanmar Oil and Gas Enterprise (MOGE), which brings in hundreds of millions of U.S. dollars in state revenue for the military every year. Chevron, the second largest oil and gas producer in the United States, which holds major stakes in Myanmar's offshore natural gas and oil fields, has lobbied against U.S. sanctions, arguing that such a move would negatively affect the livelihoods of its many employees in the country. In May the Treasury Department designated the State Administration Council (SAC) itself an official target of its sanctions, along with 13 junta officials and three immediate family members of senior generals. In

Member States of the ASEAN Alliance

*NOTE: Timor-Leste is not currently a member of ASEAN, but has established close economic ties with several of its member states.

LUCIDITY INFORMATION DESIGN, LLC

July the Treasury's Office of Foreign Assets Control (OFAC) added 22 more individuals to its list of targets for their role in supporting the military junta.

The Biden administration has consistently expressed support for ASEAN's efforts to bring about a diplomatic solution to Myanmar's political crisis. The United States and ASEAN dialogue partners such as Australia, China, and Japan have endorsed the bloc's five point consensus reached in April as the best path forward diplomatically. At July's Special ASEAN-U.S. Foreign Ministers Meeting, Secretary of State Blinken noted that the five point consensus represented an "important step forward" and urged the organization to hold the junta accountable. Blinken has also urged ASEAN to do more and responded positively to the group's designation of Bruneian diplomat Erywan Yusof as special envoy to Myanmar for crisis diplomacy. U.S. Trade Representative Katherine Tai in September repeated Secretary Blinken's call for Erywan to get on with his visit to Myanmar in order to keep the political process moving forward.

On a trip to Singapore and Vietnam in August, Vice President Kamala Harris voiced Washington's concerns with the military's violence and condemned the coup. "We condemn the campaign of violent repression. And we are committed to supporting the people there as they work to return their nation to the path of democracy," the vice president stated. Harris also reiterated U.S. support for ASEAN's diplomacy. On August 30, Secretary Blinken stated, "The United States stands with the people of Burma in their aspirations for democracy, freedom, peace, and development." Yet for all the repeated calls for strong action and vocal denunciation of the Myanmar military's subversion of democracy, the current crisis exposes the limits of U.S. power and troubling lack of sound options available to Washington policymakers. The international community remains hobbled by divisions between the great powers, particularly as exemplified in the failure of the United Nations Security Council to act decisively given Russia and China both have veto power over the group's decision making.

discussion questions

1. There is a long history of authoritarianism in southeast Asia. Knowing this trend, do you think it is possible for democracy to prevail in Myanmar? Why or why not?

2. Aung San Suu Ki has been criticized of undemocratic tendencies herself in the past. Does this fact damage her ability to be a strong opponent to the junta? Why or why not?

3. Does the reconciliation between ethnic minorities and the Burmese represent a hope for a future in Myanmar in which there is less in-fighting?

4. The United States has utilized targeted sanctions and the freezing of military assets to send a strong message to the State Administration Council (SAC). Have these policies proven effective? What other actions should the United States take toward the situation in Myanmar?

suggested readings

Mary Callahan, *Making Enemies: War and State Building in Burma,* Ithaca, NY: Cornell University Press, 2003. Callahan investigates how the military amassed power from independence in 1948 onward, and how it grew to push out other state and social institutions in order to secure a firm grasp on national power.

Michael Charney, "Myanmar coup: how the military has held onto power for 60 years," *The Conversation,* February 4, 2021. In this insightful article, Charney details the history of the military from independence in 1948 up to the coup of February 2021.

Nick Cheesman, "Post-legalism and the fear of politics: Understanding Myanmar's contradictory coup," ABC, February 9, 2021, https://www.abc.net.au/religion/post-legalism-and-myanmars-contradictory-coup/13135576 "Post-legalism "is explained by Cheesman as the rationale on which the military based their decision to launch a coup.

Aaron Connelly, "The coup in Myanmar and the threat to ASEAN centrality," International Institute for Strategic Studies, March 1, 2021, https://www.iiss.org/blogs/analysis/2021/03/coup-myanmar-asean The coup in Myanmar is a serious threat to the stability of ASEAN. Connelly examines the different ways in which the Association of Southeast Asian Nations may respond.

Hunter Marston, "Behind the coup: what prompted the Tatmadaw's grab for power," *New Mandala,* February 12, 2021, https://www.newmandala.org/behind-the-coup-what-prompted-tatmadaws-grab-for-power/ Marston explains the factors which prompted the Tatmadaw to launch a coup and dispose of the elected government.

Thant Myint U, *The Hidden History of Burma: A Crisis of Race and Capitalism,* New York, NY: W.W. Norton & Co., 2019 Myint-U explores if democracy and an equitable economy are possible in Myanmar. In so doing, he dissects how such factors as rising inequality, and tension around race and religion have come together to challenge democracy.

Don't forget to vote!

Download a copy of the ballot questions from the Resources page at www.fpa.org/great_decisions

To access web links to these readings, as well as links to additional, shorter readings and suggested web sites,

GO TO **www.fpa.org/great_decisions**

and click on the topic under Resources, on the right-hand side of the page.

Xi's China takes on the Quad
by Kevin Rudd

President Joe Biden walks to the Quad summit with, from left, Australian Prime Minister Scott Morrison, Indian Prime Minister Narendra Modi, and Japanese Prime Minister Yoshihide Suga, in the East Room of the White House, Sept. 24, 2021, in Washington, DC. (EVAN VUCCI/ AP IMAGES)

From his desk in *Zhongnanhai,* Chinese President Xi Jinping looks east with some anxiety. Over the last 180 years, all the biggest threats to China's security have come from the sea. It is therefore unsurprising that China has long seen its maritime periphery to the east as particularly hostile. Securing China's maritime periphery and maximizing the country's strategic depth into the Pacific, including by eventually pushing U.S. forces all the way back to the Second Island Chain (running from the Japanese archipelago in the north, through Guam, to Papua New Guinea and Australia in the south) is a critical component of Xi Jinping's overall strategy.

This is seen as essential for a number of reasons. First, to force U.S. reconnaissance aircraft and ships back from their decades-long practice of conducting regular operations just off the Chinese coast. Second, to assist China in its outstanding territorial claims over Taiwan, the South China Sea, and in the East China Sea. And third, to finally "break through the thistles"—as Chinese naval strategists put it—of the constricting geography that currently keeps China's naval forces effectively bottled up behind the First Island Chain

KEVIN RUDD *is an Australian politician and diplomat who served as prime minister of Australia from December 2007 to June 2010 and again from June 2013 to September 2013. After retiring from politics, Rudd was named Senior Fellow at the John F. Kennedy School of Government at Harvard University and Distinguished Fellow-in-Residence at the Paulson Institute at the University of Chicago. In January 2021, he was named the eighth President and CEO of the Asia Society.*

(Japan, Okinawa, Taiwan, the Philippines, and the Indonesian archipelago), allowing China to become a truly blue-water maritime power.

China rightly sees the forward deployments of U.S. armed forces across East Asia as indispensable to the projection and sustainment of American power in the region. China understands that these deployments are anchored in the long-standing U.S. base on Guam and its array of military, naval, marine, and intelligence facilities scattered across the territories of U.S. allies Japan, Korea, and Australia and the freely associated states in the North Pacific and supported to a lesser extent by Singapore, Thailand, and the Philippines. Under the direction of Indo-Pacific Command in Honolulu, the U.S. military's capabilities across the region are formidable in their own right. But their ability to forward deploy across the vast expanse of the Indo-Pacific is profoundly enhanced by the strategic real estate offered by these allies and other strategic partners. That is why

China has a long-standing strategic objective of fracturing U.S. alliances if at all possible. China's strategic logic is clear: America, without its alliances, would be considerably weakened, if not pushed out all together from the Indo-Pacific. Whereas China currently lacks strategic reach into the Pacific, America's allies afford the United States an extraordinary advantage. This is a state of affairs that Xi Jinping wants to reverse.

The key element of China's strategy for securing its wider maritime periphery is military—the rapid expansion of Chinese air and naval capabilities, reinforced by land-based missiles and cybersystems, which would aim to overwhelm U.S. and allied combatants. They would achieve this by sheer force of numbers and by controlling the informationized battle space. But China's military strategy is greatly reinforced by its economic strategy, leveraging the magnitude of the Chinese market with each of America's critical allies in an effort to peel them away from Washing-

ton over the long term—gradually increasing the economic costs of standing against China and so reducing over time their sense of loyalty, commitment, and obligation to the United States. In addition, China has sought to wield its political and diplomatic muscles, along with its economic power, against individual allies that have proven to be particularly recalcitrant in their insensitivity to Chinese national interests. The intention here is to make punitive examples of such states by limiting their access to the Chinese market (or, in extreme cases, interfering with their assets or even arbitrarily detaining their citizens in China) thereby warning others of the price to be paid for thumbing their nose at Beijing's political demands. The corollary, of course, is to reward those countries that increasingly reject political cooperation with America. All three parts of this strategy are designed to weaken the solidarity of U.S. alliances over time. China had some considerable success on this score over the years, such as in the Philippines.

Enter the Quad

But a critical new development in the Indo-Pacific region's alliance structures has now emerged: the rebirth since 2019 of the Quadrilateral Security Dialogue between the United States, Japan, India, and Australia—otherwise known as the "Quad." The Quad, although falling far short of a formal alliance structure with mutual defense obligations (India not being a treaty ally of the United States or Quad member states), nonetheless appears to be rapidly evolving as the most significant direct regional response to date to Beijing's increasingly assertive strategic posture. Xi's response to this important new challenge is evolving as well.

Before you read, download the companion **Glossary** that includes definitions, a guide to acronyms and abbreviations used in the article, and other material. Go to **www.fpa.org/great_decisions** and select a topic in the Resources section. (Top right)

When Japan's Shinzo Abe invited diplomats from the United States, Australia, and India to gather for a working-level meeting on the sidelines of the November 2017 Association of Southeast Asian Nations (ASEAN) Summit in Manila to discuss significantly deepening their cooperation, Beijing dismissed it as of little concern to its strategic interests. The Quad, said Chinese foreign minister Wang Yi after the meeting, was only ever a "headline-grabbing idea… They are like the seafoam in the Pacific or Indian Ocean: they may get some attention but will soon dissipate." Beijing's strategic community at this time viewed the countries of the Quad as simply too divergent in their national interests to come together with any coherence. Beijing had some good reasons to think so at the time.

The Quad had, after all, been tried once before, a decade earlier, in the mid-2000s. At that time, it never progressed

beyond informal breakfast talks among officials, having been rejected categorically by the Australian government of my predecessor, John Howard. Abe's original vision for the Quad emerged in the aftermath of the 2004 tsunami that devastated much of South and Southeast Asia, killing more than 227,000 people across fourteen countries. At the time, Japan, the United States, India, and Australia coordinated a joint—if somewhat haphazard—natural disaster response. Abe envisioned building up the four countries' capacity to work together in the region to meet shared challenges, including regional security.

In the other capitals the response was tentative at best. In Washington, Vice-President Dick Cheney was a supporter, but President George W. Bush was lukewarm from the start. He worried that the appearance of intensifying security cooperation between the four countries would alienate the Chinese support he sought in helping with nuclear proliferation in both North Korea and Iran. By December 2008, the Bush administration was privately assuring regional governments that the Quad would never coalesce—as evidenced in diplomatic cables subsequently published by another Australian, founder of WikiLeaks Julian Assange. In Delhi, Prime Minister Manmohan Singh openly ruled out any real security cooperation with the Quad, also categorizing ties with Beijing as his "imperative necessity." Indeed, before my government said anything about the Quad, Singh had publicly declared that it "never got going" and consigned it to history. Meanwhile, in Canberra, Howard's conservative government was also eager to maintain strong, economically beneficial ties with China. It adamantly opposed expanding existing trilateral strategic cooperation with the United States and Japan by adding India to the mix. His government signaled its withdrawal from the Quad at a meeting of the U.S.-Japan-Australia trilateral dialogue held in Washington in July 2007—also documented in a WikiLeaks diplomatic cable—and announced the decision in Beijing soon after. So when Abe, as the driving force behind the Quad, then unexpectedly resigned in September 2007, it delivered the death knell to Quad Version 1.0. His successor Yasuo Fukuda then consigned the Quad to history. By the end of 2007, when my government entered office, all engagement within the Quad framework had already been dead in the water for months. Taking the temperature in other capitals, we found no interest in attempting to revive it.

The rebirth of Quad 2.0

However, a decade later when Abe—back in office once more—set out to get the band back together, the region's strategic circumstances had fundamentally changed. By 2017, the U.S.-China relationship was adrift, and each of the Quad capitals was reevaluating its strategic calculus toward China. But Beijing was not yet paying serious attention to these developments.

At its first 2017 meeting in Manila,

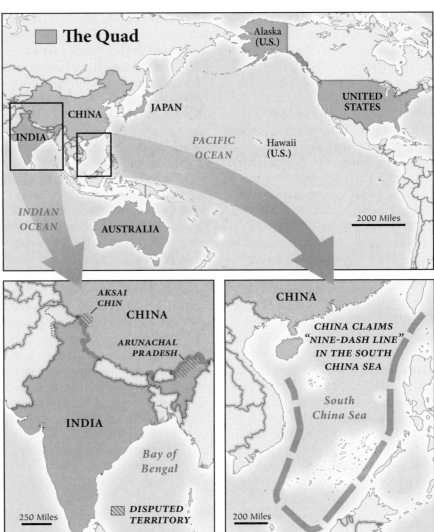

LUCIDITY INFORMATION DESIGN, LLC

the Quad countries seemed to demonstrate their previous level of internal disarray by failing to issue a unified communiqué outlining any common strategic purpose. Instead, they each released their uncoordinated statements, serving mostly to highlight divergences on key concerns. Japan left off American and Australian language on "connectivity" efforts in the Indo-Pacific (meant to offer an alternative to China's Belt and Road Initiative/ BRI) while Tokyo considered whether to cooperate with the BRI. Meanwhile, India left off all references to maritime security, freedom of navigation, and international law included by the others. The only thing the four countries did agree on was to meet once a year on a regular schedule.

It was not until September 2019

that the Quad's four foreign ministers finally met in New York for their first ministerial-level meeting. However, this time they agreed in principle to work together on what would become the Quad's mantra: to "advance a free and open Indo-Pacific." Even still, Beijing remained largely indifferent. By the time the Quad foreign ministers met again in October 2020 in Tokyo, Beijing began to pay attention. Seven months earlier, the first round of what became known as the Quad-Plus talks had also been held, with South Korea, New Zealand, and Vietnam joining the Quad countries to discuss cooperation on trade, technology, and supply chains—a development Beijing eyed with growing concern.

However, the turning point came in June 2020, when Chinese and Indian forces clashed along their shared border in what would prove to be the most significant and catalytic event in the development of the Quad. A high-altitude face-off near the disputed Pangong Lake in the Himalayan Ladakh region descended into a bloody hand-to-hand melee in which twenty Indian soldiers and at least four Chinese soldiers were killed. This was followed by mass nationalist demonstrations in India at which protesters burned Chinese goods, Xi's portrait, and the Chinese flag and called for country-wide boycotts of Chinese goods. Indian prime minister Modi promised a firm response, saying Indians could be "proud that our soldiers died fighting the Chinese." Diplomatically insensitive wolf warriors in the Chinese media, who blamed India for the clash while simultaneously mocking the Indian military's losses, helped fan the flames before Beijing finally brought them under control. While an escalation in the military conflict was averted, by September, the import of dozens of categories of Chinese products had

been blocked by Delhi and more than 250 Chinese software apps (including TikTok and WeChat) were banned from India. This was a significant setback for China's technology companies, who had viewed the Indian market as the cornerstone for future global expansion. Tensions with Delhi were only amplified further by the impact of the Covid-19 pandemic.

On the strategic front, the clash caused Delhi to fundamentally reassess its defense priorities, and India—heretofore the most reluctant of the four partners—suddenly became eager to deepen its participation in a more formal security framework that could serve as a potential strategic balance against China. Subrahmanyam Jaishankar, India's foreign minister, explained that, from India's perspective, the Quad had a "larger resonance" following the border clash and that there were much greater "comfort levels" in Delhi and Washington on a need "to engage much more intensively on matters of national security." That fall, India, for the first time in thirteen years, invited Australia

to join the annual Malabar joint naval exercises held with the United States and Japan. This was especially notable because despite growing closer to the rest of the Quad since 2017, India had refused to allow Australian participation in the Malabar exercises in 2018 and 2019, fearing it would unnecessarily antagonize China by portraying the Quad as a militarily focused partnership. But after the June 2020 border clash, all remaining political hesitation in Delhi was gone.

So when the Quad met in Tokyo that October, the geopolitical wei qi board, from Beijing's perspective, already looked far more problematic. Then U.S. secretary of state Mike Pompeo bluntly declared that Washington's goal was, ultimately, to "institutionalize" the Quad, "build out a true security framework," and even expand the grouping at "the appropriate time" to "counter the challenge that the Chinese Communist Party presents to all of us." To Beijing, it suddenly seemed as though the Quad was not only alive and well but that it might also expand.

Shifting Chinese Reactions to the Quad

Watching all these events unfold over the course of 2019 and 2020, China's strategic community had been undergoing a significant shift in its conceptualization of the Quad as a potential threat to Chinese national security interests. Tellingly, two scholars at the influential Central Party School warned of the Quad's "increasing institutionalization." Another, at the Chinese Academy of Social Sciences, noted that trends were demonstrating the Quad's transition from an "informal framework of cooperation" to a "formal regional organization." The October 2020 Quad ministerial meeting seemed to confirm these concerns.

But all such analysis appeared to point to a relatively straightforward solution: China could still use a combination of sticks and carrots to drive a wedge between the Quad countries where possible by accentuating their

conflicting national interests. In particular, the overwhelming economic reliance of each of the Asian Quad partners on the Chinese market seemed like a key weakness ready for exploitation. The simple idea was to break the Quad apart.

Beijing implemented this strategy almost immediately following the October 2020 Quad meeting. Chinese foreign minister Wang Yi dropped all nonchalant references to seafoam and changed his tone dramatically. Instead, he slammed the effort to build an "Indo-Pacific NATO" and said the Quad's Indo-Pacific strategy was "itself a big underlying security risk" to the region. China then quickly selected a target on which to use its stick. A classical Chinese axiom advises to "kill one to warn a hundred" (shayi jingbai), but in this case, the goal was to kill one (Australia) to warn two (Japan and India).

Beijing previously seemed intent on improving relations with Canberra. But without specific explanation, it suddenly imposed restrictions on imports of Australian coal—and then meat, cotton, wool, barley, wheat, timber, copper, sugar, lobster, and wine. At the same time, Chinese state media unleashed a blitz of messaging, accusing Canberra of having used the Quad meeting to "promote its own global status," asking, "How much strength does Australia own with its limited economy and population?" It warned that "if Canberra is bent on infuriating China, Australia will only face dire consequences." One analyst in China's unofficial Global Times, which is authorized to deliver hardline messages to foreign countries that the government and the party won't, declared simply: "Being a mouthpiece for U.S. aggression against China will cost Australian jobs." Then, at a press conference in Beijing, Chinese foreign ministry spokesperson Wang Wenbin urged Australians to "reflect upon their deeds" if they wanted any chance of restoring trade relations. While there were other elements at play in the Australia-China relationship beyond the Quad, the timing and content of the message from Beijing was unmistakable.

The campaign of economic retaliation against Australia continued to escalate, with China regularly using the Australian example elsewhere around the world as a warning that countries who "let themselves be led by the nose" by Washington risked being cut off from China's huge domestic market. Beijing clearly estimated that Australia was the least likely of the Quad countries to actually break with the United States; the most vulnerable to economic coercion (as the smallest of the four Quad states); and the least threatening to Chinese interests (being more distant from China's borders than Japan, India, or the long arm of American power).

The second part of China's strategy was to try to simultaneously repair relations with Japan and India—efforts also discussed at some length in the previous chapter, but which are worth summarizing again briefly here. Beijing had already been engaged in an effort to thaw relations with Japan since 2018, when Chinese premier Li Keqiang traveled to Tokyo for a trilateral summit along with South Korean president Moon Jae-in. There, Abe and Li agreed to implement a new maritime and aerial crisis communication mechanism to handle encounters in the disputed East China Sea. After a series of meetings between Abe and Xi on the sidelines of various multilateral fora, relations briefly appeared to be on the upswing, and a major visit by Xi to Japan was planned for the spring of 2020—only to be delayed by the Covid-19 pandemic.

After the October 2020 Quad meeting, Beijing stepped up its attempts to finalize the visit by Xi to meet with Abe's successor as prime minister, Yoshihide Suga. Chinese foreign minister

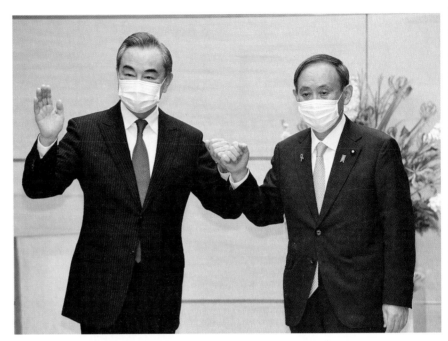

Japanese Prime Minister Yoshihide Suga (R) and Chinese Foreign Minister Wang Yi pose for a photo ahead of their meeting in Tokyo on Nov. 25, 2020. During their meeting, Suga voiced concern about Beijing's attempts to undermine Japan's administration of the Senkaku Islands, a group of East China Sea islets claimed by Beijing. (KYODO NEWS/GETTY IMAGES)

Wang Yi embarked on a visit to Tokyo in November 2020 in an attempt to re-energize the diplomatic thaw, only to be met with a frosty reception. Crowds of demonstrators, angry about human rights abuses in Xinjiang, Tibet, and Inner Mongolia gathered outside Suga's residence to protest Wang's visit, while legislators from Suga's governing Liberal Democratic Party drafted a resolution calling for an official cancellation of the summit with Xi. Meanwhile, Suga's chief cabinet secretary, Katsunobu Kato, conveyed Tokyo's "concerns about the activities of the Chinese government ships around the [Senkaku] islands," reporting that the situation was "extremely serious." By early 2021, the proposed visit to Tokyo by Xi was officially off—fatally undermined by escalating Chinese incursions into Japanese-claimed waters in the East China Sea and growing Japanese public and official concerns over human rights.

At the same time, Beijing was trying to de-escalate tensions with Delhi by seeking to defuse the border crisis and entice India with offers of economic and Covid-19 vaccine aid. But in the

end, Beijing met with little success in slowing India's embrace of the Quad. While the immediate standoff on the border may have been resolved, wariness of China had been deeply implanted in Delhi's psyche.

As the Quad continued to solidify and the scope of its activities expanded, entering into a series of new bilateral and multilateral security agreements and exercises, Beijing's confidence that the Quad could be split apart waned. China seemed not to have fully comprehended the impact of their actions in accelerating overall Quad solidarity. Moreover, China's ability to execute a coherent strategy of simultaneous targeted escalation with Australia and de-escalation with Japan and India was badly undermined by the lack of discipline of its ultra-nationalistic wolf-warrior diplomats, who succeeded in regularly offending countries across the globe. For example, a Communist Party social media post mocking India's death toll when combatting Covid-19 incited fury and disgust not only in India and the West but also from many social media users in China itself.

Finally, the election of President

Yoshihide Suga, Japan's prime minister, second right, speaks while a monitor displays U.S. President Joe Biden, Scott Morrison, Australia's prime minister, and Narendra Modi, India's prime minister, during the virtual Quadrilateral Security Dialogue (Quad) meeting at his official residence in Tokyo, Japan, on March 12, 2021. As President Biden seeks to shore up ties with allies in Asia, he's reshaping the message to avoid spooking them about America's intentions when it comes to China. (KIYOSHI OTA/BLOOMBERG/GETTY IMAGES)

Biden and his focus on allied, regional, and multilateral engagement, changed the dynamic. China lost the relative freedom of diplomatic international maneuver it had during the "America First" days of the Trump administration. The new administration was willing to quickly resolve Trump-era trade and military-basing disputes with U.S. allies such as Japan and South Korea, stabilizing relations. Whereas during the Trump period, Beijing largely pushed on an open door in its efforts to bolster its influence with other countries in the region, it suddenly faced a much more united front from Washington and its allies and partners.

Beijing's worst fears

Beijing's thinking on what to do about the Quad shifted again, coming to a head in March 2021, when the four countries held their first leader-level summit. The pivotal meeting saw the group release its first unified joint communiqué. Titled the "Spirit of the Quad," the statement agreed to "strive for a region that is free, open, inclusive, healthy, anchored by democratic values, and unconstrained by coercion," and to "facilitate collaboration, including in maritime security, to meet chal-

lenges to the rules-based maritime order in the East and South China Seas."

The Quad leaders also launched a joint vaccine-distribution initiative in the Indo-Pacific, challenging China's "vaccine diplomacy" efforts by agreeing to cooperate to produce and distribute one billion vaccines for the region. They also set up a vaccine-expert working group, a climate-change working group, and a "critical and emerging technologies" working group on securing technology supply chains, all aiming to strengthen cooperation in meeting these challenges in the region. Indian prime minister Narendra Modi spoke to what may have been Beijing's worst fears when he declared that: "Today's summit meeting shows that the Quad has come of age. It will now remain an important pillar of stability in the region."

To Beijing, the summit indeed seemed to confirm the worst: that the Quad would—by providing an alternative multilateral source of infrastructure development funding, trade initiatives, and other public goods, along with diversified regional supply chains—soon expand its competitive challenge to Chinese influence from the security realm to the economic.

Moreover, Beijing appeared to worry that the Quad would soon coordinate more closely with the Five Eyes intelligence grouping, the G7, and NATO to isolate China—a concern that turned out to be well-founded.

Full-scale attack

After the March 2021 Summit, China quickly made a third pivot in its strategy to try to deal with the Quad: full-scale political attack. There was soon an explosion in Chinese official condemnations of the Quad as a "small clique" (Xiao Quanzi) of countries. As Xi Jinping put it in a speech in May 2021, in Beijing's eyes, they were using "multilateralism as a pretext to… stir up ideological confrontation." Their collective goal, Beijing claimed, was nothing less than to "start a new Cold War." In contrast, China increasingly portrayed itself as the true champion of a "genuine multilateralism" that was "inseparable from the UN system," as well as being the leading defender and reformer of that system and of global governance in general. References by Xi and others to "great power responsibility" (daguo dandang) and China being a responsible international leader became pronounced.

Beijing's strategy transitioned to try to diplomatically isolate and marginalize the Quad by outflanking it internationally. As one Central Party School scholar argued, China should "deepen strategic interactions" and increase maritime security cooperation with ASEAN as a "type of counterweight" to the Quad. Another Chinese scholar wrote that strengthening pan-Asian economic cooperation through the Regional Comprehensive Economic Partnership (RCEP) and Comprehensive Progressive Trans-Pacific Partnership (CPTPP) trade agreements would "cushion" the Quad "and its negative impact on the regional order." In essence, the strategy aims for China to "go bigger" than the four-member Quad grouping in order to contain its influence on the regional and global stage.

Yet such denunciations have so far done little to stall the Quad's progress in galvanizing multilateral resistance to

China. In June 2021, President Biden made an extended trip to Europe, including a G7 summit in the UK that was joined by Australia and India, among others. Biden then met with both EU officials and NATO. In every case, relations with China became the top subject of discussion. Moreover, when South Korea's President Moon traveled to meet with Biden in Washington in May that year, the United States pressed Seoul to join the Quad's three new working groups and to make a statement supporting the Quad. Although Moon has been reluctant to take sides overtly with the United States in any wider strategic contest with China, in this case, Washington succeeded, and the two countries' joint statement agreed that they "acknowledged the importance of open, transparent, and inclusive regional multilateralism including the Quad"—and "the importance of preserving peace and stability in the Taiwan Strait." And, moving forward, it is possible that Seoul will find itself continuing to see more value in drawing closer to the Quad if relations with North Korea enter another period of significant tension.

Finally, in September 2021, the leaders of the Quad met in person for the first time at a summit in Washington, demonstrating the priority the four countries' leaders have now attached to continuing the group's momentum. They agreed to expand cooperation on vaccines, climate change, infrastructure financing, and supply chains for critical and emerging technologies like semiconductors and 5G, as well as cybersecurity.

All this has reinforced Beijing's worst fear: that not only could the Quad expand, for example by taking in South Korea to become "the Quint," but also that it could become the multilateral building block for a broader anti-China coalition of North American, European, and Asian liberal-democratic states. An example of this growing concern manifested itself in May 2021, when China's ambassador to Bangladesh delivered a strongly worded warning to Dhaka that it would "substantially damage" its ties with China if it joined or coordinated its actions with the Quad. The warning was striking because Bangladesh (which called the remarks "aggressive" and "very unfortunate") has retained a strenuously neutral foreign policy and had given no previous indication at all that it was planning to work with the Quad. The incident, therefore, seemed to demonstrate a level of worry bordering on paranoia that seems to have taken hold in Beijing regarding the potential expansion of the Quad and its activities.

The British invasion

It was in this context that the trilateral security partnership between Australia, the UK, and the United States known as AUKUS landed with a political and diplomatic splash in September 2021, just ahead of the first in person summit of the Quad's leadership. Negotiated in secret between Morrison, Biden, and UK prime minister Boris Johnson, the pact was billed as addressing regional security concerns which the leaders said had "grown significantly"—i.e. from China. The core of the agreement is a deal for the United States and UK to share nuclear submarine propulsion technology with Australia, which intends to build at least eight nuclear-powered attack subs in Adelaide. But the pact also includes broader security cooperation measures as well, including an agreement for Australia to explore hosting U.S. bombers on its territory, the acquisition by Australia of long-range precision strike missiles, and joint cooperation on "cyber capabilities, artificial intelligence, quantum technologies and additional undersea capabilities."

Beijing predictably reacted with alarm, calling the agreement "extremely irresponsible", a move that "seriously undermines regional peace and stability and intensifies the arms race" and one contributing to nuclear non-proliferation. Given Australia's strategic geography, and the relative weakness of China's anti-submarine capabilities, this is unsurprising from a security perspective. But the broader worry for Beijing is that the pact signifies that the Quad may not have been the last multilateral grouping to emerge in response to China's rise and its new forward-leaning strategy under Xi. .

But, for Washington's part, the AUKUS agreement also represented the result of simmering frustration with some of its European allies' unwillingness to act in a unified manner to confront China in a meaningful way. One group in particular within Europe has backed

Royal Australian Navy submarine HMAS Rankin is seen during AUSINDEX 21, a biennial maritime exercise between the Royal Australian Navy and the Indian Navy on September 5, 2021, in Darwin, Australia. Australia, the United States and the United Kingdom have announced a new strategic defence partnership, known as AUKUS, to build a class of nuclear-propelled submarines and work together in the Indo-Pacific region. (POIS YURI RAMSEY/ AUSTRALIAN DEFENCE FORCE/GETTY IMAGES)

French president Emmanuel Macron's guiding concept of "strategic autonomy," believing that Europe should remain generally neutral in Washington's global and regional struggle for ascendancy against Beijing, maximize Europe's economic opportunities, and promote Europe's strength and independence. For Washington, however, this group's equivocations are detrimental to efforts to unite more countries behind its multilateral coalition. This tension exploded into view with the AUKUS agreement.

With Australia moving to acquire nuclear submarines under the pact, it scrapped an existing $90 billion deal to buy diesel powered boats from France. Paris, which claimed it was never notified or consulted about the deal, was predictably outraged, with French Foreign Minister Jean-Yves Le Drian describing it as a "stab in the back" and something similar to "what Mr. Trump used to do." Calling the allegedly secret negotiation of the deal between the Anglosphere countries behavior "unacceptable between allies and partners," Macron took the dramatic step of temporarily recalling France's ambassadors to Australia and the United States. For Macron and those of similar mind in continental Europe, the incident only reinforced the perception that the United States could not be relied upon. Both he and EU foreign policy chief Josep Borrell declared that it reinforced the need to achieve European "strategic autonomy." Xi is likely to try to make the most of this potential opening into Europe, and in an October 2021 call with Macron he hinted that, since "recent major world events have once again demonstrated that France would be correct in advocating EU strategic autonomy," stronger Sino-French relations would "inject more stability into the world situation."

But AUKUS signified that Washington is now increasingly willing to leave those whom it perceived to be the more unreliable among the Europeans behind until they are ready to catch up. Instead, it has increasingly turned to rely on its Quad partners, along with its traditional Anglosphere allies, including the UK and the rest of the Five Eyes group. These allies have been quicker to perceive China as a potential threat to their security interests – a fact well demonstrated by Japan, whose new prime minister, Fumio Kishida, announced in October 2021 that his officially pacifist country will move to double defense spending in order to "prepare for realistic possibilities to protect our people." This has been accentuated by Tokyo's notable increased outspokenness on its willingness to act to defend Taiwan alongside the United States, and in August 2021 Tokyo and Taipei held their first bilateral security talks. Japan's deputy prime minister at the time, Taro Aso, warned that an attack on Taiwan, or "various situations, such as not being able to pass through the Taiwan Strait," would pose "an existential threat" to Japan, which would "need to think hard that Okinawa could be next." He noted that, "if that is the case, Japan and the United States must defend Taiwan together." This has represented a fundamental shift in Tokyo's diplomatic and strategic approach, which has traditionally always been extremely careful to moderate its rhetoric and its image as a regional security actor, even as it has deepened cooperation with the United States. Beijing, for its part, immediately threatened that Japan would "dig its own grave" if it joined the United States in intervening in a conflict over Taiwan, but the trend is now clear: Japan and the rest of the Quad are quickly moving to solidify security relations with Washington, despite all of China's best efforts.

The coming arms race in the Indo-Pacific

Overall, Xi Jinping has therefore achieved decidedly mixed results in securing China's maritime flank. China has had a number of strategic and diplomatic successes over the years, but the rise of the Quad has crystallized geopolitical resistance to the sustained weight of China's economic and foreign policy assertiveness into a focused institutional response. The Quad is uniquely problematic for China's strategy because its aim of unifying a multilateral coalition of resistance has the potential to stiffen spines across the whole of the Indo-Pacific and possibly beyond. For Xi, the critical question is whether the Quad will evolve to be large, coherent, and comprehensive enough to effectively balance against China, thereby undermining any sense that its dominance, in Asia or globally, is inevitable. So far, Beijing has struggled to mount an effective response to the Quad challenge. Whether Chinese officials settle on a strategy that succeeds in undermining the Quad's progress will be one of the key factors in determining the course of U.S.-Chinese competition—and the fate of China's global ambitions more generally—in what has already become a "decade of living dangerously."

China has considerable reason to worry about such developments and what they could mean for its regional and global prospects. On the security front, for example, the Quad changes Beijing's thinking about various scenarios in the Taiwan Strait and the South China Sea and, to a lesser degree, in the East China Sea, as China's sense of the likelihood of Australian, Indian, or Japanese military involvement in any conflict involving the United States grows. Especially significant would be the Quad's coordination with the United States' Pacific Deterrence Initiative. A distributed network of land-based anti-ship missiles and other precision-strike capabilities stationed in allied countries in the region could hinder Beijing's ability to threaten Taiwan with an amphibious invasion, a blockade, or land-based missiles—although political agreement on such deployments in individual Quad countries is far from guaranteed, despite the steps taken in this direction in the AUKUS pact. Another Chinese concern is that the Quad will move toward an intelligence-sharing arrangement with the Five Eyes intelligence partnership, which would allow for sensitive information on Chinese strategy and behavior to be more widely disseminated.

But the worst-case scenario from Beijing's perspective is that the Quad could serve as the foundation of a broader global anti-Chinese coalition. If the Quad were to draw other Asian countries, and eventually the EU and NATO, into efforts to confront or undermine China's international ambitions, it could over time swing the collective balance of power definitively against China. The Quad could also lay the groundwork for a broader allied economic, customs, and standards union, which could reshape everything from global infrastructure funding to supply chains to technology standards. The Biden White House's senior Asia official, Kurt Campbell, has already spoken of the need to provide a "positive economic vision" for the Indo-Pacific; Beijing fears that the Quad could become the fulcrum for such an effort.

One positive development from Beijing's perspective is the Association of Southeast Asian Nations (ASEAN), which has been perturbed by AUKUS and is likely to keep its strategic distance from the Quad, given its desire to maintain neutrality amid U.S.-China tensions. And Xi is also likely to continue to look to continental Europe to try to court potential disaffected American partners, even as China continues its current strategy of discrediting the Quad in international institutions.

Chinese officials also take comfort from continued protectionist sentiment in both Washington and Delhi, which means that neither is likely to join the CPTPP (or even RCEP) any time soon. Indeed, the gravitational pull of the Chinese economy will remain the greatest tool for weakening the Quad and subverting counter-Chinese efforts more broadly: for Beijing, China's continued economic growth and increasing share of the global economy remain its most potent strategic advantages, as they were in the past. It is for this reason that in September 2021 China formally applied to become a member of the CPTPP. The move by Beijing presents the TPP-11, led by U.S. allies Japan and Australia, with a major dilemma, particularly as China is not seeking to renegotiate standards in order to gain access to this higher-quality trade agreement. Were China to successfully join, it

Chinese President Xi Jinping, also general secretary of the Communist Party of China Central Committee and chairman of the Central Military Commission, boards the aircraft carrier Shandong and reviews the guards of honor at a naval port in Sanya, south China's Hainan Province, Dec. 17, 2019. Xi attended the commissioning ceremony of China's first domestically built aircraft carrier, the Shandong. (LI GANG/XINHUA/GETTY)

would represent a final inversion of the Obama administration's original vision of using the CPTPP to reduce regional dependence on trade with China. And without any clear alternative economic vision of its own to offer, Washington will find itself in a vulnerable position.

China will meanwhile also double down on strategic and military cooperation with Russia. Moscow and Beijing have already committed to expand bilateral nuclear energy cooperation, and in a May call with Xi, Russian President Vladimir Putin called Chinese-Russian relations "the best in history." From China's perspective, Russia serves as a useful military partner and, with respect to the Quad, offers a way to expand China's field of strategic options geographically. Russia's proximity to Japan and its continued occupation of Japan's Northern Territories, for example, could make Tokyo think twice before joining with the United States in any future military scenarios involving China.

The continued consolidation of the Quad will also serve to drive further increases in Chinese military spending. Even if some Chinese analysts

are doubtful about the actual impact of the Quad on the hard business of warfighting, military officials will argue that they must be ready for worst-case scenarios involving the Quad. Chinese officials are wary of repeating the Soviet Union's mistake of military overextension at the expense of the civilian economy. But if they see the correlation of forces with the United States and its allies shifting against China, Beijing's military spending will increase accordingly, turbocharging the regional arms race in Asia that has now begun.

Ultimately, the biggest question may be what all of this means for Xi, especially in the run-up to the 20th Party Congress, in the fall of 2022, where Xi hopes to secure his own long-term political dominance. There is some chance that the Quad's progress will offer Xi's detractors additional evidence of his inclination to strategic overreach. More likely, however, is that Xi will ultimately manage to strengthen his own hand by pointing to the Quad as proof that China's adversaries are circling the Motherland, thereby further consolidating his hold on power and ensuring U.S.-China tensions continue to climb.

discussion questions

1.) A big part of the Chinese strategy to draw Washington's allies away is leveraging the power of the Chinese economy. How successful will this play out for President Jinping's plan to break up the Quad?

2.) The Quad alliance was originally tried out in the mid-2000s but soon after died out. What factor has been most influential in initiating its revival in recent years?

3.) Is it important for the United States to maintain a powerful presence across the East Asia region? If so, to what extent will the Quad be able to fulfill this goal?

4.) As a result of the AUKUS agreement coming into creation, a French-Australia deal was scrapped resulting in Paris being outraged. What is the likelihood that President Jinping will exploit this alliance rupture, and how concerning is that possibility?

5.) The presence of the Quad will likely be exploited by President Jinping to prove that he must consolidate more power resulting in worsening U.S.-Chinese relations. Does the possibility of this turn of events invalidate the existence of the Quad?

suggested readings

Brown, Kerry. *CEO, China: The Rise of Xi Jinping.* I.B. Tauris. 288 pgs. July 2016. Brown reveals how Xi Jinping has been quietly building one of the most powerful leaderships modern China has ever seen.

Osnos, Evan. *Age of Ambition: Chasing Fortune, Truth, and Faith in the New China.* Farrar, Straus, and Giroux. 416 pgs. May 2015. Writing with great narrative verve and a keen sense of irony, Osnos follows the moving stories of everyday people and reveals life in the new China to be a battleground between aspiration and authoritarianism, in which only one can prevail.

Wright, Thomas. *All Measures Short of War: The Contest for the Twenty-First Century and the Future of American Power.* Yale University Press. 288 pgs. May 2017. In this book Thomas Wright explains how major powers will compete fiercely even as they try to avoid war with each other. Wright outlines a new American strategy—Responsible Competition—to navigate these challenges and strengthen the liberal order.

Denmark, Abraham. *U.S. Strategy in the Asian Century: Empowering Allies and Partners.* Columbia University Press. 336 pgs. August 2020. U.S. Strategy in the Asian Century offers vital perspective on the future of power dynamics in the Indo-Pacific, focusing on the critical roles that American allies and partners can play. Abraham M. Denmark argues that these alliances and partnerships represent indispensable strategic assets for the United States

Kelton, Maryanne. *More than an Ally? Contemporary Australia- U.S. Relations.* Ashgate. 226 pgs. October 2008. Maryanne Kelton introduces specific cases to demonstrate both the intensity and complexity of dealing with the United States. Through these empirical studies the government's approach is examined across trade, security, and industry sectors. The book adds to the current debate as it provides an explanatory framework for understanding the Australian government's choices in its relations with the United States across the broader spectrum of security issues.

Don't forget to vote!

Download a copy of the ballot questions from the Resources page at www.fpa.org/great_decisions

To access web links to these readings, as well as links to additional, shorter readings and suggested web sites,

GO TO www.fpa.org/great_decisions

and click on the topic under Resources, on the right-hand side of the page.

No end in sight:
a century of drug wars
by Mónica Serrano

A Mexican drug enforcement agent destroys poppies in a field in the southern state of Guerrero. (MATIAS RECART/AFP/GETTY IMAGES)

The United States has long played a key role in the set of policies that, for over half a century, have sought to eradicate illicit drug-trafficking and that have long been associated with the notion of the war on drugs. Today, as the governments of the United States and Mexico revisit the terms of their security and counter-narcotics cooperation, the concept of the war on drugs is again at the center of bilateral and regional political debates.

The chain of operations, campaigns, and plans that have been at the heart of successive wars on drugs in Latin America have failed to curb the cultivation, production, trans-shipment, and sale of illicit drugs in the U.S. drug market and increasingly, too, in Latin America. Since 1982, when President Ronald Reagan declared the second U.S. war on drugs and increased

MÓNICA SERRANO *is a professor of international relations at El Colegio de México. She is the senior fellow at the Ralph Bunche Institute, associate fellow of the International Institute for Strategic Studies IISS, and a member of the International Faculty of the Doctorate on Organised Crime at the University of Milan. She was the founding Executive Director of the Global Centre for the Responsibility to Protect (2008–11), a member of the International Advisory Board of the FRAME Project "Fostering Human Rights Among European (External and Internal) Policies" and co-editor of* Global Governance. *She has published extensively on international security and Latin America, with particular reference to international institutions, security, human rights, transnational crime, and civil-military relations.*

U.S. President Donald Trump speaks in the White House press briefing room flanked by Attorney General William Barr (3rd L), Defense Secretary Mark Esper (3rd R), Chairman of the Joint Chiefs of Staff Gen. Mark Milley (2nd R), National Security Adviser Robert O'Brien (2nd L) and Chief of Naval Operations Admiral Michael Gilday (R) April 2020 in Washington, DC. (WIN MCNAMEE/GETTY IMAGES)

the budget for narcotics control, in turn intensifying interdiction along the U.S. borders and expanding eradication and law enforcement in transit and source countries, a number of ill-fated regional trends became visible. First, throughout the region the military's involvement in drug-control efforts continuously expanded. Second, as interdiction and control at the source tightened, the incentives to bolster supplies multiplied and conflicts surrounding drug trafficking both between criminal actors and state authorities and among criminal organizations intensified. Third is the escalation of drug-related violence, from Colombia and Mexico, to Central America, to the more recent drug-related deaths in the city of Rosario, Argentina—where the drug trade has pushed the homicide rate up and in the first week of September 2021 was behind six assassinations in less than 24 hours. Fourth, the transfer of massive, never-ending illicit rents made possible the growth of powerful criminal organizations with a capacity

to infiltrate and/or dominate government institutions in countries across the region. When drug-related corruption has not guaranteed the conditions needed to conduct illicit business, drug cartels have shown their readiness to resort to ever more violent forms of behavior. Whether in Colombia, Central America, or Mexico, the effects of drug wars on chronic, unbridled violence and

widespread predatory criminality have emerged as important drivers of internal forced displacement, and increasingly of undocumented migration and asylum petitions to the United States.

Although under the Obama presidency there was talk of dropping costly repressive counter-narcotics policies, during the Trump administration the sounds of the war on drugs again resonated. In early April 2020, flanked by Secretary of Defense Mark Esper, the Chairman of the Joint Chiefs of Staff General Mark Milley and Attorney General William Barr, President Trump launched a hemispheric operation aimed at terrorists and drug cartels involving the Southern Command and 22 regional countries. The logic of war was also reaffirmed by those voices within the Trump administration claiming linkages between drug-trafficking and terrorism. More recently, the Biden administration has also made gestures toward moving beyond the war on drugs. Although Mexico's López Obrador government has been a significant force behind these changes, the explanation for the shift goes beyond the U.S. southern neighbor. What is at issue here is the dismal record of five decades of punitive drug control strategies.

The rise of prohibition and the International Drug Control Regime in the Americas

The cultivation and consumption of narcotic drugs have long been part of the culture and history of some Latin American countries, particularly Bolivia, Mexico, and Peru. But the emergence of these and other regional countries as exporters and significant players in international illicit drug circuits has been closely associated with the rise of the drug prohibition norm and the gradual consolidation of the International Drug Control Regime (IDCR).

The IDCR can be traced back to the 1909 Shanghai Opium Convention, the 1912 Hague Opium Convention, and a set of inter-war treaties and conventions that together established the principle

of international drug restriction. Since then, this principle has sought to demarcate the boundaries between legitimate production and use (i.e. for medical and scientific purposes) from illicit supply and production. As a centralized, uniform, and comprehensive global drug prohibition system, the regime only consolidated in the second half of the 20th century around three main instruments: the UN 1961 Single Convention on Narcotic Drugs (amended in 1971 and 1988), which by amalgamating eight existing international treaties and conventions reaffirmed the restrictive supply control impetus of the inter-war period; the 1971 Vienna Psychotropic Conven-

---

! Before you read, download the companion **Glossary** that includes definitions, a guide to acronyms and abbreviations used in the article, and other material. Go to **www. fpa.org/great_decisions** and select a topic in the Resources section. (Top right)

tion aimed at expanding restrictions to synthetic drugs, such as amphetamines, barbiturates and psychedelics, and the 1988 Convention against Illicit Traffic in Narcotic Drugs and Psychotropic Substances.

The consolidation of the IDCR in the postwar period, now backed by U.S. enforcing power, coincided with a more complex context. Drug supplies, trafficking routes and consumption exploded, and powerful and violent drug organizations, soon to be identified as drug cartels, also entered the scene. Although a combination of factors was behind this trend—an upsurge in consumer medical and non-medical drug demand, the spread of fashionable illicit drug cultures, and geopolitical forces associated with both decolonization and Cold War politics—the regime itself proved to be a major factor.

Thus, in the postwar decades, as critics had anticipated, the steady expansion of the illicit drug trade was in no small part the result of the "workings of the regime itself." Through various mechanisms the regime greatly incentivized actors to participate in the now global illicit trade. As the UN *2008 World Drug Report* belatedly acknowledged, the presence of international controls unavoidably entailed the emergence of "extremely problematic" illicit markets. Referring to them as "unintended consequences," the report singled out some of the mechanisms by which the IDCR contributed to the explosion of the global illicit trade. As the report stated, massive price increases "from production to retail" associated with prohibition and its enforcement created powerful incentives for countless criminals to enter and compete in these markets. Although omitted in the report, similar logic lured peasants and socially dislocated sectors into illicit drug economies, and at times also prompted poorer producer countries, desperate for sources of foreign exchange, to relax controls. The report also referred to two displacement effects that have hugely complicated drug control efforts, while simultaneously exposing the resilience of illicit drug markets. The first refers to the

"geographical displacement effect" or "balloon effect" by which tighter controls in one place produce a displacement and, often too, an increase in production elsewhere, even across continents. The second concerns "substance displacement" whereby controls to reduce supply or demand have recurrently pushed consumers and suppliers to alternative, often more powerful, dangerous, and more profitable substances. As the report makes clear, such geographical and substance displacement effects have also been evident in efforts to control chemical precursors. The report was bold in saying that the regime had relegated issues concerning demand and health approaches. And it was tepid in claiming that this was all a matter of member states' prefer-

ences. With its emphasis on prohibition and supply control, the regime itself favored criminal approaches and remained biased against public health approaches.

The United States played a key role in defining the goals, principles and norms of the regime, ultimately gearing it toward its own vision of drug control. This included the criminalization of psychoactive drugs and of drug users, a fixation with both supply control at source and interdiction, at the expense of demand reduction and public health strategies. During the second phase the U.S. role was no longer solely restricted to the normative development and promotion of prohibition norm and the regime, it also involved acting as a committed guardian and enforcer.

The onset of the war on drugs: The Nixon and Reagan years

The first U.S. war on drugs and President Richard M. Nixon's campaign to strengthen the IDCR were deployed in the middle of a heroin epidemic and rising marijuana and synthetic drug consumption in the United States, propelled by the domestic effects of the Vietnam war and the "hip-

pie" culture. Although the hardening of U.S. drug laws had already started with the institution of the first mandatory minimum sentences in 1951, and the criminalization in 1965 of psychedelic drug production and possession, under Nixon repressive drug policy escalated to new heights. With street crime on

President Richard M. Nixon turns to Attorney General John Mitchell, right, after signing a drug bill in Washington, Oct. 27, 1970, as others look on. From left: Secretary of Health, Education and Welfare Elliot L. Richardson, Narcotics Bureau Counsel Michael Sonnenreich and Special Presidential Assistant John Dean III. Others are unidentified. (AP IMAGES)

the rise and an almost doubling of the homicide rate Nixon had run for the U.S. presidency on a "law and order" platform, including a "war on drugs."

Proclaiming illegal drugs "public enemy number one" and mischievously associating hippies with marijuana, and black Americans with heroin, Nixon declared the first U.S. war on drugs in 1969. The Nixon administration then presided over a quick and massive expansion of the drug-control budget, from $66.4 million at start of his administration, to $796.3 million in 1972, to over $1 billion in the following budget.

Immediately after taking office President Nixon established a *Special Presidential Task Force Relating to Narcotics, Marijuana and Dangerous Drugs* to prepare a two-front assault on Turkish heroin and Mexican marijuana. If the Vietnam war had been a significant factor in the sudden rise in marijuana demand and Mexican supplies to the United States, the escalation of punitive drug-control policies acted as a powerful catalyst for the emergence of thriving illicit drug markets and circuits in the Americas.

Indeed, through the 1970s and 1980s, the two successive wars on drugs played a key role in the constant restructuring and relocation of illicit drug markets in the region. Thus, while the first campaigns of Nixon's war on drugs helped shift illicit opium production and trafficking from Turkey to Mexico, and marijuana from Mexico to Colombia, the aggressive clampdown on marijuana set the stage for the explosion of illicit cocaine in the region in the 1980s and the rise of powerful criminal organizations, the so called "cartels". Instead of containing the illicit cocaine boom, the battles of President Reagan's second war on drugs further fueled the illicit cocaine market. When, as a result of U.S. interdiction policies, the epicenter of cocaine trafficking shifted from Colombia to Mexico, the centrifugal effects of Nixon's war on drugs had left Mexican criminal organizations in an ideal position to seize control of changing trafficking routes.

The politics of drug control in Latin America became the other side of the coin to the war on drugs in the United States. Internal and external drug-control dynamics had in fact been linked since the early days of the IDCR, but they were significantly reinforced through the two wars on drugs. In the United States, the war on drugs soon led to the spread of mandatory minimum sentences and tough-on-crime policies that swelled the U.S. prison population and hardened the political atmosphere. While in the battle for drug control overseas, Washington sought to bolster the IDCR while increasingly relying on bilateral arm-twisting. Latin America became a key theater of this overseas war.

Shift to cocaine

Marihuana consumption, which had remained unrivalled in the United States through the 1950s and 1960 would increasingly face cocaine's competition. But what at first sight appeared as a simple shift in preferences was in fact a product of antidrug policy. The hardening of controls around cocaine followed two parallel if not synchronized routes: the enactment of national laws and controls first in Peru and by the 1960s in Bolivia, and the widening of the IDCR to coca and cocaine. In both settings the United States played a prominent role. With the 1961 Single Convention on Narcotic Drugs, Washington targeted coca leaf and cocaine and sought to criminalize these markets. With the subsequent 1972 Protocol Amending the Single Convention, a U.S. initiative pursued in the context of Nixon's war on drugs, law enforcement measures, including extradition, were reinforced.

In both the United States and the region, the imposition of controls created powerful incentives for organized illicit trades. The result was the reactivation of illicit cocaine circuits that until then had remained relatively dormant. Their subsequent evolution would more clearly expose the close interaction between tighter controls and their expansion.

Indeed, re-energized and increas-

ingly militarized under the U.S. war on drugs, drug-control restrictions acted as the opposite of a deterrent; they in fact drove and fueled cocaine illicit markets. Through the 1960s not only did the price incentives underpinning prohibition propel dynamic smuggler networks, they increasingly lured peasants into coca cultivation. As the first cocaine shadow circuits connecting Chile, Cuba, and Mexico emerged, Nixon's targeting of marijuana, amphetamines, and heroin helped induce a shift in preferences toward cocaine. By 1973, when 1–2 metric tons of cocaine entered the United States, illicit cocaine circuits already involved hundreds of skilled smugglers and thousands of peasants. Following General Augusto Pinochet's coup in Chile in 1973, and the consequent shift in cocaine routes from Chile to Colombia, the conditions were ripe for the birth of the Medellín and Cali cocaine cartels. Colombia, which in the period 1945–60 had only been mentioned once in the Annual Reports of the U.S. Bureau of Narcotics had entered the radar of marijuana and increasingly cocaine control. By 1976, the House Select Committee on Narcotics Abuse and Control had identified Colombia as "the single most important staging point for cocaine destined to the United States." At that point 20 metric tons supplied U.S. demand, and an increasing number of young Americans, an estimated 10% by 1977, had tried cocaine. As they assessed these trends, customs officials acknowledged that smuggling had become "highly organized" and interdiction "correspondingly more difficult," while Drug Enforcement Administration (DEA) officials recognized that the "great amount of money involved made it more difficult to control it than ever."

Within a decade, with cocaine seizures in the United States jumping from 2 to 27 tons in 1986, the illicit cocaine economy literally exploded. By the mid 1980s, when 22 million Americans admitted to having tried this drug, an estimated 75–100 metric tons of cocaine were entering the United States. Between 1982 and 1987 coca cultivation in the Andes doubled, and the bulk of it was still cultivated in Peru, where production increased from an estimated 33, 000 hectares in 1979, to more than 120, 000 hectares. By the early 1990s Peru´s illicit cocaine economy involved the labor of 175,000–300,000 peasants. At that point not only had processing efficiency boosted cocaine production capacity to nearly 800 metric tons but it was in the process of relocating to Colombia as a centralized vertical industrial complex. As the Medellín and Cali cartels sought to control this industry, from cultivation to importing and processing coca paste and base, to transshipment and distribution in the United States, coca cultivation in Colombia steadily expanded. Between 1988 and 1989, when the Medellín cartel controlled 80% of the cocaine consumed in the United States, coca cultivation in Colombia had already nearly doubled from 27,000 to 49,000 hectares. By then the Mexican illicit drug economy had already bounced back. In the mid 1980s Mexican drug supplies had recovered 40% of the heroin and 30% of the U.S. marijuana markets, and Mexican criminal entrepreneurs were also making significant inroads in the rising U.S. cocaine market. At that point an estimated 30% of the cocaine bound for the United States was already passing through Mexico, a volume that by the turn of the century increased to represent 85–90% of the cocaine destined for the United States. Through the next two decades, Mexico consolidated its position as the main transit route for cocaine bound to the United States.

The third pillar of the IDCR, the 1988 Convention against Illicit Traffic in Narcotic Drugs and Psychotropic Substances, was negotiated in the midst of this visible growth in illicit drug trafficking and massive cocaine consumption in the United States. Rather than offering an opportunity for a change of course, the 1988 Convention was an offshoot of the two Nixon-Reagan drug wars, the latter based on an assessment of global narcotic trafficking as a threat to the national security of the United States.

AREAS WITH MAJOR COCA PRODUCTION*

*2018 ASSESSMENT / SOURCE: UNODC-SIMCI PROJECT

LUCIDITY INFORMATION DESIGN, LLC

Andean coca cultivation in hectares

YEAR	BOLIVIA	PERU	COLOMBIA	ANDEAN
1989	53,920	119,000	49,000	221,920
1995	48,600	115,300	59,650	223,550
1999	21,800	38,700	122,500	183,000
2001	19,900	34,000	169,800	223,700
2006	25,800	36,000	157,200	219,000
2008	32,000	41,000	119,000	192,000
2012	25,000	50,500	78,000	153,500
2014	35,000	46,500	112,000	193,500
2017	31,000	49,800	209,000	289,800
2019	42,180	72,000	212,000	326,180

SOURCE: U.S. DEPARTMENT OF STATE, INTERNATIONAL NARCOTICS CONTROL STRATEGY REPORTS, VARIOUS YEARS, AVAILABLE AT HTTPS://WWW.STATE.GOV/INTERNATIONAL-NARCOTICS-CONTROL-STRATEGY-REPORTS/; THE WHITE HOUSE, UPDATED, ONDCP RELEASES DATA ON COCA CULTIVATION AND POTENTIAL COCAINE PRODUCTION IN THE ANDEAN REGION AVAILABLE AT HTTPS://WWW.WHITEHOUSE.GOV/ONDCP/BRIEFING-ROOM/2021/07/16/ONDCP-RELEASES-DATA-ON-COCA-CULTIVATION-AND-POTENTIAL-COCAINE-PRODUCTION-IN-THE-ANDEAN-REGION/

As in prior negotiations, Washington set the terms for the 1988 Convention. Various aspects of illicit trafficking were considered serious offences, and provisions which were already part of the U.S. drug-control arsenal were adopted and internationalized. The upshot was the universalization of a penal approach and the widening of penalization resulting from new provisions on money laundering, asset seizure, and the diversion of precursor chemicals. The convention also introduced the potential criminalization of individuals and groups. Thus, in addition to large-scale traffickers, individuals linked to the illicit market chain—from peasants and manufacturers to couriers, dealers, and consumers—were also targeted.

The explosion of the illicit cocaine economy would have profound implications for countries in the region. By and large, illicit drug markets tend to be competitive, organized around flexible networks, and are rarely if ever monopolized. However, the booming of the cocaine industry in Latin America points to some degree of coordination and organization behind production and trafficking operations. Indeed, the capacity to store and move large loads across long distances and continents, often involving dozens of metric tons of cocaine, suggests the presence of "more durable, bureaucratic, violent and strategic" organizations.

By multiplying the economic stakes in the illicit drug marketplace, in both Colombia and Mexico the cocaine industry helped propel the rise of a new generation of criminal organizations, ready to exploit lax arms markets and to turn drug-trafficking into a global and increasingly violent enterprise. Whether loosely organized around independent entrepreneurs or more centrally coordinated, through their smuggling operations—the sector where great fortunes tend to be made—criminal actors were able to accumulate massive wealth and power and to put governments on the defensive. With justice and security institutions unable to cope with either the massive corruption and/or intimidation and vicious violence that accompanied the cocaine boom, state authorities in the region were confronted with unforeseen and formidable challenges. In Colombia members of the Medellín cartel, most prominently Pablo Escobar, sought out a role in politics, while the Cali cartel endeavored to cultivate solid alliances with the police and politicians. Meanwhile, with the acquisition of vast amounts of rural land, the Medellín cartel propelled the expansion of violent paramilitary groups. These developments, coupled with the effects of intensified antidrug campaigns, opened wars with multiple fronts and fueled atrocities, while handing over lucrative opportunities to armed actors in both Colombia and Peru. By extending their protection to peasants, guerrilla groups *Sendero Luminoso* (Shining Path) in Peru and the FARC (Fuerzas Armadas Revolucionarias de Colombia) in Colombia were able to extract significant revenues and to lay down valuable political bases. This, ultimately at the price of the stability of both these countries.

In Mexico, the opening and constant shifting of cocaine routes across the territory radically altered the size, value and organization of its illicit drug economy. As in Colombia, not only did the criminal organizations seem more powerful, violent and defiant, but their ability to peacefully coexist, coordinate and share the spoils of the cocaine transshipment economy waned. As U.S. interdiction efforts pushed the cocaine route deeper into Mexican territory, tighter market competition intensified. Open-ended and violent competition was also exacerbated by Mexican law-enforcement pressures. Then, as now, these pressures would always favor one criminal organization over the other. At an average fee of $1,250 per kilo of cocaine transported into the United States, estimates of the income accumulated by one single Mexican intermediary between 1985–86 came in at around $75 million. With such margins, the disputes over turf, routes, and territory became ever more frequent, fuelling in turn systemic drug violence and paving the way to an ever more intractable humanitarian crisis.

In Colombia, in the period 1984–90, a brutal war escalated over political participation and extradition between the government and the Medellín cartel. Five years after the assassination of Colombia's Minister of Justice Rodrigo Lara Bonilla, and the attack on the Justice Palace, a chain of "narco-terrorist" attacks in 1989 took the lives of presi-

A Colombian paramilitary soldier patrols the streets December 14, 2000, in San Isidro, in the Guamuez Valley, Colombia. (CARLOS VILLALON/GETTY IMAGES)

dential candidates, officials, judges, policemen and over 100 civilians on a commercial flight. By the mid 1990s, when both the Medellín and Cali cartels were finally dismantled, the cocaine industry had been transferred to both the right-wing paramilitary and the leftist FARC in Colombia, while control over the most profitable part of the business, the smuggling sector, had passed to ever more brutal Mexican drug cartels. As Colombia collapsed into a protracted civil war, Mexico was about to descend into a three-decade period of escalating drug-related violence and mass atrocities. In Peru, the bulk of coca cultivation relocated to Colombia and the Shining Path was finally defeated, but arms and drug-related corruption scandals also rocked the government at the highest level.

The war on drugs, here to stay:
From Plan Colombia to Mérida Initiative

With their stability lost at the turn of the century Colombia and soon Mexico were left with no option but to escalate their military responses by turning to Washington. The United States stepped up to provide key strategic resources. The Plan Colombia and the Mérida Initiative helped the two countries to recover some of their stability, but this came at the cost of compromising their fragile democracies.

By the turn of the century Mexican drug organizations had internationalized and were actively bidding for greater control of cocaine smuggling operations. This had been partly achieved by extracting from Colombian traffickers an increasing portion of their payment in cocaine rather than cash. Over time, this boosted the profits of the Mexican cartels. By the mid 1990s, their control over the smuggling sector was finally consolidated by the impact of unyielding U.S. anti-drug pressures on the Ernesto Samper administration, which led to the dismantling of the Cali cartel. By then U.S. officials estimated the value of Mexican drug exports at around $10 bn, whereas Mexican official estimates put the value as high as $30bn. To these revenues were soon added the profits of a methamphetamine export industry that Mexican criminal organizations readily developed, taking advantage of a regional consumption wave in the United States and the vacuum left by a clampdown on laboratories in California.

The confluence of internal and external pressures radically altered the autonomy of both Colombia and Mexico to choose their own drug-control policies. On the one hand, in both

A U.S. special forces soldier, rear, helps train a Colombian anti-narcotics battalion, in Larandia, a military base about 235 miles southwest of Bogota, Colombia, May 4, 2001. The training is part of the U.S.-backed Plan Colombia, a $1.3 billion aid package that aims to help Colombia eliminate drug production. (SCOTT DALTON/AP IMAGES)

countries the boom of thriving illicit economies coincided with and helped fuel thorny political pressures and the weakening of state institutions. On the other, the 2001 terrorist attacks on 9/11 transformed the context in which Colombian and Mexican officials calculated their policy options, and their respective drug relations with the United States. In both Colombia and Mexico, the realities of rising and uncontrollable drug-related violence ultimately forced the governments to finally acquiesce to portrayals of problems of narcotics and crime as a "terrorist threat" and to reach out to the United States for help.

In Colombia drug revenues had empowered armed actors, from left and right, providing them with resources to open other illicit outlets, including extortion, and to increasingly control territory. Whereas the FARC protected coca growers, the paramilitaries, with their connections to the Medellín cartel, while actively participating in the drug trade, extended their protection instead to landowners. As the illicit drug economy became entangled with these actors, it unleashed and fueled new forms of violence, in turn opening a multiple front war and critically weakening the state. The peace plan originally envisaged by the Andrés Pastrana government proved unfeasible in a context where the FARC, with nearly 20,000 rebels, was at the peak of its power, and in control of nearly a third of the country, had more incentives to keep their power and profits than to barter for peace. The efforts to draw a line between the war on drugs and war with the FARC and to "denarcotize"

Revolutionary Armed Forces of Colombia (FARC) guerrillas guard the location of talks between Manuel Marulanda, Marxist rebel chief of the FARC, and Colombian President Andrés Pastrana in Los Pozos, Caqueta, 466 miles south of Bogota, February 9, 2001. The two began a second day of talks in an attempt to relaunch the fragile peace process in the violence-torn South American country. (LUIS ACOSTA/AFP/GETTY IMAGES)

relations with the United States came to an end after the assassination in 1999 of three American activists at the hands of the FARC. The prospects of renewed U.S. drug-war pressures prompted the Pastrana administration to turn its "economic program for peace" into a U.S.-funded security initiative: Plan Colombia. In July 2000 the U.S. Congress approved a request by the Clinton administration for $1.3bn in "emergency" aid to Colombia and its neighbors. Through the next 10 years, additional disbursements approved by successive administrations amounted to $6.5bn. The logic established by the first package, which allocated 75–80% of the funds to Colombia's armed forces, prevailed until 2007, when resources started to shift to economic and institutional aid. During 15 years of Plan Colombia (2000–16), U.S. aid to Colombia totaled nearly $10 bn.

By 2002, with Washington's active support, the Alvaro Uribe administration in Colombia embarked on a twin strategy that sought to roll back the FARC and also to prepare the ground for the demobilization of the country's right-wing paramilitary groups. The

FARC were effectively cornered: Colombia's National Police, with the support of the armed forces, regained control of major roads and reestablished its presence in numerous municipalities that had been lost to armed groups. Between 2003 and 2006 these efforts then coincided with a controversial peace negotiation with the paramilitary. Pressure from human-rights groups and victims would eventually force the Uribe government to revisit its initial unconditional rendition terms, and to replace them with the 2005 Law of Justice and Peace. The new law, which granted minimum dignity to victims, led to the collective demobilization of 31, 671 paramilitary irregulars, and between 2003 and 2009 of 19, 553 insurgents surrendering their arms on an individual basis.

As had been the case with the dismantling of the Medellín and Cali cartels, the strategic cornering of the FARC and the demobilization of the paramilitary proved critical for the survival of the state. There is a broad consensus that the plan—by boosting the moral of Colombian security forces and providing them with cutting edge

military hardware and additional significant financial resources in secret "black-budgets"— marked a turning point in the conflict and helped the government recover its strategic superiority.

Eventually, Plan Colombia, together with Uribe's 2003 Democratic Defense and Security Policy (DDSP) enabled the Colombian government to regain and maintain significant portions of the territory. Violence, in terms of homicides, massacres, kidnappings or internally displaced population, fell. Whether, however, this can be attributed to the coercive measures of Plan Colombia and the DDSP, or to the demobilization of the paramilitary remains moot. Moreover, these achievements came at significant costs: Colombia experienced increased and sustained militarization; serious human rights violations at the hands of the military went up; and the conflict entered the "gray conflict zone"—in which the lines between the active and post-conflict phases tend to blur. As a counterinsurgent strategy Plan Colombia secured important successes, but its contribution at ending the illicit drug economy can safely be set at zero. As the table below shows, two decades after the start of Plan Colombia coca cultivation in Colombia had in fact doubled.

As with Colombia, Mexico's decision to reach out to Washington through the Mérida Initiative in 2006 was in no small part motivated by an escalation in criminal violence. The gathering momentum for transition to democracy was accompanied by a chain of vicious criminal wars in cities along the U.S.-Mexico border. In Tijuana, under sustained DEA pressure and criminal competition from the Sinaloa cartel, the hegemony of the Arellano-Felix cartel over the Tijuana-San Diego corridor waned. The decay of the Tijuana cartel was accompanied by marked increases in the homicide rate and episodes of shockingly gruesome violence. In Ciudad Juarez, the sudden and unexpected death of the leader of the Juarez cartel, Amado Carrillo, in 1997 brought to an end a decade long "narco-peace" there. In the period between 1997 and 2005, internecine strife over the organization's leadership and criminal competition from the Sinaloa organization resulted in greater instability and violence. As the Juarez and Sinaloa cartels outsourced and mobilized gangs, disappearances, mass killings and feminicides exploded. By 2005 uncontrolled violence in Juarez forced federal authorities to intervene. Meanwhile, in 1999, along the North-East border, the Zetas—14 or so ex-elite military officers—had been recruited by the Gulf cartel as the armed branch of the organization. In 2003, the arrest of Osiel Cárdenas and the ensuing crisis over the leadership of the organization allowed the ascendance of the Zetas. Their violent paramilitary tactics were soon in full display, first in 2001, as they expanded their presence into Michoacan and Guerrero, and then in 2003 as they fiercely resisted the Sinaloa cartel's challenge for the control of Nuevo Laredo. Following the intervention of federal troops in Nuevo Laredo in 2003 Mexican and U.S. authorities provided evidence of the Zetas' military capabilities.

Rising levels of drug-related violence provided the Mexican President Felipe Calderón with a powerful justification to consider the use of military force. When Calderón assumed power in December 2006, 2,000 Mexicans had been killed in drug-related violence, doubling the number of deaths attributed to drug violence. Equally alarming were the implications of the proliferation of criminal armies, which had been catalyzed by the Zetas' paramilitary tactics, for overall levels of violence.

As had been the case with Presidents Pastrana and Uribe in Colombia, for President Calderón the war was not a war of choice, but of necessity, and the requirements of national security made closer cooperation with Washington a top priority. By the end of 2007, Washington and Mexico had agreed to a $1.4 billion, three-year package in U.S. aid. As in Plan Colombia, 75% of these resources were allocated to bolster the capacity of the military (mostly the Navy) and police forces.

Although the Calderón administration was at pains to emphasize that the Mérida Initiative was in no way inspired by Plan Colombia, the parallels were striking. As with Plan Colombia, this initiative fell under the broader framework of the war on terror. A first glance at both initiatives reveals a common security paradigm, one in which distinct threats converge in a "lethal nexus" bringing together organized crime, drug-trafficking and terrorism. Both plans also shared a key assumption: to restore stability and state authority coercive force was indispensable.

The definition of drug-trafficking as a national security threat, embodied in President Ronald Reagan's 1986 National Security Decision 221, had paved the way to the increasing militarization of drug control policies in both Colombia and Mexico. For decades, the governments of these countries had sought to resist this trend, that in their view was partly responsible for exacerbating their drug problem. Yet, the increasing viciousness and escalation of drug violence would force them to reconsider their courses of action and to privilege the military option.

In both Plan Colombia and the Mérida Initiative the initial proportion of funds assigned to the armed forces and the police massively outweighed those allocated to the rule of law and institutional reform. In both countries, the decision to prioritize military responses resulted in a massive injection of national resources to their respective armed institutions. In Colombia strong military action succeeded in rolling back the FARC but hardly offered an answer to the complex challenges associated with a thriving illicit economy. Through peace negotiations, leading first to the demobilization of the paramilitary in 2005 and subsequently in 2016 to the FARC's disarmament, the Colombian state was able to restore stability. But one of the underlying questions is at what price?

Decades of intensive and costly drug control campaigns had failed to reduce coca cultivation and production. In 2019 coca cultivation increased by 2% to reach 212,000 hectares and, at 951 metric tons, cocaine production had increased by 8%. It is true that in the period between 2006–10 cocaine use in the United States decreased by 50%, and with a slow steady decline through 2015, the value of the U.S. cocaine market was halved. Nonetheless, at an estimated annual value of $25bn in 2016 this market remained attractive. To this must be added the relevance of expanding cocaine markets in Latin America.

In Mexico, before long, it became painfully clear that President Calderón's war on drugs would not close the chapter of illicit drugs, nor offer an effective solution to drug violence. Not only did the aggressive deployment of the military fail to act as a deterrent, the response of criminal organizations was ever more defiant. By the end of 2008, drug-related deaths escalated to 6,000 a year, and an increasing proportion of those killed were police and members of the armed forces. There were also signs indicating the readiness of criminal organizations to inflict casualties on civilians and to increasingly target civilian local authorities and politicians. In the period between 2002 and 2019 an estimated 264 mayoral candidates and former mayors were murdered by criminal organizations.

In the last two decades a rapidly evolving opiod epidemic in the United States and the policy responses adopted by U.S. authorities added to the complexities of Mexico's drug problems. The tighter opiod prescription rules introduced by the Obama administration had rippling effects in Mexico. Deprived of legally available opiods and treatment, drug users in the United States increasingly shifted to heroin. Between 2006 and 2016, amid the opiod crisis, heroin consumption in the United States increased by 45%, with its chronic use expanding across the nation, and into rural areas, among an estimated 2.3 million Americans. The annual value of the U.S. heroin market was then estimated at $43bn. Mexico soon replaced Colombia as the main heroin supplier to the United States. In the years 2011–14 seizures of processed opium and poppy eradication doubled, and two years later Mexico accounted for nearly 50% of the illicit heroin found on U.S. streets. By then, not only had the number of plantations discovered outpaced eradication efforts, but local criminal fragmentation exacerbated violent competition and homicidal violence.

Although Colombia and Mexico have followed different trajectories, they have clearly converged on a number of issues related to illicit drugs. For many decades, both Colombia and Mexico were pressed into criminalizing narcotic drugs and implementing ever more punitive policies. And while public concern over the impact

of these substances among Americans was allegedly a major motivation behind these decisions and pressures, the antidrug crusade also imposed a massive toll on specific sectors of the U.S population. To mention only one harm, since 1980 drug arrests in the United States tripled and through the next three decades more than 31 million Americans would be arrested for drug offenses.

After the Reagan administration declared a second war on drugs Colombian and Mexican leaders were forced to resort to previously unthinkable uses of force. Yet, the violent evolution of their illicit markets strongly suggested that the logics of international drug prohibition and national stability were clearly at odds. While the imperatives

of stability and state survival have pushed governments in the region to resort to military solutions, these have proved deeply problematic. In Mexico, Colombia, and in many other Latin American countries, decades of punitive and coercive anti-narcotic policies have clearly failed to stem and have most likely fueled the expansion of illicit drug economies. Intensified criminal competition in turn fueled violence in rapidly changing regional illicit markets. With rising levels of criminal violence came atrocities and the signs of humanitarian crises. By the 21st century, the legacy of decades of militarization and military responses to the drug problem has altered civil-military balances as well as the quality of Latin America's fragile democracies.

UNGASS, and future scenarios

In September 2012, in three consecutive statements delivered at the United Nations General Assembly, the presidents of Colombia, Guatemala, and Mexico called on the UN to lead a far-reaching debate on the scope and limits of drug policy. Identifying illicit drug trafficking and related illicit markets as major drivers of violence and violent deaths in Latin America, the three presidents called for a long-overdue international debate on the drug problem. In requesting the 2016 General Assembly Special Session on the World Drug Problem Colombia, Mexico, and Guatemala sought to address these problems with a view to reform the IDCR and to establish a new basis for drug policy.

In the course of the last decades, campaigns on behalf of drug treatment and harm reduction, together with trends toward decriminalization and marijuana legalization, have driven drug-policy reform in many countries, including the United States. And while some of these airs of change have reached Latin America, it is important not to overestimate the prospects for drug-policy change in the region.

A number of factors point to a continuity with drug prohibition and its pu-

nitive enforcement in this region. Harm reduction—which gained salience with the HIV/AIDS pandemic—may now be an important part of the drug-policy agenda of many advanced countries, and distribution programs are now a feature of drug policy in Europe, Canada, Australia, New Zealand, China, Brazil, Armenia, Kyrgyzstan, and Iran, among others. However, its new standing has not always been reflected in actual drug-policy budgets. Moreover, as both the politics of harm reduction in the United States and the refusal to explicitly refer to it in the UNGASS' final document make clear, in some quarters, the primacy of punitive prohibition remains practically unchallenged.

Although marijuana reform has made advances in Latin America, with many countries moving toward decriminalizing possession of small doses of cannabis, the inertia of punitive criminal justice systems and unruly police agencies prevails. The same views expressed since the 1960s by commissions and reports in the United States, Europe, and Australia that questioned the psychoactive dangers of marijuana and concluded that the costs of criminalization outweigh the benefits have long been present in Latin America.

Yet, the waves that in the 1990s spread from Europe, to Australia and New Zealand in the Pacific, to Israel in the Middle East and that gathered force at the subnational level in the United States—with 35 states approving the use of medical marijuana, 15 states (plus the District of Columbia) allowing recreational adult use, and in Oregon decriminalizing possession of hard drugs—have not made significant inroads in Latin America.

The contrast among various U.S. administrations cannot disguise the fact that at the national level, the U.S. federal government has kept in place its deterrent-law enforcement approach to illicit drugs, based on the threat of arrest and incarceration. It is true that different administrations have handled these subnational decriminalization trends in different ways, but there is little doubt that the bureaucratic interests of law enforcement agencies, including the DEA and the U.S. Immigration and Customs Enforcement (ICE), remain closely attached to their commitment to prohibition and its enforcement at home and abroad.

It is important to reflect on why the economic costs of mass incarceration, or the social and democratic costs of criminalizing substantial numbers of the population have been overlooked. The same applies to decisions that have led to ignoring the potential benefits to be gained from drawing clear boundaries between relatively harmless and more dangerous drug markets. What is at issue here is the way in which a paradigm that had always been an article of faith—that the evil of illicit drugs lay in their supply from abroad—entrenched itself and developed an elaborate institutional base.

It would be wrong to underestimate the harm caused by drugs, but it would be equally misleading to ignore the difficulties that prohibition has entailed. The long record of drug prohibition suggests that punitive approaches to drug control do not work, and come at a huge cost. In the course of over four decades, the legacy of successive wars on drugs has been abundantly clear. The connections between these legacies within the United States and countries in Latin America appear to be stronger than has sometimes been suggested. They include the diversion of resources and budgets from prevention, education, and treatment to law enforcement; the enlistment, through significant budgetary allocations of local and state police corps in anti-drug operations; DEA training of police forces and their diversion from more pressing crimes; the adoption of ever more punitive legislation involving both the creation of new civil penalties and the expansion of criminal punishment, from mandatory sentences to greater use of the death penalty; erosion of constitutionally protected civil liberties; increasing reliance on irregular practices such as the admission of illegally obtained evidence in drug trials; the dismantling of legal restrictions on policing, the militarization of police forces and greater dependence on the armed forces; massive arrests and mass incarceration propelling in turn the expansion of the prison systems and police forces. This has clearly been the case in the United States despite the fact that by 2005 the great majority of arrests were for possession and of these, the great majority were for marijuana possession.

April 21, 2016. Bolivian President Evo Morales Ayma displays a leaf from a coca plant while addressing the General Assembly. At the morning session on the final day of the United Nations General Assembly Special Session on the world drug problem, three South American Presidents from Peru, Bolivia, and Columbia addressed the Assembly at UN Headquarters in New York City. (ALBIN LOHR-JONES/PACIFIC PRESS/ALAMY)

Although the experience of many countries suggests that when it comes to responding to the drug problem there is a spectrum of choice, for reasons related to ideology and to racial politics, prohibition and punitive enforcement, including drug wars, prevailed in the United States. These choices were then exported under duress to Latin America.

Colombia, Guatemala, and Mexico came to UNGASS 2016 in the hope of reforming drug policy and the IDCR. The session revealed that many African countries were ready to admit to facing the same intractable drug control problems as Latin America. It also made clear that Latin American and European countries converged around the themes of drug policy and human rights. Yet, their views did not result in a uniform trend and their perspectives varied. While European countries emphasized the human and health rights of drug users, Latin American representatives called attention to the implications of prohibition and punitive enforcement for violent dynamics and human rights in their countries. As a result, no common front emerged to seriously challenge the regime and punitive drug policies.

Instead in the polarized atmosphere of UNGASS 2016 two realities became clear. While democratic countries, across regions, reiterated their commitment to human rights, and at minimum acknowledged the need to harmonize drug policy and human rights, autocratic and authoritarian governments lent their unconditional support to punitive enforcement, including through the death penalty. All governments, including authoritarian regimes, may find it impossible to totally suppress consumption, but what these positions appeared to confirm is that authoritarian states, with their intrusive and repressive role in most aspects of daily life, have a greater ability to suppress illicit drug market activity.

The Latin American countries may have failed in their efforts to inspire a true and honest debate about drug policy and drug control. But owing to their experiences we may now know something about the tensions that underpin the relation between drug control and human rights that we did not know decades ago. Addressing this global problem, in a manner consistent with human rights and democratic standards, would require a major and honest restructuring of U.S. and international drug-control policies and of the punitive logic that has long informed the IDCR.

discussion questions

1. Should the punitive enforcement of drug prohibition continue to be used or is it time to change tactics? Why or why not?

2. From its inception in 1909, the International Drug Control Regime has been dominated by the United States. Why has the United States sought to enforce its desire for punitive enforcement in the regime? Has this been beneficial?

3. Members of the poorer segments of Latin American society have come to rely on the drug trade as a means to financially support themselves, having been denied work in official sectors. Does this reliance justify the presence of the drug trade? Why or why not?

4. To what extent have human rights been sacrificed during the war on drugs?

suggested readings

Lukasz Kamienski, *Shooting Up. A Short History of Drugs and War,* Oxford, Oxford University Press, 2016. Shooting Up: A Short History of Drugs and War examines how intoxicants have been put to the service of states, empires and their armies throughout history.

William B. McAllister, *Drug Diplomacy in the Twentieth Century,* London and New York, Routledge, 2000. Drug Diplomacy in the Twentieth Century is the first comprehensive historical account of the evolution of the global drug regime. The book analyses how the rules and regulations that encompass the drug question came to be framed and examines the international historical aspects of this global problem.

William O. Walker III, *Drug Control in the Americas,* Albuquerque, University of New Mexico Press, 1981. Walker examines the origins and development of drug control from WWI to the present. Why drug dealers are undeterred by US policy is the central question addressed in this book.

Mónica Serrano "A Humanitarian Crisis in the Making" in Wil G. Pansters, Benjamin Smith and Peter Watt, eds., *Beyond the Drug War in Mexico. Human Rights, the PublicSphere and Justice,* N.Y. and London, Routledge, 2018. This volume aims to go beyond the

study of developments within Mexico's criminal world and their relationship with the state and law enforcement. It focuses instead on the nature and consequences of what we call the 'totalization of the drug war,' and its projection on other domains which are key to understanding the nature of Mexican democracy.

Marco Palacios "A Historical Perspective on Counterinsurgency and the 'War on Drugs' in Colombia" in Cynthia J Arnson ed., *In the Wake of War. Democratization and Internal Armed Conflict in Latin America,* Stanford, Stanford University Press, 2012. In the Wake of War assesses the consequences of civil war for democratization in Latin America, focusing on questions of state capacity. Contributors focus on seven countries—Colombia, El Salvador, Guatemala, Haiti, Mexico, Nicaragua, and Peru—where state weakness fostered conflict and the task of state reconstruction presents multiple challenges.

Annette Idler and Juan Carlos Garzón eds., *Transforming the War on Drugs: Warriors, Victims and Vulnerable Regions,* Oxford University Press, 2021. The contributors trace the consequences of the war on drugs across vulnerable regions, including South America and Central America, West Africa, the Middle East and the Golden Crescent, the Golden Triangle, and Russia. It demonstrates that these consequences are 'glocal.' The war's local impacts on human rights, security, development, and public health are interdependent with transnational illicit flows.

Don't forget to vote!

Download a copy of the ballot questions from the Resources page at www.fpa.org/great_decisions

To access web links to these readings, as well as links to additional, shorter readings and suggested web sites,

GO TO www.fpa.org/great_decisions

and click on the topic under Resources, on the right-hand side of the page.

Foreign policy, economic power, and U.S. industrial policy

by Jonathan Chanis

*President Joe Biden tours the Ford Rouge Electric Vehicle Center in Dearborn, Mich., May 18, 2021. (*DOUG MILLS/THE NEW YORK TIMES/REDUX)

America has debated vastly increasing state intervention in its economy three times in recent history. These debates, like the one we are now experiencing, were caused by perceived economic distress and concerns that self-regulating markets will not facilitate economic prosperity or national security. Although the Biden administration has avoided the term "industrial policy," the "Infrastructure Investment and Jobs Act," and the "Fiscal Year 2022 Budget Resolution" clearly contain industrial policy solutions, i.e., government efforts to promote a sector or industry identified as critical for economic competitiveness or national security.

The first two attempts at industrial policy (IP) in the late 1970s/early 1980s and early 1990s ended with policies that were diametrically opposed to its goals: privatization, deregulation, increased financialization, and significantly more open foreign trade. The third attempt after the 2008 Global Financial Crisis (GFC) resulted in some interventionary solutions, particularly the Dodd-Frank Act financial reform and the Affordable Care Act, but relative to the size of the

U.S. economy these interventions were small. The current IP initiative, however, is different because of the size of intervention sought and the degree of support it has from the governing administration. A number of other conditions also have changed.

First, there is a broad-based rejection, including in the Biden White House, of much mainstream American economic thought. The dominant free-market paradigm that came by many, especially critics, to be labeled neoliberalism cre-

JONATHAN CHANIS *has worked in investment management, emerging markets finance, and commodities trading for over 25 years. Currently he manages New Tide Asset Management, a company focused on global and resource trading. He previously worked at Citigroup and Caxton Associates where he traded energy and emerging market equities, and commodities and currencies. He has taught undergraduate and graduate courses on political economy, public policy, international politics, and other subjects at several education institutions including Columbia University.*

ated politically destabilizing inequality and exacerbated intergenerational and class conflicts. This led many to question neoliberalism's utility. Second, China's spectacular economic development over the last 30 years has made it harder to deny the constructive role governments can play in economic development. This in no way excuses China's human rights abuses; it just acknowledges its unrivaled success in reducing mass poverty. The China experience, as well as new research on IP's role in other Asian development successes, has caused some economists to take a more sympathetic view of IP. Third, China's economic success has created a new and major national security problem for the United States. An economically powerful China is increasingly more capable of competing for global dominance. As discussed below, enduring political and military power can only be built upon a strong economic foundation.

In an effort to enact its IP agenda and compete with China, the Biden administration is attempting to harmonize U.S. domestic and international economic policies. As Jake Sullivan, U.S. National Security Adviser said: "We've reached a point where foreign policy is domestic policy, and domestic policy is foreign policy." The policy separation that began under the Nixon administration and accelerated under the Clinton administration helped to justify and create the neoliberal world in which we all now live. The Biden administration wants to reintegrate these policies and bring them back under the purview of foreign policy in order to facilitate its domestic economic agenda. If this reintegration and reunification is successful, it would represent a sweeping U.S. foreign policy reconfiguration.

The commingling of company/industry specific assistance arguments with foreign policy arguments makes evaluating industrial policy proposals more difficult. National security and economic efficiency are two very different standards by which to judge a policy. However, how the United States harnesses or does not harness economic power to secure its national security is arguably the most critical foreign policy issue confronting the United States for the next decade. And this raises a host of questions about the appropriate role for multinational companies (MNC) at home and abroad. In particular, should the power of these corporations be made at least partially subservient to U.S. government efforts to promote domestic welfare and secure vital foreign interests?

The current IP debate is more than a debate over specific government actions to favor or not favor a company or industry. It also is about popular trust or mistrust of government and questions about government's competency; it is about China's rise and how the United States responds to a country practicing deliberate mercantilist policies; and, most of all, it is about what type of capitalism America wants, or for some, if America should even have a capitalist economy. In order to evaluate the merits of these issues, one needs to examine how economic power relates to foreign policy; define industrial policy and detail the administration's actions; and, assess the arguments of IP critics and supporters.

Economic power and foreign policy

Political power often is defined as the ability of one actor to manipulate the behavior of another actor against its preferences. Political power is ultimately a psychological relationship between at least two people, and at the international level it is built upon on a multitude of factors ranging from geography, demography, and the size of a country's economy, to the quality of a state's leadership and armed forces, and social cohesion of its population.

Economic power is the ability to obtain one's preferences through the production, consumption, purchase, or sale of a good or service. It is closely related to financial power, or the ability to satisfy a preference through the use of money. Economic and financial power are both foundational and instrumental in international politics. They are foundational because they serve as the basis for other types of power such as political and military power, and instrumental because they often can be used to pursue discrete goals, e.g., harm or help another state.

The relationship between economic and political power is complex because, as the political scientist Robert Gilpin wrote, "politics determines economics, but economics tends to redistribute power and wealth." Economic and political power are deeply intertwined and it is difficult to see how either can exist isolated from the other.

Although international political power is notoriously hard to quantify, its most essential characteristic is its relative nature. If something debilitating happens to two states equally, such as a devastating pandemic, and their responses are similar, then there most likely will not be a change in their relative power positions. However, if the states are afflicted unequally or their responses differ greatly, then their relative power position likely will change. In politics, power is relative, not absolute.

In economics, absolute gains are more important than relative gains. Trade is built upon the notion that even if one side benefits disproportionately, exchange still should occur as long as the other party gains something. Moreover, according to neoliberal logic, if a less economically developed state begins to grow and closes the economic gap with another more advanced state, this is positive and to be desired. Neoliberalism, like classical liberalism, views economic development positively because it believes more prosperous and commercially oriented societies are less belligerent.

The neoliberal view valuing relative economic gain and minimizing the importance of absolute gain means

Before you read, download the companion **Glossary** that includes definitions, a guide to acronyms and abbreviations used in the article, and other material. Go to **www.fpa.org/great_decisions** and select a topic in the Resources section. (Top right)

that the United States should not be threatened by China's rapid economic growth. Political "realists" such as John Mearsheimer reject this perspective because, as noted, economic power is a crucial element upon which political and military power rests. An industrious, prosperous, and technologically advanced country is better able to afford and develop the military and other capacities necessary for competing in the international system. Prosperity and wealth allow a state to fund higher defense budgets; increase the potential for weapons production self-sufficiency; support more innovated technologies for defense and general welfare; and, if it wishes, carry out a range of economic actions to induce or coerce others to follow its will, while reducing is own vulnerability to such pressure.

To political realists, the United States should be prepared to forgo beneficial economic interactions with a rising power such as China if those interactions adversely change *the relative balance of power* against the United States. This means actions that enhance prosperity may undermine security and vice versa.

Global economic integration over the last three decades has heightened realist security concerns because the cost of competing with China has increased as China's economy grew and its economy became more efficient. For realists, security always trumps prosperity, at least if people want to avoid foreign domination. Realist security concerns also have been undermined because military power has become less useful over the last 75 years. Changes in military technology (e.g., development of nuclear weapons and asymmetric warfare), enhanced communication technologies and the impact of new media, the spread of nationalism, among other things, have elevated the role of economics in international competition. But to realists this has not changed the nature of the international system; it has only shifted the emphasis from military competition, to economic competition. As President Biden said: "…in today's world, economic security is national security."

Mercantilism and China

Economic power always had a critical role in international politics, especially through mercantilism, a.k.a. "merchant capitalism." For many, mercantilism is associated with tariffs, protectionism, and "bullionism" or the accumulation of gold. Even sophisticated observers often think of it only as an anachronistic trade policy based on positive trade balances. Part of this perception can be attributed to the popularization of neoclassical (essentially neoliberal) economics with generations of American college students and the public at large, but to many historians and political scientists, and even a few economists, mercantilism was about a great deal more than this. In fact, mercantilism was, and has remained for many states including China, an indispensable source of economic power and a potent tool for development.

Historically, mercantilism had many problematic ideas such as the zero-sum nature of trade and an obsession with a positive trade balance. But its *political importance as a continuing system of thought* resides in how state authorities were and are able to extract resources from their societies to build the economic foundations of state power. Under mercantilism, the political authorities generally did not interact with the new merchant and entrepreneurial classes through coercion. Rather they

gave these groups privileges and incentives (especially monopolies) that allowed them to enrich themselves while helping the state grow stronger and more secure. Mercantilism used private individuals and private property to achieve public aims. This allowed states to finance their defense and foreign military ambitions while, perhaps unknowingly, advancing the transition to an industrial economy and a higher standard of living for its citizens.

Even after the Napoleonic Wars, when Great Britain began to establish the contemporary global trading system, many states, including the United States, pursued unabashedly mercantilist policies. Similarly, after the Second World War when the United States became the leading advocate for global trade, numerous countries including Japan, Korea, Singapore, Taiwan, and eventually China economically modernized using mercantilist policies. While some still dispute the role of state intervention in promoting the development of these countries, it is notable that the greatest economic development examples of the last 60 years deemphasized many standard Western economic development recommendations.

Current discourse tends to avoid the word mercantilist, so we say "state capitalist," or in more market-oriented systems "industrial policies," but they are similar phenomena. Economic lib-

Workers assemble Air China's first ARJ21 aircraft, a regional passenger jetliner developed and manufactured by the Commercial Aircraft Corporation of China (COMAC), on May 21, 2020, in Shanghai, China. (YIN LIQIN/CHINA NEWS SERVICE/GETTY IMAGES)

eralism's intellectual victory, as Harvard University economist Dani Rodrik has written, "has blinded us to the great appeal—and frequent success—of mercantilist practices. In fact, mercantilism remains alive and well…. But it is more accurate to think of mercantilism as a different way to organize the relationship between the state and the economy…. Mercantilist theorists… were in fact strong proponents of capitalism; they just propounded a different model than liberalism."

China is closing the economic gap with the United States by following mercantilism, or "state capitalism." Regardless of nuanced differences between the terms, this strategy enables China to place the state's resources behind selective companies and industries, and buttress them in ways that ignore traditional market mechanisms, particularly the need to earn a short-term profit. China has not primarily been concerned with economic efficiency, but rather with building state power and longer-term domestic prosperity. One can argue that this is just instrumental for keeping the Chinese Communist Party in power, but that is largely beside the point.

China's economic rise initially began in 1977 with Deng Xiaoping's "Four Modernizations," but it was not until its turn toward greater global integration in the 1990s that economic development really accelerated. (See Graph 1.) During this period, China undervalued its exchange rate to promote export competitiveness, and it created numerous incentives for foreign corporations to relocate to China while allowing millions of peasants to move from the countryside to cities and work in export-oriented factories. The government provided local firms with tax incentives, subsidies, advantageous lending rates, privileged access to land and foreign exchange, and other inducements, which in turn attracted international investment and partnerships. According to the Peterson Institute's Nicholas Lardy, China spends approximately 3% of its annual output underwriting these subsidies.

China's full ambitions became clear in 2015 when it announced the "Made in China 2025" (MIC-25) program. MIC-25 is a mercantilist blueprint for economic and eventual military development. It is designed to turn China

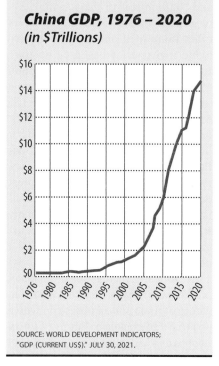

GRAPH 1

China GDP, 1976 – 2020
(in $Trillions)

SOURCE: WORLD DEVELOPMENT INDICATORS; "GDP (CURRENT US$)." JULY 30, 2021.

into a superpower over the coming decades by fostering growth in ten key areas including supercomputing, artificial intelligence, and new energy vehicles. (See Figure 1.)

Combined with existing economic practices, MIC-25 subsidizes uncompetitive industries until they gain competitiveness, acquires foreign technology, as the U.S. Trade Representative has documented, in any way possible including intellectual property theft, extortion, and espionage, and makes it difficult for U.S. and foreign firms to gain access to China's domestic market on equal terms with local firms. MIC-25 aims to make China "the leader among the world's manufacturing powers." That this is a euphemism for global economic dominance is especially clear since President Xi Jinping is reported by China scholar Andrew Nathan to have told people his country will surpass the United States in economic and military power by 2049.

If one assumes a political realist, as opposed to neoliberal, view, this is alarming because China is increasingly a competitor, if not an outright U.S. adversary. Its rapid economic growth is financing a substantial military buildup and it is increasingly using economic policies such as the Belt and Road Initiative to induce or coerce other countries to accommodate themselves to China's interests. Moreover, China is a revisionist power. It already overturned the status quo in Hong Kong by taking de facto control of the city,

FIGURE 1

China's Industrial Priorities (2015-2025)
"Made in China 2025" plan targets 10 Sectors:

00101110 10110010 11101100 01011101 — Next generation information technology	Energy-saving motor vehicles
High-end computerized machines and robotics	Energy efficient industrial equipment
Aerospace development	Agricultural equipment
Maritime equipment and high-tech ships	New materials and processes
Advanced trains and railway equipment	Biopharma and state-of-the-art medical devices

SOURCE: "NOTICE OF THE STATE COUNCIL ON ISSUING MADE IN CHINA 2025. MAY 8, 2015, GUOFA [2015] NO. 28" and among other things, it is actively working to: absorb Taiwan, dominate the South China Sea, and change the Kashmiri border with India. Secretary of State Antony Blinken warned China in April 2021 that it would be a "serious mistake" if it tried to change the status quo by force.

Some already believe that the United States would lose a military confrontation with China over Taiwan were it to occur. This relative and increasing military decline makes U.S.-China relations increasingly unstable, and it places more pressure on the United States to compete with China economically. However, China's mercantilist strategy makes competing problematic. As Director of the National Economic Council Brian Deese said: "We should be clear-eyed that China and others are playing by a different set of rules…. We cannot ignore or wish this away." The Biden administration sees industrial policy as a way to address China's economic strategy.

Definitions

There is no single accepted definition for the term "industrial policy." As noted, in common usage it refers to government efforts to promote (or not promote) a sector or industry identified as critical for economic competitiveness or national security. However, IP proponents and opponents frame discussion of the subject by limiting or expanding their definitions in ways that best advance their positions. In particular, IP proponents have created a plethora of terms to describe the nuances of their perspective and to distance their proposals from past IP controversies, and from each other. Some terms are: soft industrial policy, true industrial policy, smart industrial policy, productive development policy, green industrial policy, innovation policy, competition policy, industrial strategy, developmental state, and even common good capitalism.

Rodrik, one of the foremost industrial policy proponents, says industrial policy "…refers to policies that stimulate specific economic activities and promote structural change. As such, industrial policy is not about industry."

Under this definition, besides manufacturing, IP concerns services, education, labor force and immigration policies, as well as just about anything touching upon development or economic transformation. This expansive definition makes industrial policy almost a synonym for any state intervention, and it buttresses a key proponent argument that industrial policy is already widely practiced in the United States. Trade policy, tax policy, regulatory policy, immigration policy, energy policy, agricultural policy and a host of other state choices all contain biases that favor or disfavor various companies and sectors. So why not just recognize this and try to make the whole process more coherent and transparent?

IP opponents tend to want to keep the definition limited. In an expansive and negative critique titled *Questioning Industrial Policy: Why Government Manufacturing Plans Are Ineffective and Unnecessary,* Scott Lincicome and Huan Zhu of the Cato Institute argue that IP has four essential features: it focuses solely on manufacturing; it targets specific firms or industries; it is a direct government action to fix a market failure; and, the policy outcome is to be generated within national borders. This limited definition enables opponents to focus on what is considered IP's most egregious error: the government trying to "pick winners and losers."

Narrowly construed, the main IP instruments are: 1) tariffs, import quotas and other trade restrictions; 2) direct subsidies, tax credits, or exemptions for producers or consumers; 3) domestic procurement requirements; 4) direct state investment; and 5) currency manipulation. In contrast to these "vertical" interventions targeting specific firms or industries, there also are "horizontal" or wider interventions that look to improve the overall business environment. These measures include: increased public spending on research and development (R&D); strengthening education and worker training; improving the infrastructural network; "flexibilizing" labor markets (i.e., making it easier to hire and fire workers); working through public-private partnerships; steering investment through national development banks not directly controlled by the government; and reducing corporate taxes.

Biden administration actions

While there are major economic policy differences between the Trump and Biden administrations, both rejected the notion first popularized by economist Paul Krugman that "it is simply not the case that the world's leading nations are to any important degree in economic competition with each other." To liberals, as Robert Gilpin wrote, the state, "has no meaning as an economic entity." People and corporations compete, not states. However, as Biden sees it (and Trump saw it), nations do compete with each other and the United States is losing the competition.

For Biden and others, China used and continues to use unfair trade and other policies to reduce American economic wellbeing and international power. Consequently, this administration has continued, and in some cases reinforced, Trump policies on tariffs,

trade treaties, "buy-American" procurement provisions, individual and company sanctions, and efforts to re-shore critical manufacturing. The Biden administration's stated intention is to revitalize America's domestic economy by creating "the industries of the future." Biden wants better paying jobs, especially in manufacturing, more educated and capable workers, more geographically balanced economic development, and greater technological and manufacturing innovation. In order to achieve this, the President wants to increase government intervention into the economy.

In the first Biden administration speech on its new approach to economics and foreign policy at the Atlantic Council in June 2021, economic adviser Brian Deese studiously avoided the words "industrial policy." While panelists and audience questioners used the term, Deese did not. Given America's controversial history with IP, distancing the current policy from past debates may make it easier to defend this "industrial strategy."

Deese's speech also was notable because the only economist mentioned in the presentation was Dani Rodrik. Although Rodrik, especially over the last few years, has defended his profession and by extension its deep connection to neoliberalism, he has been an early and harsh critic of globalization. Rodrik's mention, together with the fact that there are no prominent neoliberal senior economists serving in the administration, confirms the administration's break with mainstream American economic thought as developed since the late 1960s. This rejection of neoliberalism is common among other senior administration figures.

In a February 2020 *Foreign Policy* article, Jake Sullivan, before joining the Biden administration as National Security Adviser, and Jennifer Harris wrote that "…economists got a number of things wrong and significant correctives are overdue…." Over "…the past 30 years, foreign-policy professionals have largely deferred questions of economics to a small community of experts who run international economic affairs…. [T]his deference has come from a view that economics and foreign policy ought to be kept distinct…." Moreover, the "foreign-policy elite," like much of U.S. society, "internalized this economic orthodoxy" and adopted a "…reflexive confidence in competitive markets…and a corresponding belief that the role of government is best confined to securing…competitive markets through enforcing property rights, only intervening in the supposedly rare instance of market failure…."

Dovetailing with this neoliberal rejection is faith in government action. IP is about the power and purported effectiveness of government intervention, and President Biden clearly believes in this. In many ways he is the anti-Ronald Reagan. While Reagan was famous for rhetoric like: "Government is not the solution to our problem, government is the problem," Biden highlights what he sees

as government's constructive and necessary role. In March 2021, he said: "We need to remember the government isn't some foreign force in a distant capital. No, it's us…. America thrives when… we turn our hands to common purpose." In an address to a Joint Session of Congress also in April, he said: "Throughout our history…public investment and infrastructure has literally transformed America — our attitudes, as well as our opportunities." He highlighted, among other accomplishments, government support for the transcontinental railroad and interstate highway system, and the space program.

The administration has identified numerous areas that it thinks warrant forceful state intervention. Some of these, such as repairing U.S. highways, modernizing U.S. ports, and providing support for pre-K education, fit the broader IP transformational (horizontal) definition and are less controversial. Others, however, are more narrowly construed as assisting particular companies or sectors, especially in the alternative energy and automotive sector, and are more controversial. Several of these proposals from the "Infrastructure Investment and Jobs Act" (IIJ), signed by the President in November 2021, are below. (See *Insert 1*.)

In addition to these IIJ Act appropriations, the Fiscal Year 2022 budget sent to Congress in June 2021, and the ongoing negotiations for the Build Back Better (BBB) plan contain a num-

ber of IP type appropriations. Even if the BBB passes at a reduced level, the total costs for IP related expenditures in 2022 and beyond could run into the hundreds of billions of dollars. This is a huge amount of money, even for the multitrillion dollar U.S. budget.

In order to justify these expenditures, the administration in June 2021 released *Building Resilient Supply Chains, Revitalizing American Manufacturing, and Fostering Broad-Based Growth*. In this document, the administration identified four industries for significant state support: Semiconductor Manufacturing and Advanced Packaging; Critical Minerals and Materials; Pharmaceutical and Active Pharmaceutical Ingredients; and Large Capacity Batteries. In all four areas, the administration wants to "double down" on investing in the U.S.'s "innovation ecosystem with world-class universities, research centers, start-ups and incubators…." Importantly, the administration will require any products developed from this funding and cooperation be manufactured in the United States.

Semiconductor manufacturing in the United States over the last 20 years declined from 37% of global production to approximately 12%. This foreign sourcing creates extreme supply chain risk, especially given the high concentration of production in Taiwan, and China's increasing belligerence toward that country. The report identifies other risks including depen-

INSERT 1

Infrastructure Investment and Jobs Act Provisions
(in $ billions)

$21.5	Energy Department's Office of Clean Energy Demonstrations
$8.0	Clean hydrogen
$8.0	*"48C tax credit"* promoting advanced clean energy manufacturing
$7.5	Electric vehicle charging stations
$7.5	Electric and "low emission" buses and ferries
$5.0	Projects demonstrating "innovative approaches to transmission, storage, and distribution infrastructure"
$3.5	Carbon capture
$3.0	Battery material processing grants
$3.0	Battery manufacturing and recycling grants
$2.4	Advanced nuclear reactor projects

dence on legacy (outdated) products, and minimal private incentives for manufacturing in the United States. In order to rebuild U.S. manufacturing capability, the U.S. Senate passed the "United States Innovation and Competition Act." It includes $52 billion for incentivizing companies to increase domestic semiconductor manufacturing, and $195 billion for research and development.

Critical Minerals and Materials (CMM) are materials not found or produced in the United States in sufficient quantities "…to supply the military, industrial, and essential civilian needs… during a national emergency...." The CMM supply chain is at "serious risk of disruption" from natural disasters, political intervention, distortionary trade practices, and other factors. Trade liberalization and implementation of global, just-in-time supply chains caused this vulnerability by eroding U.S. manufacturing capabilities and labor-force skills. The administration will identify U.S. sites where critical minerals can be produced and processed "while adhering to the highest environmental, labor, and sustainability standards." It will "identify gaps in [mining] statutes and regulations that may need to be updated." Various departments, including Defense and Energy, and agencies will use grants, loans, loan guarantees, and offtake agreements to support U.S. production. Precise programs and funding requirements are still being determined, but the cost could easily be in the tens of billions of dollars.

Large Capacity Batteries are used in electric vehicles (EVs), stationary facilities (e.g., electric utilities), and defense products. The administration thinks the U.S. opportunity "…to secure a leading position in the global battery market is still within reach if the Federal Government takes swift and coordinated action…." including by stimulating end product demand through subsidizing EVs sales and building charging infrastructure. Besides stimulating end demand, the administration, wants to facilitate/create the entire supply chain from minerals production and processing, to battery

cells fabrication and battery pack manufacturing, to end of product life recycling or disposal. This is an extremely ambitious task and total funding requirements are still being determined, but it should easily be in the scores of billions of dollars.

Pharmaceutical and Active Pharmaceutical Ingredients (APIs) vulnerability was painfully revealed during the Covid-19 pandemic when various antibiotics, painkillers, hormones, antiviral drugs, and even vitamins were in short supply. The inability to source APIs, 90% of which are produced overseas, revealed a major weakness in the American public health system. The administration "…will establish a public-private consortium for advanced manufacturing…of domestic essential medicines...." They start by selecting 50–100 critical drugs for domestic manufacturing. Proposed expenditures for this sector in the report were small ($60 million), but the evolving "American Jobs Plan" contains a $50 billon request for the National Science Foundation and a substantial part could be used for pharmaceutical and API support.

Assessing the Arguments

A feature of the American IP debate is the extensive disagreements between supporters and opponents. These disagreements involve not only policy prescriptions but basic economic principles, and assessments of current economic conditions and of IP's historical experience. Regarding the above-mentioned government-private sector cooperation, for example, some libertarian opponents consider IP a "synonym for fascism" since they think civil liberties are fatally undermined when the government and private sector cooperate. Proponents like Robert Atkinson and Michel Lind see the entire libertarian perspective and its "radical theory of cosmopolitan individualism" as "unrealistic" and a "recipe for national decline."

A common belief among opponents is that IP does not work. It will not promote growth, create jobs, or transform the economy in any positive way. To many, the United States should return

to what they think made it great: increasing high-skilled immigration, reducing taxes and regulations, and securing new trade agreements.

For decades, many opponents pointed to "import substitution industrialization" (ISI), particularly in Latin America, as empirical evidence of IPs failure. ISI tried to promote domestic manufacturing by protecting local companies from foreign competition through tariffs and import licensing, subsidized credits, and foreign exchange manipulation. By the 1970s, these policies often were seen as failures since most ISI countries did not grow vigorously or transform their economics. IP proponents, however, disagree with this assessment.

Joseph Stiglitz and Bruce Greenwald argue that labeling Latin America ISI a failure is "at best, a contention, and at worst simply wrong." They note that Brazil, the most "ardent adopter" of ISI, had very high growth prior to 1980, and the problem after 1980 was not ISI, but excessive debt and macroeconomic shocks.

The sides also disagree over IP's economic impact in Europe and Asia, and, due to definitional differences whether some countries now follow IPs. While all accept that most West European countries pursued IP after 1945, some argue that they repudiated these policies as European integration increased after 1993. Others, such as political scientist Fabio Bulfone, argue that state intervention merely morphed from vertical IP to horizontal IP. Similarly with Japan, some argue that IP interventions were greatly reduced, while others note how the government still "strongly persuades" companies to follow its directions through financial system dominance and other forms of "administrative guidance."

IP's role in the success of the Asian "miracle" economies of Hong Kong, South Korea, Singapore, and Taiwan is especially contentious. The original IMF IP view was negative, but new research is causing a reconsideration. A 2019 IMF study by economists Reda Cherif and Fuad Hasanov summed this work up by writing "…the success of the Asian miracles cannot be disentangled from that of their industrial policies." Opponents, however, stand by their assessments that these "miracles" would have happened without IP.

Even regarding China, there is stark disagreement. Given China's high growth rate and extensive use of interventionary policies, IP's role in promoting economic success might seem self-evident. Opponents disagree. Lincicome and Zhu write: "…China's rapid growth since the 1980s can be largely attributed to market-based domestic reforms…and its general liberalization of trade and investment policy, including its accession to the WTO, not industrial policy." Paradoxically, they highlight how China's continuing interventions have misallocated resources, exacerbated corruption, and created investment bubbles and industrial overcapacity. They particularly highlight corruption and warn of the dangers of copying Chinese policy in the United States.

Many IP opponents see any government economic involvement as a major source of corruption. Lincicome and Zhu argue that IP in the United States would increase corruption by allowing special interests and others to "capture" the budget and regulatory process, defraud consumers, and loot the treasury. Stiglitz, however, argues that not having an IP "…opens the possibility that

Commerce Secretary Gina Raimondo holds a silicon chip wafer with Micron Technology CEO Sanjay Metrotra at the company's fabrication facility in Virginia. (COMMERCE DEPARTMENT.)

the structure of the economy is set, or at least greatly influenced, by special interests. Such an economy is likely to be beset by rent seeking and the resulting pervasive inefficiencies…the economy will be characterized by lower growth and more inequality than would be the case if the government were more self-consciousness in their direction of the economy."

Similarly opposing assessments characterize evaluation of the U.S. economy. Using the example of manufacturing jobs, Lincicome and Zhu argue that economic conditions in the United States are not as dire as IP proponents assert: "…U.S. manufacturing data reveal a flexible and dynamic sector that is generally responsive to free market forces. [The] offshoring or automating of low-wage, low-skill [jobs] is an important part of a healthy, dynamic economy…." Trying to bring back low-skilled manufacturing jobs would destroy "high-productivity, high-innovation industries…."

Proponents, however, stress the importance of low-skill manufacturing. Oren Cass, a conservative IP proponent, stresses that low-skill manufacturing provides work for those at the lower end of the income distribution. Cass approvingly cites a 2010 argument by Andy Grove, who many consider the "father" of Silicon Valley, that "…transferring manufacturing and a great deal of engineering out of the country has hindered our ability to bring innovations to scale at home. Without scaling, we don't just lose jobs — we lose our hold on new technologies." Cass and others assert that if this manufacturing takes place in China or other foreign countries, then the United States will not capture any positive spillovers, including future innovation. IP opponents, citing Fredrich Hayek's "knowledge problem," retort that governments can never be smarter than the market and that efforts at redirecting investments will be counterproductive. Stiglitz thinks this problem is surmountable, especially since governments, like firms, get better at making IP decisions as more policies are tried and results studied. He writes: "…the

only way to learn how to do industrial policies is to carry out industrial policies [and] learn…from one's successes and failures." He also stresses that in order to gage IP's success, one needs to evaluate how IP affected the performance of the overall economy, not just a single company or industry.

The primary rationale for IP rests on the existence of market failures, i.e., the inability of an economy to deliver the optimal amount of a good or service. Market failures occur when individually rational behavior does not lead to rational group outcomes. Insufficient provision of national defense (a public good), or failure to control a polluting factory (an externality) are classic market failures. IP proponents see the offshoring of American manufacturing, given China's economic policies, as a market failure. IP opponents accept that market failure can exist, but they think that the cure, IP, is worse than the disease.

The notion by opponents that IP would make conditions worse is based on an optimistic view of existing economic conditions. Lincicome and Zhu write that American living standards "…cannot justify U.S. industrial policies…. Americans today are absurdly rich as compared to only a few decades ago." They and others want to know what is so bad about the current situation?

The retort from IP proponents is scathing. Cass writes: "Libertarians often posit an ideal world of policy non-intervention as superior to the messy reality of policy action. But that ideal does not exist…and we should not give preference to our existing mess, built on an incorrect understanding of our economic challenges, over one that at least aims closer to the right direction. [Market] fundamentalists who insisted on eliminating the barriers between our market and China's have, by their policy choices, introduced massive distortions into our market. Insisting on allowing the distortions, and then announcing that a dislike of distortions precludes any response, is irrational."

Beyond partisan IP battles, some are concerned about the ability of the United States to pay for large IP initiatives. Enormous pandemic spending may have accustomed many to the size of proposed government IP outlays, and some offer "Modern Monetary Theory" as a justification for the accompanying deficits. Many are uneasy, however, with risking so much on a novel theory. Others, like Jake Sullivan and Jennifer Harris, argue that while debt matters, it matters more on what it is spent.

What's different now

Besides the previously noted factors distinguishing this IP debate from previous ones, there are two other important differences. First, some current IP proposals have bipartisan support. Previous IP consideration had no meaningful Republican support; now competition with China has elevated many IP proposals into national security issues many Republicans can endorse. Consequently, it is much easier to give government money to companies, if it is a way to meet a perceived threat from China. As Senator John Cornyn, a conservative Texas Republican and past critic of government funding of industry, said: "Frankly, I think China has left us no option but to make these investments."

Second, the domestic U.S. lobby supporting closer economic relations with China is weaker than five years ago. Many multinational corporations are disappointed with how China now treats them and this has reduced pro-China business sentiment. The supply chain vulnerability revealed by the Covid-19 pandemic also prompted a call for reducing economic dependance on China. While some U.S. financial service companies still are trying to expand in China, there is little or no Biden administration support for these efforts. There is a new appreciation that what is good for U.S.-based multinational corporations is not necessarily good for U.S. prosperity and security. National Security Adviser Sullivan even called out JPMorgan and Goldman Sachs for their China investments and asked "… what does that have to do with jobs and wages here in the United States…?"

Third, attitudes toward capitalism have changed. While it is unclear how well many Americans understand the meaning of socialism or even capital-

GRAPH 2

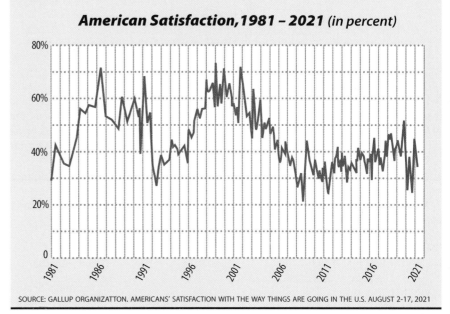

American Satisfaction, 1981 – 2021 (in percent)

SOURCE: GALLUP ORGANIZATTON. AMERICANS' SATISFACTION WITH THE WAY THINGS ARE GOING IN THE U.S. AUGUST 2-17, 2021

ism (especially given its many varieties), it is clear that a large and growing segment of the public, especially among Millennials and Gen Z (or those born between 1981 and 1996, and after 1997 respectively) are increasingly hostile to what they think capitalism represents. According to an Axios/Momentive June 2021 poll, only 42% of Americans aged 18–24 surveyed had a positive view of capitalism, while 54% have a negative view. This was a sharply negative swing from the 58/42% split two years earlier. Other polls across all age groups and going back further in time also indicate similar attitudinal shifts, although not as drastic as the recent shift among younger Americans.

Younger Americans, in particular, are frustrated and angry about their economic situation and they blame Boomer policies adopted from the Reagan administration onward. According to Bruce Gibney, author of *A Generation of Sociopaths*, Boomer "… policies of under-investment and debt accumulation…made it very hard to deal with our most serious challenges going forward." They destroyed "…social solidarity [and] a sense of commitment to fellow citizens [and] replaced [it] by a cult of individualism." (Individualism is, of course, at the heart of neoliberalism.) Helen Andrews, author of *Boomer,* said the "uberization" of the post-Boomer work force gave her

generation less job security and lower incomes, made it virtually impossible for her generation to get ahead, and, led to enormous wealth concentration among older Americans. Both Andrews and Gibney think that "trickledown economics" has been a particularly pernicious failure. Given such views, many Gen Z and Millennials are predisposed toward market intervention and industrial policy.

Even if public understanding of "socialism" and "capitalism" miss precise textbook definitions, most Americans recognize problems when they see them. According to the Gallup Organization, very few Americans are satisfied with "the way things are going in the U.S." (See Graph 2). In contrast to the first two U.S. IP experiences, satisfaction after the 2008 GFC IP debate has never really recovered. Events like the Surfside, Florida, condominium collapse and the February 2021 Texas electricity interruption continue to raise questions about the utility of unfettered markets and about minimizing government's economic role. The Great Decision for America is: will it pursue more interventionary economic policies, i.e., industrial policy, or will it try to reconfigure neoliberalism? The foreign policy implications are profound, and it will affect not just competition with China, but the entire array of U.S. relationships world-wide.

discussion questions

1. "Industrial policy" emphasizes substantial government intervention in a nation's economy. What are the benefits and consequences of this intervention?

2. How would increased government intervention in the economy affect U.S. relations with allies and other countries?

3. Which U.S. industries, if any, are most suitable for industrial policy?

4. Neoliberal economic theory has been prominent in several U.S. administrations. President Biden's push for "industrial policy" represents a stark break from this theory. What factors have caused this change? Is it warranted?

5. There is disagreement over what contributed to China's economic growth, i.e. liberalization or industrial policy. Which do you think is the reason for this growth and why?

suggested readings

Atkinson, Robert and Michael Lind. *National Developmentalism: From Forgotten Tradition to New Consensus.* American Affairs Journal. May 20, 2019. A detailed critique of the "five distinct schools" concerned with how the U.S. should govern its own economy and fit into the global economy.

Blackwill, Robert and Jennifer Harris. "The Lost Art of Economic Statecraft: Restoring an American Tradition." *Foreign Affairs.* March–April, 2016. The case for reintegrating economic statecraft back into foreign policy and an explanation of how it was originally separated.

Heilbroner, Robert. *The Worldly Philosophers: The Lives, Times And Ideas Of The Great Economic Thinkers.* Touchstone, 1999. Although the book ends with John Maynard Keynes, it is still one of the best examinations of the origin and evolution of capitalism and how views of it changed over time.

Lincicome, Scott and Huan Zhu. "Questioning Industrial Policy: Why Government Manufacturing Plans are Ineffective and Unnecessary." *Cato Working Paper.* June 16, 2021. A detailed and highly critical review of industrial policy.

Building Resilient Supply Chains, Revitalizing American Manufacturing, and Fostering Broad-Based Growth. The White House. June 2021. A deep dive into the structure, vulnerability, and opportunities of the four priority sectors targeted by the Biden administration for industrial "strategy."

Sullivan, Jake and Jennifer Harris. "America Needs a New Economic Philosophy." *Foreign Policy.* February 7, 2020. A detailed look at the thinking behind the Biden industrial strategy agenda and foreign policy can support it.

Mearsheimer, John J. "The Inevitable Rivalry: America, China, and the Tragedy of Great-Power Politics." *Foreign Affairs.* November/December 2021. The collapsing neoliberal global world order will leave the United States and China to compete with each other in a new multipolar world.

Don't forget to vote!

Download a copy of the ballot questions from the Resources page at www.fpa.org/great_decisions

To access web links to these readings, as well as links to additional, shorter readings and suggested web sites,

GO TO **www.fpa.org/great_decisions**

and click on the topic under Resources, on the right-hand side of the page.

Biden foreign policy in the age of strategic competition
by G. John Ikenberry

U.S. President Joe Biden delivers a speech on stage during the World Leaders' Summit of the COP26 UN Climate Change Conference in Glasgow, Scotland, on November 2, 2021. (BRENDAN SMIALOWSKI/AFP/GETTY IMAGES)

The Biden administration confronts a world in turmoil. The system of rules and institutions built in the decades after 1945 and expanded after the Cold War is in disarray. Cooperation among the advanced industrial democracies—the so-called G-7 countries—has ebbed, even in the face of a global pandemic and economic recession. Western democracies have struggled to cope with rising inequality, political polarization, and ethnic and anti-immigrant populism. Meanwhile, China is quickly emerging as a global superpower, poised to overtake the United States as the world's largest economy. Under the leadership of President Xi Jinping, China has begun to challenge American leadership and the liberal-oriented global order. American

strategic thinkers have announced the return to "great power competition," signaling a transition from a grand strategy designed for a unipolar world system to one oriented toward U.S.-Chinese strategic competition and the balance of pow-

G. JOHN IKENBERRY *is the Albert G. Milbank Professor of Politics and International Affairs at Princeton University in the Department of Politics and the School of Public and International Affairs. Ikenberry is also a Global Eminence Scholar at Kyung Hee University in Seoul, Korea. In 2018–19, Ikenberry was a Visiting Fellow at All Souls College, Oxford University. In 2013–14, Ikenberry was the 72nd Eastman Visiting Professor at Balliol College, Oxford. Ikenberry is a Fellow of the American Academy of Arts and Sciences.*

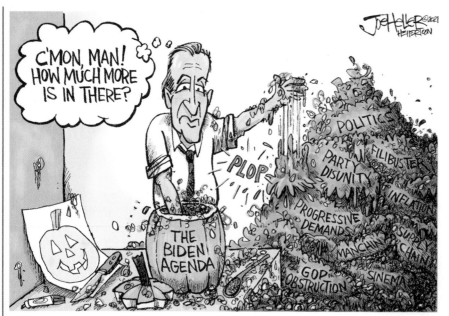

er. Amidst these upheavals, the world looks starkly ill-equipped to cope with the global-scale problems of climate change, pandemic disease, nuclear weapons proliferation, and emerging 21st century challenges of cyber warfare, bioengineering, and artificial intelligence. The demand for leadership that can solve global problems is growing, but its supply—including in the United States—is deeply uncertain.

The Biden administration's foreign policy seeks to respond to these deteriorating circumstances at home and abroad. Its message to the world is: "America is back." But is the United States back—and what precisely is the Biden administration's strategic vision and grand strategy for reasserting American leadership?

At the outset, President Biden has defined his foreign policy as a counterpoint to the Trump administration. It seeks to repair the damage of the Trump era. For four years, Trump took the United States down a dangerous path, attacking and undermining the architecture of the postwar American-led liberal international order. Trade, alliances, arms control, environment,

Before you read, download the companion **Glossary** that includes definitions, a guide to acronyms and abbreviations used in the article, and other material. Go to **www. fpa.org/great_decisions** and select a topic in the Resources section. (Top right)

human rights, public health, democratic solidarity, multilateral problem solving—across the full spectrum of policies and commitments, the Trump administration acted as a wrecking ball. The Biden administration has seen as its first mission to reverse gears and return to the postwar U.S. tradition of liberal internationalism and foreign policy leadership. On its first day of office, it announced America's return to the Paris Climate Agreement and it moved to reaffirm security commitments to allies in Europe and East Asia. More generally, the Biden administration promised a return to a cooperative style of American leadership, with its emphasis on diplomacy, multilateralism, security cooperation, and support for the liberal democratic world. In effect, the new administration announced its return to the seventy-five-year-old "playbook" of American foreign policy—tying the country's power to institutions, partnerships, and cooperation with like-minded states.

Thus, in its first year in office, the Biden administration has sought to rebuild American leadership by reaffirming old allies and forging new ones. The goal is to rebuild liberal democracy at home and abroad, and by so doing show that democracies and open societies can in fact solve problems. Biden seeks to draw a direct contrast with

illiberal and autocratic states, starting with China. The world will see that the United States and its democratic allies are capable of providing a better life for their people than their autocratic and authoritarian rivals. In this sense, the Biden administration sees domestic and foreign policy challenges as deeply linked. The American society and economy need to be rebuilt, and this will strengthen the country's global position and reputation. If the U.S. system is "broken" and allies and partners do not think it can be trusted, the entire American edifice of leadership is jeopardized. Biden's focus in on the decaying foundations—both physical and political—of the American system at home and abroad, seeking to rebuild them to deal with the central emerging problems of the 21st century.

The Biden administration seeks to refurbish the modern liberal state and the liberal international coalition. But it faces powerful headwinds in pursuing this foreign policy of renewal. In this essay, I will do three things. First, I will look at what I argue are the three crises of international order that shape the challenges of Biden-era foreign policy. These are the crises of geopolitics, modernity, and liberal democracy. Second, I offer a portrait of Biden's emerging foreign policy vision, which is focused on strategic competition with China. The Biden administration—and the American foreign policy establishment more generally—increasingly sees China as a "systemic rival." China is not just a growing geopolitical rival; it is also competing with the United States as a model for navigating the 21st century challenges of modernity. The China challenge provides a sort of unifying frame of reference for the Biden administration's larger domestic and foreign policy agenda. Finally, I will draw parallels between Biden's vision of American renewal and the defense of liberal democracy with Roosevelt-era thinking of the 1930s and 40s. As in FDR's day, liberal democracy is in peril. The question is: can the United States once again rise to the occasion and make the world safe for democracy?

The geopolitical crisis

The Biden administration is seeking to rebuild America's global position, but it is doing so in the middle of three world political storms—crises of geopolitical, complex interdependence, and liberal democracy.

For the first time since the early years of the Cold War, the United States finds itself confronted by a powerful—and increasingly powerful—superpower rival. The American-led order was built in an era when the United States and the other postwar industrial democracies were the most powerful states in the system. The Soviet Union was dominant within its sphere of influence. But the United States and its allies and partners were the most powerful and dynamic states in the system, preponderant in economic, political, technological, and military capabilities. The postwar world economy was organized around the rapidly-expanding American economy, creating opportunities for the United States to use its market to invite other states into its geopolitical orbit. The postwar system of alliances was also anchored in outsized American military power and technological capabilities to project force across oceanic distances. In the first decades after the end of the Cold War, the United States emerged as a "unipolar power," overshadowing other major states. It was a world order in which one powerful state held sway, underwriting a system that was safe for democracy.

The rise of China to peer competitor status with the United States has upended a century of American global dominance. It is a once-in-a-century world-historical power shift—what scholars call a global "power transitions." A leading state that has dominated world order and shaped its rules and institutions is under challenge from a rising state. China is rising up and seeking to replace the United States as the world's leading state—and to reshape or reorient the rules and institutions of global order. This has happened before. Great Britain rose up in the 18th and early 19th century to challenge and replace France and other European states as the leading power in the Western imperial world. In the early 20th century, the United States similarly grew powerful and challenged Great Britain for leadership of the postwar world. The Chinese-led global power transition may be even more far-reaching and consequential. It may be a "triple" power transition -- a transition from a world dominated by the United States, the West, and liberal democracy to a world dominated by China, the East, and state socialism.

Power transitions are dangerous moments for world order. The leading state that has upheld the international order is in decline, while a newly powerful rising state seeks to establish its leadership. A struggle ensues, and conflict—and the risks of war—increases. This dynamic can be seen in the escalation of competition and conflict in U.S.-Chinese relations. As China's trade and investment relations have spread outward through East Asia, Africa, and Latin America, its strategic interests in shaping global and regional rules and institutions grow. In the meantime, the United States seeks to maintain its hegemonic position in East Asia as well as its overall global influence and leadership. The clash between China and the United States is made worse because the two countries are also ideological rivals. China has risen up outside the old Western world, bring with it a "century of humiliation." It offers the world its own civilizational values and orientations. Its communist ideology and state socialist regime also clash with American and Western liberal democratic values and institutions. The United States has also established itself over the postwar decades and the leading alliance partner and security provider in East Asia. As China's military buildup continues, the two countries are increasingly in a contest for hegemony in the region. Together, these aspects of the global power transition are destabilizing old rules and institutions of regional and global order.

The crisis of modernity

The world is also entering into a new era of cascading interdependence, and this is the second crisis of international order. This is the ongoing global transition that over the last two centuries has defined the modern era. Beginning in the early 19th century, the industrial revolution and waves of scientific and technological change on an increasingly global scale have globalized human life on this planet.

Members of the Communist Party of China (CPC) review the oath of joining the party in front of the party flag on April 13, 2021 in Luoyang, Henan Province of China. (JIA FANGWEN/VCG/GETTY IMAGES)

In this Sept. 8, 1945, file photo, only a handful of buildings remain standing amid the wasteland of Hiroshima, the Japanese city reduced to rubble following the first atomic bomb to be dropped in warfare. On Aug. 6, 1945, a U.S. plane dropped an atomic bomb on Hiroshima.Japan surrendered on Aug. 15, ending World War II. (AP IMAGES)

Some states and societies have been at the vanguard of modernity's pathway, while other societies and peoples have lagged behind. The scientific and technological revolutions of the modern era are markers of this global transformation—steam power, the railroad, the telegraph, airplanes and automobiles, satellites and computers, ballistic missiles and the internet. Across two centuries, all peoples across the world have seen their lives transformed—both for better and worse—by these staggering upheavals of modernity.

At each stage of this industrial revolution, new and complex forms of economic, military, and environmental interdependence have posed challenges to global governance. Revolutions in military technology, creating increasingly lethal and global-scale violence capacity, have triggered repeated efforts at arms control and disarmament diplomacy. The nuclear revolution, which began during World War II with the horrific atomic bombing of Hiroshima and Nagasaki, has been one of the most dangerous manifestations of modern interdependence. Technological advances in nuclear energy and ballistic missiles and near-catastrophes such as the Cuban missile crisis galvanized efforts by the

United States and the Soviet Union to negotiate arms control agreements. The unfolding industrial revolution and the rise of global capitalism in the 20th century have created similar challenges for the management of the world economy. After World War II, the United States and other industrial countries found new ways to stabilize trade and investment flows. Starting in the 1960s, environment degradation and pollution rose in significance, and various international agreements were negotiated—such as in the area of ozone depletion—that addressed global ecological dangers. In all these ways, modernity has generated complex linkages, dangers, and externalities that in each era has set the stage for struggles over global governance.

In recent decades, the world has seen an intensification of security, economic, and environmental interdependence. Nuclear proliferation has taken a new turn as North Korea has built its arsenal and Iran has threatened to cross the nuclear weapons threshold. In the meantime, Russia and the United States have continued to modernize their nuclear capabilities and China has engaged in a rapid military buildup. As *The New York Times* recently reported, "There is little arms control; modern

technologies are unrestrained; and the players are more numerous and rapidly building up nuclear stockpiles." Economic interdependence is also taking a new and unstable turn. The old multilateral system of rules and dispute settlement mechanisms has largely broken down, while conflicts within and between regions have intensified over technology standards, production platforms, intellectual property rights, trade preferences, and industrial policy. The 2008 financial crisis was the worst economic crisis to shake the world economy since the Great Depression, but rules and cooperative agreements to manage the next financial crisis have not been put in place.

More recently, the Covid-19 pandemic has shaken the world, leaving millions of people dead and little global cooperation to manage the aftermath. The World Health Organization (WHO) has shown itself to be a weak instrument for monitoring and responding to the outbreak and spread of the virus. Covid nationalism—not internationalism—has been the dominant response to the crisis. Scientists make it clear that the Covid-19 pandemic is not a once-in-a-century phenomenon, but something that will inevitably reappear more regularly in the future. The international community has an overwhelming shared interest in strengthening global public health institutions. Indeed, there are proposals for a "pandemic treaty" to strengthen the WHO and global disease monitoring and containment protocols. But there is little momentum for such a grand pivot towards building standby capacities for future outbreaks. The political incentives for leaders in most countries are overwhelmingly short-term and national in orientation. The European Union has stumbled in its response to the pandemic, while China has pursued vaccine diplomacy within its spheres of influence.

An even more ominous global-scale crisis is climate change and global warming. Only a few years ago the problem of climate change appeared to be a problem for future generations, but the multiple and complex effects of a warming earth are already manifesting. Draughts, floods, fires, extreme weather, ocean acidification, rising sea levels—these are many of the early signs. Unless greenhouse gas emissions are massively reduced, this degradation of global ecosystems—already locked in to some degree—will spiral out of control, producing a global-scope civilizational catastrophe. The growing endangerment of life on earth is at the heart of the crisis of modernity. It is industrial modernity itself—the so-called Anthropocene age—that imperils humanity. The relentless release of carbon emissions into the atmosphere is the ultimate externality of industrial society and world economic development. Global movements for clean energy and environmental protection have grown larger and louder in recent years. The Biden administration has led the United States back into the Paris agreement on climate change. China and other countries are also seeking to establish their leadership in this area, but governments are mostly offering promises of future actions.

The crisis of liberal democracy

The third crisis of international order is the weakening of the established Western liberal democracies, including in particular the United States. The countries that did the most to build the postwar liberal international order are now divided and less willing and capable of providing global leadership. The United States and the major states of Europe were the great beneficiaries of the postwar Western system. This system provided the rules and institutions for these countries to simultaneously build modern social democracies at home and cooperative relations abroad. Growing middle classes in the advanced democracies were the core constituencies for the American-led postwar liberal order. It is all the more perilous for the global system that it is precisely these countries that are now faltering. To many observers, 2016 was the dramatic moment that revealed

the depth of the problems facing the Western liberal democracies, the year when Great Britain voted to leave the European Union and the United States elected Donald Trump. These two countries—the oldest and most respected liberal democracies—had led the way in building the postwar liberal order, but in 2016 they were seemingly in full-scale retreat.

Inside the United States and other Western societies, the postwar politics and institutions of liberal democracy are under stress. For the middle classes in these societies, the postwar era of steadily rising incomes and social advancement has stalled. For decades, the advanced democracies enjoyed the security and gains that came from social democracy. Postwar liberal democracy was built around growth coalitions, class compromise, and political pluralism embraced by both the left and the right. Postwar governments enlarged their roles in managing the economy and directing public investments in education, social security, and economic safety nets. These postwar decades of rising economic opportunity and social consensus have largely come to an end. In its place, Western industrial societies have experienced rising economic inequality, political polarization, and an erosion of trust in basic institutions.

These problems have been long in the making. Beginning in the 1980s, a

neo-liberal counter-movement in Western democracies began to attack the postwar foundations of social democracy. With the coming to power of Margaret Thatcher in Britain and Ronald Reagan in the United States, these efforts intensified. Conservative governments rapidly began undermining labor unions, diminishing the progressivity of taxes, deregulating market activity, and cutting social welfare services. With rising concern over environmental degradation, conservative and neo-liberal parties were in the forefront in resisting environmental regulation as infringements on private property and individual liberty. The last two decades have seen growing struggles within these countries to rebuild political majorities around modern social democracy, but economic stagnation and divisive "backlash" politics have undercut these efforts. Under these depressed conditions, Western democracies have seen an outbreak of nationalism, xenophobia, and anti-immigrant sentiment. These societies have turned inward and become increasingly divided.

This crisis of liberal democracy has had the effect of weakening the rules and institutions of global order. The United States and other liberal states have been less inclined to underwrite an open, rules-based system. The political incentives of national leaders in these countries make it difficult for

U.S. President Ronald Reagan sits with British Prime Minister Margaret Thatcher at 10 Downing Street, London, on June 5, 1984. (ROGERS/EXPRESS/GETTY IMAGES)

them to champion global cooperation. The middle classes in these countries have come to see the liberal international order—and the "globalization" it has produced—as a threat more than an opportunity. For many people the open, rules-based system primarily benefits capitalists, bankers, and other internationalist elites. In these various ways, the old postwar consensus within Western liberal democracies on the virtues of liberal internationalism has eroded. The challenges of modernity and interdependence are growing, but the political impulse within liberal democracies to step forward to organize and lead a cooperative global order have waned.

Biden's strategy of strategic competition

Faced with these crises, the Biden administration is giving shape to a grand strategy of strategic competition with China. It begins with a conviction that China is increasingly a full-spectrum challenger to the U.S. global position and the U.S.-led liberal democratic world. "China and other countries are closing fast," President Biden said in an April 2021 joint session of Congress. Chinese President Xi Jinping is "deadly earnest about becoming the most significant, consequential nation in the world." Earlier, in February, Biden said that the world is "at an inflection point between those who argue that. . ... autocracy is the best way to go forward, and those who understand that democracy is essential." To be sure, China is deeply embedded in the global system and world economy, and U.S.-Chinese cooperation will be essential to manage problems of security, economic, and environmental interdependence. But the United States and China are also hegemonic rivals with very different visions of world order, rooted in increasingly divergent developmental and order-building interests and values. The United States wants to make the world safe for democracy and China wants to make the world safe for the Chinese Communist Party (CCP) and political autocracy. The United States believes—as it has for over two centuries—that it is safer in a world where the liberal democracies hold sway. China contests such a world. Therein lies the grand strategic rub.

The Biden administration has thus moved to place long-term strategic competition with China at the center of its foreign policy. The abrupt and chaotic ending of the American war in Afghanistan was seen by many as a decision by Biden to step back from global security leadership. But it is better seen as a strategic rebalancing of resources and commitments, repositioning the United States to focus on East Asia and competition with China. The post-9-11 grand strategy of fighting a global war on terror has ended, giving way to a China-centered grand strategy organized around the balance of power, hegemonic competition, and a struggle to shape the organizing logic of the global system. The Biden administration's efforts to build counter-weights to China in the Indo-Pacific—the Quad and the AUKUS agreement—are harbingers of this strategic reorientation. As Julian Borger of *The Guardian* writes: " AUKUS and an invigorated Quad are the two central pillars of the U.S. president's signature foreign policy, which some are calling the Biden doctrine: bolstering the world's democracies against the spread of authoritarianism by building a web of alliances."

Several convictions inform this new grand strategy. First, as China grows in wealth, power, and global influence, it is increasingly turning into a "systemic rival" of the United States, offering alternative leadership and order-building agendas. As Gideon Rachman notes, "the Biden team believes that China is determined to displace the United States as the world's preeminent economic and military power, and they are determined to push back." Fundamentally, China seeks to contest, weaken, and shrink America's liberal hegemonic presence in the world, paving the way for the elevation of its hegemonic leadership that champions an international order more congenial with its own illiberal regime principles and interests. President Xi seems to share this view, telling legislative officials in Beijing in April 2021 that "China can already look at the world on an equal level," suggesting that China no longer sees the United States as a superior force. China is a "systemic rival" because it challenges the full spectrum of American power, interests, and values. This competition will play out over many decades and across a wide array of areas—military power, alliances and alignments, markets and trade, money and finance, next-generation technology, science

An aerial photo taken on Sept. 11, 2021, shows large container ships loading and unloading cargo at Yangshan Deep-water Port in Shanghai, China. In August 2021, the container throughput of Shanghai Seaport reached 4.318 million TEUs (20-foot equivalent units), setting a new monthly production record since the establishment of the port. (COSTFOTO/ BARCROFT MEDIA/GETTY IMAGES)

and research, and democratic versus autocratic ideology and values.

Second, the engagement strategy of the 1990s that sought to integrate China into the liberal international order mostly failed. Welcoming China into the U.S.-led system—capped by its membership in the World Trade Organization (WTO) in 2000—did not lead to the hoped-for liberal outcomes. China became more integrated into the world economy, and mutually beneficial trade and growth followed, but Beijing did not continue on its path of reform, opening, and liberalization. 2018 was a turning point, when the Deng-era term limits on the Chinese presidency were dropped, making President Xi Jinping, in effect, "ruler for life." The attack on democracy in Hong Kong, the oppression of the Uyghurs, the intimidation of Taiwan, the territorial aggrandizement in the South China Sea, the internal crackdown on Western influences, the cult-like elevation of "Xi Jinping thought"—these are markers of the pathway China is traveling. Under President Xi, China has become more autocratic, anti-liberal, anti-democratic, and internationally aggressive. Glimmerings of openness, reform, the rule of law, and civil society outside the reach of the communist state have essentially disappeared.

Third, the United States is not capable of balancing against China's illiberal hegemonic ambitions on its own. It will need to work with a coalition of like-minded states and associated partners to create alignments that strengthen the underpinnings of the liberal international order. In his recent UN General Assembly speech, Biden mentioned "allies" eight times and "partners" sixteen times. After all, the China challenge is not just aimed at America's global position. It is a challenge to the wider world of liberal democracies and their long-standing military, economic, and ideological dominance in the global system. By working together, liberal democracies can leverage their power to shape global rules and institutions. This strategy of fostering cooperation

U.S. President Joe Biden meets with China's President Xi Jinping during a virtual summit from the Roosevelt Room of the White House in Washington, DC, November 15, 2021. (MANDEL NGAN/AFP/GETTY IMAGES)

among the democracies is not a project to build a unified Cold War-era "free world" bloc—this is not possible or even desirable. The goal is to build a wide variety of ad hoc groupings to aggregate military, economic, and diplomatic capabilities in various zones of competition. Within East Asia, as Kurt Campbell and Rush Doshi have argued, the "purpose of these different coalitions—and this broad strategy—is to create balance in some cases, bolster consensus on important facets of the regional order in others, and send a message that there are risks to China's present course."

Fourth, the most important step in countering Chinese ambitions is to make liberal democracy work at home. Demonstrating that liberal societies can function effectively and solve problems—this is the goal upon which everything else depends. American internationalism is only sustainable if it advances the life opportunities of the middle-class. This means a New Deal-type effort to renew and rebuild American society and institutions, investing in a modernized economy, infrastructure, research and technology, and clean energy. The competition between China and the United States is really a competition over "modernity projects," alternative models and ideologies of global development and socio-economic advancement. America suc-

ceeded as a global power in earlier eras because its capitalist democratic model seemed to outperform its rivals. We are entering an era where this competition will again play out.

Fifth, the struggle between China and the United States will also center on competition to shape global rules, regulations, technological platforms, and the values and principles enshrined in global institutions and regimes. Multilateral institutions and regimes are not value neutral. They can be more or less friendly to liberal democracy and human rights and more or less friendly to authoritarianism and autocracy. Technology platforms and their network externalities also can give one side or the other advantages. This struggle favors first movers and countries that work together with other countries to create "critical mass" coalitions. The United States will seek to build coalitions with liberal democracies to strengthen their position in these diverse, technology-driven areas of global rule and regime-making.

The Biden administration has made clear that the United States will need to build working relations with China, even as it competes. There are critical and growing "problems of interdependence" that can only be tackled through superpower cooperation. After all, even during the Cold War, the United States and the Soviet Union worked together

A woman holds a protest placard during an election rally for Taiwan's current president and Democratic Progressive Party presidential candidate, Tsai Ing-wen, ahead of the presidential election on January 10, 2020, in Taipei, Taiwan. Tsai Ing-wen, who campaigned on defending Taiwan from China, did win the election. (CARL COURT/GETTY IMAGES)

through the WHO on finding a cure for small pox, and the two countries engaged in sustained efforts at arms control. The United States should not need to "buy" cooperation from China on solving problems such as global warming by pulling its punches on issues such as human rights and Taiwan. The two superpowers will need to identity red lines and establish crisis diplomacy mechanisms to keep competition from spiraling out of control. Both sides will have incentives to build restraints and guard rails into their regional and global rivalry.

Grand strategy begins at home

With the Biden administration, the United States has continued this pivot to Asia, while largely abandoning its earlier efforts at engagement in favor of expanded efforts to build geopolitical counterweights. It has kept the Trump administration's heavy tariffs on Chinese imports, and sought to limit Chinese economic penetration, especially in high-technology areas. It is a strategy that combines active counterbalancing across military, economic, and ideological fronts, with continued and renewed efforts to find areas of common agreement with China in solving problems of interdependence, especially climate change. The Biden strategy borrows from the classic realist playbook that emphasizes the importance of active maintaining a military balance of power in East Asia and strengthening alliances with countries potentially in the shadow of Chinese domination. Deterrence, forward basing, and security cooperation are the essential tools. So too are regional security pacts such as the Quad and the AUKUS security agreement. These are classic realist-inspired strategic moves, creating counter-weights to growing Chinese power. "These were big moves on the chessboard in Asia," argues Michael Green, an Asia specialist at Georgetown University. "What they show you is that the effort to engage China isn't working the way everyone expected, and a recognition there has to be a lot more muscle in how we deal with China."

In the meantime, the Biden efforts to strengthen bonds of solidarity among democratic states across the region— and the promotion of human rights—is meant to push back against the spread of autocratic states with affinities to the Beijing model. Beyond this, the strategy seeks to build trade relations that bias the rules in favor of human rights and liberal values. Here the Trans-Pacific Partnership (TPP), negotiated by President Obama, and rejected by Trump, is a model. It restricts state-owned enterprises from subsidized dumping, protects intellectual property rights, outlaws human trafficking, and requires the legalization of independent trade unions and collective bargaining. The world trade system will have rules, and the question is whether they will or will not incorporate human rights and liberal democratic protections. This piece of the Biden strategy still hangs in the balance, endangered by anti-TPP factions on both the left and the right.

The emerging "systemic rivalry" between the United States and China will shape world politics for decades. But there are restraints that will limit its intensity and dangerous consequences. One is on the Chinese side: the growth of Chinese power and its aggressive "wolf warrior" actions have triggered a regional and global backlash. If China's foreign policy continues to become more aggressive and belligerent, it will generate even more pushback. In effect, China faces the problem that post-Bismarck Germany faced, and what historians call the problem of "self-encirclement." Germany under Bismarck undertook elaborate efforts to reassure and diplomatically engage its neighbors. But by the turn of the century, post-Bismarck Germany began to destabilize and threaten Europe through its economic growth and military mobilization. For the same reasons, China should worry about how it exercises power and look for ways to avoid backlash and self-encirclement. At some point, China will want to moderate its ambitions and signal restraint.

For the United States, restraint comes from the fact that most of its alliance partners are deeply tied economically to China. Across both Northeast and Southeast Asia, countries are simultaneously dependent on China for trade and investment and the United States for security protection and the maintenance of the military balance. Remarkably, one hundred countries in the world have twice as much trade with China as they do with the United States. The United States needs to worry that if its pushes too hard on its allies to confront or contain China, they will jump off the American bandwagon. The United States will have incentives to pursue a "not too hot, and not too cold" strategy in East Asia. It will need to reassure allies that America "is back," and that it intends to remain a provider of regional security and the military balance. But it will also need to convey reassurance in the other direction, that it will not push frontline states into a war with China—or even force these states to make existential choices about which side they are on.

Stepping back, a revitalized American-led liberal international order will only happen if it reestablishes the connections between domestic, social, and economic well-being and international cooperation. Fundamentally, this means resisting the idea that liberal internationalism is simply an agenda for "globalization." Globalization is about reducing barriers and integrating economies and societies. Liberal internationalism is different—it offers a vision of how to manage interdependence. Trade does generate efficiency and welfare gains for countries, but it also is a disruptive threat to workers and communities. Liberal internationalism must be defended as a project to manage the trade-offs between openness and social stability. This was a seminal innovation of the postwar Western system. In giving national governments space and policy tools to pursue economic stabilization and development, the architects of this order tried to reconcile open trade and free-market capitalism with social protections and economic security.

In the same way, the success of the Biden grand strategy ultimately hinges on developments at home. Can the United States get its own house in order? Inside the United States and other Western societies, the postwar politics and institutions of liberal democracy are under stress. For the middle classes in these societies, the postwar era of steadily rising incomes and social advancement has stalled. For decades, the

Rust is visible on the Theodore Roosevelt Bridge, which connects Washington, DC, to Virginia across the Potomac River, on April 7, 2021. In April 2020, the American Road and Transportation Builders Association listed the heavily trafficked bridge as structurally deficient, the worst rating. (DREW ANGERER/GETTY IMAGES))

advanced democracies enjoyed the security and gains that came from social democracy. Postwar liberal democracy was built around growth coalitions, class compromise, and political pluralism embraced by both the left and the right. Postwar governments enlarged their roles in managing the economy and directing public investments in education, social security, and economic safety nets. These postwar decades of rising economic opportunity and social consensus have largely come to an end. In its place, Western industrial societies have experienced rising economic inequality, political polarization, and an erosion of trust in basic institutions.

The ambitious proposals of the Biden administration—with massive funding proposals for infrastructure, research and development, education, the social safety net, and the transition to a low-carbon economy—are driven by this deep worry about the future of liberal democracy in the United States and abroad. In particular, the Biden administration's elevation of a comprehensive national crisis-response to climate change is driven by the linkage it sees in the three crises of geopolitics, interdependence, and liberal democracy. In this sense, Biden's grand strategy is an echo of Roosevelt's New

Deal-era agenda for domestic renewal and the rebuilding of international order. "The achievement of basic national interests requires making difficult domestic reforms in response to shifting global challenges," as Daniel Deudney and I argue. "Just as the United States in World War II quickly and dramatically ramped up production, the Biden program recognizes that responding to climate change requires far-reaching domestic innovations. The mobilization to defeat the Axis powers and then the Soviet Union left no aspect of American life untouched and unchanged. So too, effectively responding to the climate crisis will remake America. If this reconstruction serves liberal democratic values, the United States will be made stronger and more capable—and more liberal and democratic." Today, as in the 1930s, the future of liberal open societies is uncertain. The emerging hegemonic rivalry between the United States and China is really a competition to see which superpower can lead in solving the great problems of the 21st century. The viability for American and Chinese hegemony depends, in the final analysis, on the solutions and public goods that each generates for the world. It is a contest to see who can offer the world a better hegemonic deal.

discussion questions

1. Should the United States return to the postwar tradition of liberal internationalism and global leadership?

2. What effect has the Trump years had on the standing of the United States in the international community? Has it been beneficial or detrimental?

3. What has the Covid-19 pandemic exposed about the faults of the international community?

4. Both the United States and China are competing to offer the world a better selection of solutions and public goods. Which country will be able to provide the more attractive offer and thus obtain hegemony?

suggested readings

Kaufman, Joyce. *A Concise History of U.S. Foreign Policy.* Rowman and Littlefield Publishers. 368 pgs. July 2021. Kaufman focuses on the major actors involved in the making of foreign policy and the changing relationships among them. She also explains the major theoretical perspectives within international relations and contextualizes key foreign policy decisions as they fit these frameworks.

G. John Ikenberry. *A World Safe for Democracy: Liberal Internationalism and the Crises of Global Order.* Yale. 352 pgs. 2020. G. John Ikenberry argues that in a 21st century marked by rising economic and security interdependence, liberal internationalism—reformed and reimagined—remains the most viable project to protect liberal democracy.

Kurt M. Campbell and Rush Doshi. "How America Can Shore Up Asia Order: A Strategy for Restoring Balance and Legitimacy." *Foreign Affairs,* January 12, 2021. Campbell and Doshi lay out a strategy for how the United States can restore balance and legitimacy in Asia.

Jake Sullivan. "More, Less, or Different? Where U.S. Foreign Policy Should—and Shouldn't—Go from Here." *Foreign Affairs,* January/February 2019. Sullivan explores the debate over how U.S. foreign policy should be conducted after the election of Donald Trump in 2016.

Thomas Wright. *All Measures Short of War: The Contest for the 21st Century and the Future of American Power.* Yale. 288 pgs. 2017. In this book Thomas Wright explains how major powers will compete fiercely even as they try to avoid war with each other. Wright outlines a new American strategy—Responsible Competition—to navigate these challenges and strengthen the liberal order.

Mira Rapp-Hooper. *Shields of the Republic: The Triumph and Peril of America's Alliances.* Yale. 252 pgs. 2020. Rapp-Hooper argues that America's national security requires alliances that deter and defend against military and non-military conflict alike. The alliance system is past due for a post–Cold War overhaul, but it remains critical to the country's safety and prosperity in the 21st century.

Don't forget to vote!

Download a copy of the ballot questions from the Resources page at www.fpa.org/great_decisions

To access web links to these readings, as well as links to additional, shorter readings and suggested web sites,

GO TO www.fpa.org/great_decisions

and click on the topic under Resources, on the right-hand side of the page.

About the balloting process...

Dear Great Decisions Participants,

As you may already know, my name is Dr. Lauren Prather and I have been working with the Foreign Policy Association (FPA) for the last five years on the National Opinion Ballot (NOB). A version of this letter has appeared in previous briefing books, so I'm only writing a quick hello this year.

My research is primarily focused on international relations. I am a faculty member at the School of Global Policy and Strategy at the University of California, San Diego (UCSD) and have research projects on a range of public opinion topics, from foreign aid to climate change to national security issues. I also teach a class on public opinion and foreign policy for my university.

One of the key difficulties in my research is that the public is often uniformed or misinformed about the topics. This is where you come in! The Great Decisions participants continue to be some of the most informed Americans about foreign policy issues, and the NOB is the perfect opportunity to voice those opinions.

The NOB is also one of the only public opinion surveys in the United States that attempts to gather the opinions of the educated public. Thus, it has great value to researchers and policymakers alike. Some of the questions in which researchers are interested include the following:

- Are the opinions of the educated public significantly different from those of the average American?
- How does public opinion about foreign policy change over time?
- How does public opinion on one foreign policy issue relate to public opinion on other foreign policy issues? For example, are people who support U.S. government policies to mitigate climate change more or less willing to support drilling in the Arctic?
- How do different segments of the population, men or women, liberals or conservatives, view foreign policy choices?

In order to answer the types of questions researchers are interested in, such as how do people's opinions change over time, the NOB needs to have certain attributes. We need to have a way to organize the ballots by participant across all topics. That way, we know, for example, how participant #47 responded to the question about climate change mitigation and how he or she responded to the question about drilling, even if those were in different topics in the NOB. Your random ID number is the **only thing** connected to your responses and **never** your e-mail address. In fact, as a researcher, I must receive the approval of my Institutional Review Board by demonstrating that your data will be protected at all times, and that your responses will be both confidential and anonymous.

If you have any questions or comments, I am always happy to respond via e-mail at LPrather@ucsd.edu. To learn more about my research and teaching, you can visit my website at www.laurenprather.org.

Thank you again to everyone who has participated in the NOB over the years. I have learned a tremendous amount about your foreign policy views and it has greatly informed my own research. In the future, I hope to communicate to the scholarly world and policy communities how the educated American public thinks about foreign policy.

Sincerely,

Lauren Prather

Don't forget to vote!
Download a copy of the ballot questions from the
Resources page at www.fpa.org/great_decisions

AFRICA
'21—China in Africa
'20—Red Sea Security
'18—South Africa's Fragile Democracy
'15—The U.S. and Africa: The Rise and Fall of Obamamania
'14—Islamic Awakening
'13—China in Africa
'11—The Horn of Africa

ASIA
'21—The Two Koreas
'20—India and Pakistan
'20—The Philippines and the U.S.
'18—China and America: The New Geopolitical Equation
'17—Prospects for Afghanistan and Pakistan
'17—Conflict in the South China Sea
'16—Korean Choices
'15—India Changes Course
'14—China's Foreign Policy
'13—Myanmar
'12—Indonesia
'12—Exit from Afghanistan & Iraq

LATIN AMERICA
'20—U.S. relations with the Northern Triangle
'19—U.S. and Mexico: Partnership Tested
'17—Latin America's Political Pendulum
'16—Cuba and the U.S.
'15—Brazil in Metamorphosis
'12—Mexico
'11—Rebuilding Haiti

MIDDLE EAST
'21—Persian Gulf Security
'19—The Middle East: regional disorder
'18—Turkey: Partner in Crisis
'17—Saudi Arabia in Transition
'16—The Rise of ISIS
'16—The Future of Kurdistsan
'16—Shifting Alliances in the Middle East
'15—Syria's Refugee Crisis
'15—Sectarianism in the Middle East
'14—Israel and the U.S.
'14—Turkey's Challenges
'13—Egypt
'13—Iran
'12—Middle East Realignment

RUSSIA AND EASTERN EUROPE
'18—Russia's Foreign Policy
'15—Russia and the Near Abroad
'11—The Caucasus

WESTERN EUROPE
'21—Brexit and the EU
'19—The Rise of Populism in Europe
'17—The Future of Europe: Coping with Crisis
'13—Future of the Euro
'11—Germany's Ascendancy

DEFENSE AND SECURITY
'20—Artificial Intelligence and Data
'19—Nuclear Negotiations: Back to the Future?
'18—U.S. Global Engagement & the Military
'17—Nuclear Security: the Enduring Challenge of Nuclear Weapons
'14—Defense Technology
'13—Intervention
'13—NATO
'13—Threat Assessment
'12—Cybersecurity
'11—American National Security Since 9/11
'11—Sanctions and Nonproliferation

ENVIRONMENT
'20—Climate Change and the Global Order
'16—Climate Geopolitics: The Road to Paris and Beyond
'14—Food and Climate
'12—State of the Oceans

ECONOMIC ISSUES
'21—Global Supply Chains
'19—Decoding U.S.-China Trade
'17—Trade, Jobs and Politics
'17—U.S. Foreign Policy and Petroleum
'14—U.S. Trade Policy
'11—Banks, Governments and Debt Crises

U.S. FOREIGN POLICY
'21—End of Globalization?
'21—The Arctic
'20—China's Road into Latin America
'19—State of the State Department and Diplomacy
'18—Media and Foreign Policy
'18—The Waning of Pax Americana?

OTHER CRITICAL ISSUES
'21—Role of the WHO
'20—Modern Slavery and Human Trafficking
'19—Refugees and global migration
'19—Cyber conflicts and geopolitics
'18—Global Health Issues
'16—The UN's Post-2015 Development Agenda
'16—International Migration
'15—Human Trafficking: A Serious Challenge to Humanity
'14—Energy Independence
'12—Energy Geopolitics
'12—Promoting Democracy
'11—Making Sense of Multilateralism

Global Discussion Questions

No decision in foreign policy is made in a vacuum, and the repercussions of any single decision have far-reaching effects across the range of strategic interests on the U.S. policy agenda. This Great Decisions feature is intended to facilitate the discussion of this year's topics in a global context, to discuss the linkages between the topics and to encourage consideration of the broader impact of decision-making.

1. Consider "Outer Space" in the context of the "Quad Alliance." As shown in both articles, geopolitical tensions are rising between the United States and China. What is similar about the power struggle in space and in the Pacific? How should the United States be responding to heightened tension in both of these realms?

2. Consider "Changing Demographics" in the context of "Drug Policy in Latin America". How are the demographics of the United States impacted by the issue of drug related violence in Latin America? Is this a positive or negative change taking place?

3. Consider "Climate Change" in the context of "Industrial Policy". How is President Biden's push for increased government spending related to the fight against climate change? Should the government be taking an increased role in this fight?

4. Consider "Russia and the U.S." in the context of "Myanmar and ASEAN". How is Russia's support for the military junta in Myanmar a result of U.S.-Russia tensions? What is the best way for the United States to respond to this new alliance?

5. Consider "Biden's Agenda" in the context of the "Quad Alliance". How does the revitalization of the Quad reflect President Biden's foreign policy? What are President Biden's goals when it comes to the position of the United States in global affairs?

Don't forget to vote!
Download a copy of the ballot questions from the Resources page at www.fpa.org/great_decisions

Become a Member

For nearly a century, members of the Association have played key roles in government, think tanks, academia and the private sector.

As an active participant in the FPA's Great Decisions program, we encourage you to join the community today's foreign policy thought leaders.

Member—$250

Benefits:
- Free admission to all Associate events (includes member's family)
- Discounted admission for all other guests to Associate events
- Complimentary **GREAT DECISIONS** briefing book
- Complimentary issue of FPA's annual *National Opinion Ballot Report*

Visit us online at

www.fpa.org/membership

FOREIGN POLICY ASSOCIATION 1918

Make a Donation

Your support helps the FOREIGN POLICY ASSOCIATION's programs dedicated to global affairs education.

Make a fully tax-deductible contribution to FPA's Annual Fund 2020.

To contribute to the Annual Fund 2020 visit us online at **www.fpa.org** or call the Membership Department at

(800) 628-5754 ext. 333

The generosity of donors who contribute $500 or more is acknowledged in FPA's *Annual Report*.

All financial contributions are tax-deductible to the fullest extent of the law under section 501 (c)(3) of the IRS code.

FPA also offers membership at the SPONSOR MEMBER and PATRON MEMBER levels. To learn more, visit us online at www.fpa.org/membership or call (800) 628-5754 ext. 333.

Return this form by mail to: Foreign Policy Association, 551 Fifth Avenue, 30th Floor, New York, N.Y. 10176

ORDER ONLINE: WWW.FPA.ORG/GREAT_DECISIONS

CALL (800) 477-5836

FAX (212) 481-9275

☐ MR.　☐ MRS.　☐ MS.　☐ DR.　☐ PROF.

NAME _____

ADDRESS _____

_____ APT/FLOOR _____

CITY_____ STATE _____ ZIP _____

TEL_____

E-MAIL _____

☐ AMEX　☐ VISA　☐ MC　☐ DISCOVER
☐ CHECK (ENCLOSED)

CHECKS SHOULD BE PAYABLE TO FOREIGN POLICY ASSOCIATION.

CARD NO.

☐☐☐☐☐☐☐☐☐☐☐☐☐☐☐☐

SIGNATURE OF CARDHOLDER

EXP. DATE (MM/YY)

☐☐☐☐

PRODUCT	QTY	PRICE	COST
GREAT DECISIONS 2022 Briefing Book (FPA31715)		$35	
SPECIAL OFFER TEN PACK SPECIAL GREAT DECISIONS 2022 (FPA31722) *Includes 10% discount		$315	
GREAT DECISIONS TELEVISION SERIES GD ON DVD 2022 (FPA31716)		$40	
GREAT DECISIONS 2022 TEACHER'S PACKET (1 Briefing Book, 1 Teacher's Guide and 1 DVD (FPA 31718) E-MAIL: (REQUIRED) _____		$75	
GREAT DECISIONS CLASSROOM-PACKET (1 Teacher's Packet & 30 Briefing Books (FPA31719) E-MAIL: (REQUIRED) _____		$775	
MEMBERSHIP		$250	
ANNUAL FUND 2021 (ANY AMOUNT)			

SUBTOTAL	$	
plus S & H*	$	
TOTAL	$	

For details and shipping charges, call FPA's Sales Department at (800) 477-5836.
Orders mailed to FPA without the shipping charge will be held.